SWEET AND SOUR EXPERIENCE IN LIFE

Lessons Learned From LIFe's Highs and Lows

Ashok Kumar khanna

BlueRose ONE
Stories Matter
NewDelhi • London

BLUEROSE PUBLISHERS
India | U.K.

BlueRose ONE.com
Stories Matter
NewDelhi • London

For permissions requests or inquiries regarding this publication, please contact:

BLUEROSE PUBLISHERS
www.BlueRoseONE.com
info@bluerosepublishers.com
+91 8882 898 898
+4407342408967

ISBN: 978-93-7139-649-3

Cover design: Shubham Verma
Typesetting: Sagar

First Edition: July 2025

INTRODUCTION

The Sweet and Sour experiences in life are a reflection of Ashok kumar Khanna's journey, born in 1954, his life has been a testament to the unpredictable nature of existence. Through the lens of personal, as explored in these pages, is a complex tapestry of uncertainty. It presents challenges that test our resilience, moments of joy that remind us of its beauty, and instances of humour that lighten the load of even the heaviest burdens. The book dives into diverse themes—stories of achievements that inspire, anecdotes filled with laughter, and profound messages rooted in spirituality and divinity. Each chapter is designed to resonate with readers, providing not just a glimpse into a man's life but also a take on the universal truth(s) that bind us all. Whether it's navigating the unpredictable tides of life, cherishing its lighter moments with heartfelt jokes, or seeking solace in the wisdom of divine teachings, Sweet and Sour Not Easy serves as a companion and guide. It reminds us that while the path may be challenging, it is our spirit and perspective that shape the journey.

The book dives into diverse themes—stories of achievements that inspire, anecdotes filled with laughter, and profound messages rooted in spirituality and divinity. Each chapter is designed to resonate with readers, providing not just a glimpse into a man's life but also a take on the universal truth(s) that bind us all.

Whether it's navigating the unpredictable tides of life, cherishing its lighter moments with heartfelt jokes, or seeking solace in the wisdom of divine teachings, *Sweet and Sour Not Easy* serves as a companion and guide. It reminds us that while the path may be challenging, it is our spirit and perspective that shape the journey.

Sitting with grand father

I was sitting with my grandfather and said, "Dada Ji, tell me about your life in Pakistan."

He looked at me, smiled, and said, "Why do you want to know about my life in Pakistan?"

He continued, "We had a good life–a big house, a farmhouse, and a joint family of 12 people. Everything was going well. We not only respected our family but also our neighbours and the entire town. Everyone knew us well, and it felt like we were all members of one big family. There wasn't much entertainment back then, but people used to meet each other warmly and participate in each other's joys and sorrows. It was a close-knit community."

I asked, "You mean all religions, including Muslims?"

"Yes," he replied. "We were all like brothers and sisters. There was no question of any difference. We celebrated each other's religious functions, exchanged gifts, and shared dishes during festivals."

Just then, his old friend entered with his grandson. "Hello, Papa Ji! Brother, how are you?"

My grandfather exclaimed, "Oh, what a surprise to see you after such a long time!" Both hugged each other, and my grandfather kissed his friend's forehead. "Lovely to see you, my old friend and brother. How did you find my address?"

"I got your address from Chotu Ram. Do you remember him? He was our neighbour in Gujranwala, Pakistan."

"Yes, the son of Pishori Lal," my grandfather said.

"Yes, Papa Ji."

"And where is he now?" my grandfather asked.

"Sadly, he and his wife were killed during the partition," his friend replied.

My grandfather's face fell. "Oh, I'm so sorry to hear that. It's very sad."

Pointing to the young boy, his friend said, "This is my grandson."

"Lovely, smart boy," my grandfather said with a smile. "What's your name, son?" Shy and hesitant, the boy replied, "My name is Neeraj."

My grandfather turned to me and said, "Go inside and ask your grandmother to bring tea. Tell her Mahesh Uncle has come—he was with us in Pakistan."

As I got up, my grandfather added, "Take Neeraj with you and play with him."

I held Neeraj's hand, took him to another room, and conveyed the message to my grandmother.

Hearing the message, my grandmother was overjoyed and whispered in my ear, "How many people are there?"

I said, "Only one." This is Neeraj, my grandfather's friend's grandson, and we are going to play cricket.

My grandmother hugged him and placed her hand on his head as a blessing.

My cricket partner came to pick me up for the game and introduced me to Neeraj, saying, "He also plays cricket. He's from Sarojini Nagar School."

He looked at both of us and said, "But we are already eleven. Sorry, we cannot include him in the team."

There was a pause for a moment before Neeraj said, "You both go. Don't worry about me."

I requested my partner, "Let's take him along, or else he'll get bored here." He agreed, and we all proceeded to the ground for the 20-over game.

At the field, my partner handed Neeraj a scorebook and asked him to keep score. I could tell from his expression that he wasn't thrilled, but he accepted the task.

We began batting, and in the second over, our opening batsman slipped while running, got injured, and had to be taken to a doctor as he was unable to walk. Our captain approached me and asked, "What does your friend do—batting or bowling?"

I replied, "I just met him today, so I don't know what his expertise is."

I quickly went to Neeraj and asked, "Would you like to play? Do you bat or bowl?"

"I'm an all-rounder and usually bat at No. 4," he answered confidently.

I told him to put on the batting pads and be ready.

Our second wicket fell in the 5th over, and we were struggling at 20 for 2. Neeraj stepped in and made a valuable 40 runs, helping us post a total of 130 runs.

When it was our turn to bowl, the captain handed me the ball for the opening spell. I was shocked but stepped up. In my first over, I conceded 20 runs but managed to take one wicket. Neeraj bowled three overs, giving away only 10 runs. By the 10th over, the opposition had scored 80 runs for 4 wickets, and it looked like we might lose.

I was given the ball again for my second over. This time, I took two wickets and gave away only 5 runs. By the 16th over, the opposition needed just 10 runs with 4 overs left. Neeraj was asked to bowl again, while I was sent to field at deep long-on.

The batsman hit a high shot toward me. I jumped and caught the ball mid-air. Everyone thought it was a six, but when I held up the ball, they were shocked and surprised. My teammates hugged and praised me, saying, "Well done, Ashok!"

In the last over, the opposition needed just 4 runs to win. I was handed the ball. On the first delivery, the batsman charged forward but missed, and our wicketkeeper stumped him. The last batsman came in, with five balls remaining. He defended my second ball and hit a low shot on the third, which Neeraj caught skilfully.

We won the match, but the opposing team began shouting, claiming it wasn't a clean catch and that the ball had touched the ground. Suddenly, they started fighting and attacked Neeraj, injuring him badly. He was rushed to the hospital, and a police case was filed.

I was scared as my family began arguing with me about why I had taken Neeraj to the match. Neeraj's grandfather, however, hugged me and defended me, saying, "Why blame him? These things happen. Don't worry, everything will be resolved." His support comforted me, and eventually, my family calmed down too.

Neeraj was released from the hospital, and the police case was eventually withdrawn. The parents of the opposing team apologized and requested we drop the case, fearing it might ruin their children's careers.

Old days

In those days, phones were a rarity in Mehrauli. I remember there were only two phone connections in the entire town–one belonged to a wealthy businessman, and the other to my father, who had received it as a priority due to his work with the UN. Our number was widely circulated in Mehrauli, and it was both a blessing and a burden. If we responded to calls, people appreciated it; if we didn't, they criticized us, claiming we were arrogant and uncooperative.

At that time, owning a bicycle was considered a luxury. Then scooters came along, but even those were distributed through a quota system.

We were fortunate to get one. Today, such things hold little value—even cars are common now.

First invitation of the cricket tournament

One day, I received a call from Neeraj inviting me to play in a cricket tournament at Asiad Village the following Saturday. I told him I was excited but needed to check with my father first.

That evening, I asked my dad, "Can I go to Asiad Village for a cricket tournament?"

He looked at me and said, "It's better if you focus on your studies. This game won't help you in your career."

I pleaded, "Dad, please let me go!"

But he replied firmly, "No means no."

Feeling upset, I went to another room angrily. My grandmother was there and comforted me. She approached my dad and said, "Let him go. Why upset him over this?"

After thinking for a moment, my dad said, "Let me consider it."

Later, my grandmother reassured me, saying, "Don't worry. I'm sure he'll let you go." She placed her hand on my head and kissed my forehead lovingly.

The next day, to my surprise, my father said, "You can go. I'll drop you off and pick you up." I was thrilled and immediately called Neeraj to share the good news. However, I added, "I don't have a cricket kit."

Neeraj replied, "Don't worry! I have a spare kit you can use."

On the day of the tournament, my dad dropped me off at Asiad Village and handed me ₹100. I said, "Why are you giving me money? I don't need it." But he insisted, "Keep it and enjoy yourself."

The game began, and to my surprise, Madho Rao Scindia was on the opposing team. We chose to field first, and I was given the opening spell, even though I was a spinner specializing in googlies. In my first over, I took two wickets. Then, Maharaj (Madho Ji) came to bat. He played cautiously and couldn't score much against my bowling.

Some of his friends approached me and said, "Give Maharaj some easy balls so he can score runs." I started tossing flighted deliveries, but he misread them and was clean-bowled. Afterward, he came over, appreciated my bowling, shook my hand, and gifted me a beautiful pan.

That day was unforgettable–a fantastic game, great exposure, and meeting Shri Madho Rao Scindia, who was a kind and charming personality. I took six wickets that day, and the next morning, the newspapers carried the headline: "*Ashok Shines and Wrecks Opposing Team.*"

I went to a public telephone booth (since mobile phones weren't available at the time) and called my dad to share the good news and ask when he would pick me up. He replied...

He would come after two hours and suggested I go with Neeraj to his residence in Sarojini Nagar, where he would pick me up later.

A visit to Neeraj's house and met his sister

Neeraj and I decided to take a three-wheeler since he had two cricket kit bags, and carrying them on a bus wasn't practical. We reached his house in about 30 minutes. On the way, he showed me his school in Sarojini Nagar and said, "Why don't you take admission here? It's a good school with an excellent reputation, and students here score well."

I replied, "My dad won't allow it, though I know this school has a good reputation."

When we arrived at his house, Neeraj introduced me to his mother. I touched her feet, and she blessed me warmly. She offered me sweets and a Coke. I politely said, "Aunty, I don't drink Coke. Can I have lemon water with salt instead?"

She paused for a moment, then smiled apologetically and said, "Sorry, son, we don't have lemons. But I can make tea for you."

I quickly replied, "No, Aunty, don't worry. I'll drink Coke." She smiled and went to another room.

Neeraj and I sat discussing the match. He seemed even more excited than me. "You know," he repeated, "you've done so well! That team was much stronger than us, yet we won."

I smiled and said, "Thanks for the compliment. Honestly, I didn't even expect I could bowl that well."

Suddenly, there was a knock at the door. Thinking it was my dad, I told Neeraj, "I think my dad's here. I'll get it."

When I opened the door, I was taken aback to see a beautiful girl standing there. She glanced at me and then at the flat number before asking, "Who are you, and what are you doing in my house?"

I quickly replied, "Oh, I'm Ashok, Neeraj's friend."

She looked puzzled. "But I've never seen you here before."

I explained, "I'm from Mehrauli. Your grandfather and mine are old friends from Pakistan. After our cricket match today, Neeraj brought me here to wait for my father, who's coming to pick me up."

She smiled slightly and said, "If you don't mind, may I come into my house?"

Embarrassed by my distraction, I stepped aside, saying, "Sorry, of course, please come in."

Inside, Neeraj greeted her, "Hi Reeta! How was your day?"

"Not good," she replied. "The teacher was on leave, so it felt like a waste of time going and coming."

Neeraj gestured toward me and said, "Oh, by the way, meet my friend Ashok. He took six wickets in four overs, and we won the match!"

She looked at me, smiled, and extended her hand for a handshake. I nervously stepped forward and shook her hand. She said, "Congratulations!"

Blushing, I stammered, "Th-thank you. It was just a fluke."

She smiled again. "I don't agree. Anyway, all the best for the future. It was nice meeting you."

"Same here," I replied, still flustered.

It was my first handshake with a girl, and I felt like I was flying. Her smile and voice stayed with me as I kept thinking about her.

Soon after, my dad arrived on his scooter. I got on behind him but couldn't stop glancing back at the door. Neeraj and his mother came to see me off, but Reeta wasn't there. My eyes searched for her face, and I felt a strange emptiness.

As we rode home, my dad said something to me, but I didn't respond. Lost in my thoughts, I didn't even realize he was speaking to me.

He stopped the scooter and asked, "What's the matter? Why aren't you answering?"

Startled, I replied, "Sorry, Dad. I was thinking about the cricket match. I played really well today! All my teammates lifted me up and cheered, shouting, 'Hip hip hurray!'"

Smiling, he said, "That's exactly what I was asking about–how your game went."

I proudly replied, "I was the hero, Dad! Even Madho Rao Scindia came over to appreciate my bowling."

“Wow, that’s great to hear! Congratulations,” he said. From that day onwards, my dad never stopped me from playing cricket. However, he always reminded me to focus on my studies as well.

One day, I told my dad that I wanted to change schools from Qutab High Secondary to Sarojini Nagar, where Neeraj studied in the same class. "We’re very good friends now," I explained. "He’s more intelligent and better in studies. His company will improve my academics and games, and give me more exposure."

My dad asked, "What do you mean by 'more exposure'?"

"Dad, I mean moving from the village to the city. I’ll learn so many new things and experience a different life," I said eagerly.

He looked at me seriously. "At your age, this 'exposure' can ruin you too. I’ve been telling you repeatedly to focus on your studies, but you’re dreaming about exposure. You’ll have plenty of opportunities for that in the future. For now, concentrate on your education."

How could I tell him that by "exposure," I meant meeting Reeta? I didn’t know what happened during our first meeting, but my mind was neither on my studies nor on cricket. It could have been my first crush. The thought of seeing her frequently if I changed schools occupied my mind.

One day, Dad questioned, "Why did you take Sanskrit? You should’ve chosen Math; it will get you more marks."

Without thinking, I replied, "I can change if you shift me to Sarojini Nagar school. Neeraj told me their math teacher is excellent."

Dad looked at me and smiled. "I’ll consider it for your future. A friend of mine is the principal at Sarojini Nagar. I’ll talk to him and get his views before deciding."

Hearing this, I was thrilled and excited. I prayed to God, hoping for admission to that school.

A couple of weeks later, Dad said, "I met the principal at Sarojini Nagar. He's willing to accept your admission."

I was overjoyed. Finally, I got into the school, and luckily, Neeraj was in the same class.

Everything was going well until one day when three teachers were on leave. Most of my classmates decided to watch the movie *Pakeezah* at Kamal Cinema. We had a great time, enjoyed the movie, ate food nearby, and returned home late.

When I reached home, I saw my parents waiting at the gate, worried. Dad asked, "Where were you?"

Realizing they already knew about our class skipping, I confessed, "I'm sorry. All my friends decided to see a movie, and I couldn't stop myself from joining them."

Dad's face hardened. "So, this is the 'exposure' you were looking for? You're still under 16. I trusted you, and you broke that trust. It's better you return to your old school so we can keep an eye on you."

I was speechless and quietly moved to another room.

Dad called out loudly, "I'm talking to you! Why are you walking away? I need an answer. Why did you go, and with whose permission?"

I turned and said, "I'm sorry. I didn't hide anything and told you the truth. I promise I won't go anywhere without informing you."

Dad replied sternly, "How can I trust you? You've broken that trust."

I raised my thumb and said, "Dad, I promise I won't break the rules again. Trust me."

After a pause, he softened. "This time, I'll accept your apology. But in the future, no excuses or explanations will be tolerated."

Relieved, I promised him again. The matter was settled, and I breathed a long sigh of relief.

The next day at school, the principal called an assembly and said, "Raise your hands if you went to watch the movie at Kamal Theatre."

About 20 of us raised our hands, including me.

"All of you," the principal said firmly, "meet me at the playground at 12 o'clock."

We nodded, speechless, and chorused, "Yes, sir."

At noon, we gathered nervously in the playground...

The principal and some teachers accompanied him. The principal said, "When you are in school, it is the school's responsibility to ensure your safety. You are not mature enough, and you don't know what is good and what is bad for you. This is the first time in this school that you went to a movie instead of going home. If anything had gone wrong, the blame would have fallen on the school. I've called you here to understand why you all decided to go to the theatre instead of going home."

We all stood silently with our heads bowed. He spoke loudly, "Look ahead; no need to bow your heads." We all raised our heads and said, "Sorry, sir. It will not happen again. We have already been scolded by our parents."

One of our classmates spoke up, "After school hours, we can go anywhere. Why are we being treated like this? How can the school management be responsible? As we said earlier, we've already been scolded and apologized to both our parents and you."

On hearing this, the principal got annoyed and asked, "What is your name?"

"My name is Ankit," he replied.

"Ankit, you come tomorrow with your father. You don't know how to speak to teachers and the principal," said the principal. "We have decided to appoint a psychologist for you so you can learn some basic manners and improve your personality. You need to learn more about yourself." He continued, "Now, everyone else can go back to class. Ankit, you take two rounds of this playground as punishment."

We all rushed to our classes, and in class, everyone was shocked by Ankit's response. About 30 minutes later, he came back, looking neither sweaty nor tired. We asked him, "What happened? How was your punishment? You don't look tired at all." Another student added, "He looks fresher than before."

Ankit smiled and said, "I told the peon that my father is a politician, and if I get sick, everyone will be in trouble, including him. I asked him to let me do only half a round slowly, and he agreed." Some students in his group laughed loudly, saying, "Yaar, friend, you are really great!"

A few of us decided to stay away from Ankit's group, as they could create problems for us. I narrated the whole incident to my father, and he applauded me. "Very good! I'm proud of you."

Later, Neeraj told me, "Let's go to our house for lunch today, as it's my birthday, and my Dada Ji (grandfather) specially asked me to invite you. He really likes you."

I replied, "I can go, but only if we return before lunchtime. I don't want to miss class, and since the principal knows my father, I don't want any misunderstanding or distrust between us. I promised him that I won't bunk any classes and will go straight home after school."

Neeraj said, "It's good to be obedient to your parents, but you are coming to our house, and your dad knows us."

Inside, I was eager to go during lunch hours just to catch a glimpse of his sister, Reeta, but I pretended to be uninterested. "No, I'm not interested in going during school hours," I said.

Finally, Neeraj said, "Alright, we'll return during lunch, but you promise that tomorrow evening you'll come with me to our house to celebrate my birthday. Tomorrow is Sunday, and you can take permission from your parents."

I told him, "I can't decide right now. Let me speak to my dad, and if he permits, I'll come."

We both walked to his house, and I prayed to God, wishing I could see Reeta that day. Neeraj pressed the doorbell, and his grandfather opened the door. We entered the house. I touched his Dada Ji's feet as a sign of respect. He put his hand on my head and kissed me, blessing me, "May you live long, my child. How is your dad, and my old friend from Pakistan, your grandfather?"

I said, "Sir, both are fine. They often ask about you because they know I'm studying at Sarojini Nagar with Neeraj."

He smiled and said, "Oh, such kindness from them. Your grandfather was very hard-working. He earned a lot of name and reputation in Pakistan. He had everything there, but the great thing is, when he came here, he started from scratch." And he reached the same heights. All his siblings are also well settled. My attention was on another room. Finally, I said, "Neeraj, let's go to school in time before the next class starts." Neeraj replied, "Yes, come, let's move."

I asked, "Where is Aunty? Can I say hello to her?"

Dada Ji replied, "My son, she and Reeta have both gone to the market for birthday preparations. I hope you are coming tomorrow. Has Neeraj invited you?"

"Yes, UNCLE, he told me, but I need to take permission from my dad."

"Don't worry; I'll speak to him and ask him to send you here."

"Thank you, uncle. Please speak to my dad, and then I can come."

Neeraj said, "Grandpa, please don't tell his dad that he visited here. He wasn't planning to come, but I brought him. Otherwise, he would face unnecessary trouble."

I reached class on time but felt uncomfortable, knowing I had violated my promise to my dad. The reason I had gone wasn't even there, and I felt like I was missing out on a dream I had in my mind. I tried to console myself, thinking, "Never mind, tomorrow my dream will come true."

My father gave permission and told me to take his scooter, drive carefully, and not drive too fast. I had just gotten my driver's license right after turning 18. I was excited to ride the scooter on my own; it felt so different to drive it outside town for the first time. I took a deep breath, started the engine, and left for Sarojini Nagar. I drove carefully and slowly, and finally, I reached their house.

There were a lot of people there, including some classmates. I met them, and Neeraj took me to a neighbouring room where some liquor was being served. Outside, tents were set up for dinner. I told Neeraj, "Wow, Yaar, this is a big celebration. I'm happy to be here for your birthday."

One of the uncles said, "Hope you're not kids anymore. If you're an adult, you can enjoy a drink." My classmates looked at each other and gave eye signals, suggesting we should try it. I was hesitating, not sure whether to start, as I had never consumed alcohol before, but curiosity made me think, "Let's try it and see what happens."

Just then, someone brought beers, and everyone picked one up. When the bottle reached me, I hesitated, looking at the bottles and my friends. Neeraj looked at me and said, "Take it, dear. It's your friend's birthday. Enjoy." I picked up the bottle, and everyone said, "Cheers! Happy birthday, Neeraj!" All of them sipped their beer, and I did too. It had a bitter taste, and soon I started feeling a little intoxicated. I only drank half the bottle and left it on the table.

After a while, they turned on the music, and everyone started dancing, doing Bhangra. Reeta also came in and started dancing. She came to me, held my hand, and began dancing with me. I was shy, but it felt like my dream had come true. I felt like I was in seventh heaven.

One of Reeta's friends shouted over the loud music, "Who is this guy?" It was so loud that it was hard to hear anything. Reeta introduced me to her, saying, "Ashok Bhai, this is my friend Alka." I was about to leave when I heard her call me "brother." My world crashed down, and the intoxication wore off immediately. I grabbed the leftover beer and gulped it down quickly.

Alka, noticing, said, "Wow, great, what a speed!" I thought for a moment, "Should I stay or leave immediately?" Alka added, "You look like you go to the gym." I wasn't in the mood to reply, so I ignored her.

In the meantime, Reeta entered, and Alka said, "I was praising him for his good physique, but he ignored me." I changed the subject and said, "Actually, I'm drunk and trying to figure out how to drive my scooter home."

I felt the effects of the beer and gathered some strength. I turned to Reeta and said, "Can I make a request?"

She smiled and replied, "Yes, brother. No formalities, go ahead."

"When we first met, and you congratulated me for winning the cricket match, I was the man of the match. I was attracted to you at first sight."

She was speechless and said, "I'm sorry, Ashok, I have a boyfriend. My family knows about him, and we've already decided to get married."

Alka looked at me and Reeta and smiled, saying, "Reeta, don't break his heart. He's a cute guy." Then she added, "Don't worry, Ashok. Treat her as your friend, and me too. Friendship is a common thing. We can meet and remain friends. This is your crush, and it happens at this age. Don't take it too seriously—just stay friends."

At first, I felt like everything was falling apart, but I realized she was right.

I felt like my life had been robbed and that nothing was left. Later, my conscience realized that I may have been wrong, and I needed to regain control of my senses. I said, "I am sorry for my feelings, and I hope I haven't hurt you. Please don't tell Neeraj or Grandpa; otherwise, I won't be allowed to come here again."

She looked at me, promised she wouldn't reveal anything, and said, "Stay in touch."

"Sure," I replied, and left for home. On the way, I thought about how foolish I had been to get carried away so quickly without knowing all the facts. "Thank you, God, for giving me clarity," I thought, feeling lighter and not so depressed.

Next day in class

The next day, we were informed that there would be a psychology class every Wednesday, and we were waiting for the teacher to arrive. Neeraj nudged me with his elbow twice. I asked, "What's the matter?"

He replied, "Look at the door."

A beautiful woman, around 32 years old, tall and slim, wearing a printed yellow and red saree, entered and said, "Hello, boys. I am Anjali, your psychology teacher. How are you all?"

"We're fine, madam," the boys responded.

"Any questions from the class?" she asked.

Neeraj stood up and said, "Madam, I am the class monitor, and I welcome you to our class. We hope that we will all benefit from your suggestions and guidance. Please show us the right path, so we can move forward without difficulties. Enlighten us."

She smiled and said, "I will not be doing any enlightenment, but I will give you simple tips on how to cope with life, particularly student life. Most of you here must be under 18."

Some students said, "Yes," while others said "17" or "16," and so on.

"Right, at your age, focus is very important," she continued. "You are not yet mature, and you see so many new things that curiosity plays an important role. Everyone wants to enjoy new experiences and feels that they are important. Sometimes, this leads us to fall into addictions. Addictions to anything are very harmful."

Neeraj raised his hand and asked, "Madam, are focus and concentration the same thing, or...?"

"Good question, Neeraj," she replied.

"Actually, focus is the ability to direct your attention to a specific task, and concentration is the ability to maintain that focus over time."

Neeraj followed up, "Madam, it is often seen that we focus and concentrate during exams, and when we revise, we gain confidence that we're ready for the exam. But when we start answering, our minds get puzzled, and we might make mistakes. Later, we realize, 'Oh, the answer was this, not what I wrote."

Stress is something all human beings experience, especially when preparing for exams, interviews, or other important tasks. Let me give you some tips that can help you cope with stress and perform better in any task:

All students replied, "Yes, Madam," while Neeraj added, "You've raised an important topic. Please guide us on how to handle stress and tension effectively."

I explained, "Some people may experience anxiety disorders, but in general, we can manage anxiety by incorporating mindfulness, relaxation techniques, and proper breathing exercises into our routine. While this is a vast subject, I'll guide you on how to handle exam stress and improve focus and concentration."

Tips to Manage Stress:

1. **Physical Activity:** Go for a walk or engage in some form of physical activity like playing a game. This will help clear your mind and reduce stress.
2. **Breathing Exercise:** Try this technique:
    - Inhale deeply for a count of 4.
    - Hold your breath for a count of 4.
    - Exhale slowly for a count of 4.
    - Hold your breath again for a count of 4. Repeat this cycle for 5 minutes. As you get comfortable, increase the count: inhale for 4, hold for 7, and exhale for 10. This practice is incredibly effective in calming the mind, boosting energy, and reducing stress.

If your mind is calm, you will feel confident, composed, and free from anxiety or panic.

3. **Bhramari Pranayama:** This breathing technique involves making a humming sound like a bee.
    - Sit in a comfortable position, either on a chair or in a cross-legged posture.
    - Relax the muscles of your face and jaw.
    - Close your eyes and block your ears with your thumbs.
    - Inhale deeply through your nose, and as you exhale, create a humming sound like "hmmm" or "Om."

Benefits of Bhramari Pranayama:

- Reduces stress, anxiety, and depression.
- Improves sleep quality.
- Calms throat irritation or infections.
- Helps regulate blood pressure.
- Beneficial for students, adults, and even older people.

1. **Anulom Vilom (Alternate Nostril Breathing):**
    - Gently inhale through your left nostril while keeping your right nostril closed.
    - Exhale through your right nostril while keeping your left nostril closed.
    - Alternate and repeat: inhale through the right nostril and exhale through the left nostril.
    - If either nostril feels blocked, try **Nadi Shodhana Pranayama** to clear the air passages.

These practices will not only help you manage exam stress but also improve your focus, concentration, and overall well-being.

Start incorporating them into your daily routine to experience the benefits.

Teacher: "Breathing exercises offer the following benefits:

- **Reduces Stress and Anxiety:** By calming the nervous system and regulating cortisol levels.
- **Strengthens the Lungs:** Helps treat respiratory issues like asthma and chest infections.
- **Improves Heart Health:** Supports cardiovascular function.

- **Boosts Digestion and Metabolism:** Stimulates digestive organs.
- **Enhances Concentration and Focus:** Keeps the mind sharp and attentive.
- **Purifies Blood and Improves Skin Glow:** Promotes overall vitality."

Neeraj: "Madam, your skin is also glowing. It seems you are practising these breathing exercises!"

The teacher smiled gently and then laughed loudly, and the entire class burst into laughter. "I do practice them," she admitted, "but good skin is also hereditary."

"Now, let's return to the subject," she continued. "Breathing exercises also:

- **Boost the Immune System:** Enhances the body's defense mechanisms.
- **Improve Mental Clarity:** Sharpens thinking and decision-making.
- **Balance Hormones:** Reduces mood fluctuations and keeps emotions in check.

One very important tip: **Get 7-8 hours of sleep daily.** Proper sleep is essential for staying fresh and healthy."

Neeraj: "My mother has trouble sleeping; she suffers from sleep apnoea."

Teacher: "I suggest taking her to a neurologist who specializes in sleep disorders. In the meantime, here are some general tips for improving sleep quality:

4. Have a light dinner.
5. Drink a glass of warm milk at night.

6. Try chamomile tea before bed.
7. Take a shower before sleeping.
8. Walk for 10 minutes after dinner.
9. Meditate before going to bed.

But remember, self-treatment can only go so far; always seek expert advice when necessary."

She paused and added, "For stress relief, you can also listen to light music or watch comedy Shows, whenever you feel uneasy. This can improve your concentration and help calm your mind."

Teacher: "That's all for today. Next time, we'll discuss another topic. If any of you are dealing with family issues that are affecting you, feel free to bring them up."

The class nodded appreciatively.

As the teacher began to leave, Neeraj rushed to her and grabbed her bag, which looked heavy. "Let me carry this for you, Madam," he offered earnestly.

Madam, I will drop you, and I will take care of this bag. How to handle this bag? It is quite heavy.

Yes, I am staying in Mumbai, and here I was on a visit only for your class, as your school principal invited me for a lecture in your school. I am doing practice in Mumbai and visiting professors in the schools and Hospitals and institutes. I always keep my belongings in this bag, which is enough for three days.

She boarded the taxi for another visit, and Neeraj kept her bag on the back seat near her and said, Madam, I am grateful to you for your visit in our class; we all have been given very good advice and tips, which will certainly help us and in your next class we get more opportunity to improve our way of life and personality. She smiled and waved and the taxi sped away. He watched till the taxi disappeared from his eyes.

Neeraj thought, I should have taken her contact number in case my mother needs her consultations.

Neeraj came back to class, all the students staring and smiling. Some came to him and gheraoed him and said, “Tellus Neeraj, what did you gossip with Madam?” Another said chamcha /spoon, other said

He has a crush on her; she was so beautiful. Neeraj lost his temper and shouted, “Will you guys keep quiet?” She gave us wonderful advice and Tips and I cannot extend the courtesy to drop her. This was only a courtesy and nothing else, please don’t make stories which have no legs. Everyone kept quiet and went to their desks.

Ashok to Neeraj, you gave another befitting reply to them. Some people's minds always go on the wrong side. I know you very well, you are a good human being and have good manners. This courtesy was required and we can get more advice and tips from her in the future.

Neeraj, you are my good and friend and hug him and say thanks for your compliments;

I narrated the whole story to my mother, and she smiled and pinched my cheek and smiled and spoke, “Well done by Neeraj but in this age, girls are the attractions, how you say, He might have been attracted.”

Mom, you are also having the same views, it is not fair, shesmiled and said, I was joking. Go to the dining table and take your favourite food, rajma chawal is there.

Our exam came near, and there was no news of her for our next session on Phycology and I went to the principal and enquired about herprincipal, she was very busy and could not give us any date, you liked her session, principal questioned. Yes, sir, she gave very good advice and tips, and our confidence has boosted a little bit.

Principal, I am sorry, now your exams are near and concentrate on study and forget about cricket for the time being, I know you play very well.

The exam went very well, and I got only 45% marks and Neeraj got 60%; at that time these were considered good marks in 1970. He decided to do Chartered Accountancy and took B.com (P).

I did my graduation and got the same 45% marks, and the connection with Neeraj was almost discontinued.

An attempt to find him

Once I visited Sarojini Nagar at his house and came to know that they had already shifted to Mumbai, and his neighbour Akash, who was also in our cricket team told me that he got the job in Mumbai.

After learning that Neeraj had become a Chartered Accountant on his first attempt and now worked as a finance advisor in the government, I couldn't help but feel proud of him.

Akash, his neighbour, invited me for a cup of tea, and I gladly accepted.

As we sat down, I was curious to know more about Neeraj's sister but wasn't sure how to broach the topic. Eventually, I asked, "What about Neeraj's family?"

Akash replied, "His mother has passed away, and his father has fallen into depression. He's shifted to Noida."

I cautiously continued, "And his grandfather and sister?"

Akash smiled. "His grandfather is still active–he must be over 90 now. As for his sister, she's married to an engineer and settled in Madhya Pradesh."

"Did she marry the same person she had an affair with?" I asked hesitantly.

Akash shook his head. "No, that boy went to the USA for further studies. She had no choice but to marry someone else. Fortunately, he's a good man and well-known to the family. She's living a happy life."

I sighed, reflecting on life's unpredictability. *You make plans, but life–and sometimes God–has a different path in store for you.*

By chance, met Neeraj's grandfather

Later, I visited Noida to attend a family wedding and was shocked to see Neeraj's grandfather there. I immediately touched his feet, and he recognized me.

"God bless you!" he said warmly. "How's your family?"

He specifically asked about my grandfather, and I hesitated before replying, "I'm sorry, Dadaji. He's no longer with us."

The news visibly shook him. "Oh my God! He was fine. I spoke to him not too long ago!"

"Yes, Dadaji," I said gently. "He was well and worked until his last breath. Suddenly, he felt uneasy. We called a doctor, but he passed away before anything could be done. According to our Hindu customs, we placed him on the floor, lit a diya, and performed his cremation the next day. More than a thousand people attended his funeral."

Tears welled in his eyes. "Oh, my dear old friend! You've left before me. You were such a good and spiritual person–my inspiration. I learned so many good things from you."

Overwhelmed with grief, he lost his balance and was about to fall. I quickly supported him, helping him to a chair and offering him a glass of water. "Are you alright, Dadaji?"

He couldn't speak at first, but after a while, he nodded. Soon, other relatives came to assist, and I accompanied them to make sure he was comfortable.

After some time, he felt better. I took his address and promised to visit him, eager to learn more about his memories of Pakistan—stories I hadn't been able to gather from my grandfather.

Before I left, he hugged me tightly, kissed my forehead, and said, "May God bless you, my child. May all your desires come true, and may happiness fill your life."

I touched his feet again, overwhelmed by his kind words. "Thank you, Dadaji. I'll always cherish your blessings."

As I walked away, I noticed a faint smile on his face. The sadness from the news of my grandfather's passing seemed to have lifted slightly, replaced by the warmth of sharing fond memories and extending heartfelt blessings.

UPSC exam

Once, I visited my cousin, Rajni Sabharwal, one day and noticed she was busy filling out a form for the UPSC examination for an assistant post. Intrigued, I asked her about the exam, and she explained everything in detail. She suggested that since I had learned typing and shorthand, I should consider applying for the stenographer exam. She also mentioned that some competitive classes were about to start and encouraged me to join, saying it would help with my preparation.

Since I wasn't earning, I approached my father to ask for money to register for the UPSC exam and the competitive classes. He seemed pleased with my initiative. "I'm happy you're planning your future and thinking about settling down," he said. "Although I left a government job to join UNDP, I still feel that government jobs are secure, even if the salary isn't high. Why don't you aim for the IAS exam instead?"

I was confused about what to do or say to my father. I finally said, "Dad, let me first take this assistant or steno exam. If I succeed, I can then consider appearing for the IAS exam."

He simply replied, "Do whatever you wish. Take the money you need from your mother."

I decided to start preparing for the UPSC exam and joined competitive classes. My cousin was more intelligent and knowledgeable than me; she consistently scored higher marks in school. I often had to hear my parents compare me to her, saying, "Work harder and learn from her." However, my real interest lay in cricket.

In the meantime, my father didn't want me sitting idle. He told me, "During these summer holidays, join this packer-movers company. You'll stay busy, learn something useful, and avoid wasting time with friends, which might lead to bad habits. We shouldn't have regrets later."

I felt torn between preparing for the UPSC and taking the job. But as a dutiful son, I joined the company and began working during the day while attending competitive classes in the evening.

Before the exam, my father suggested, "There's a vacancy in the UNDP for a stenographer. You should apply for it. In the mornings, join steno classes to improve your skills. It'll help you get the job."

My schedule became incredibly tight–shorthand and typing classes in the morning, work during the day, and competitive classes in the evening. From 6 a.m. to 10 p.m., I was on the move, working more than 16 hours a day. But I never felt tired or frustrated because I believed I was gaining valuable knowledge and experience.

When the UPSC exam results were announced, I missed qualifying by a few marks. My cousin and her siblings, on the other hand, all passed and secured government jobs. I felt disheartened.

Support of Dad

Sensing my disappointment, my father said, "Don't get upset. I have bigger plans for you. I spoke to a freight forwarder looking for a good packer-mover, and you've got the experience now." He introduced me to the company, and I began handling packing and domestic movements for them.

Opportunity awaiting at family get-together

At a family get-together, my brother-in-law introduced me to his uncle, Mr. Chawla, who worked in the Ministry of External Affairs. During our conversation, Mr. Chawla learned about my business in packing and shipping. He asked, "Are you interested in working for the ministry?"

Mr. Chawla mentioned that there was significant business in handling personal effects and government supplies for missions abroad. I was thrilled and replied, "Why not? When can I start?" He said, "It's not entirely in my hands, but I can introduce you to the right people in Establishment and Administration."

One day, I visited the Ministry with him. He first introduced me to the Attaché of Establishment. S.P., who expressed dissatisfaction with the existing packers. He suggested I quote for a shipment of shoes to be sent abroad. I submitted a quote, which was approved, and successfully handled my first shipment for the ministry. The shipment reached safely and on time. This opened the door for more assignments.

I aimed to expand into handling personal effects as well. Mr. Chawla later introduced me to Ms. Sibal, the admin in charge. Unfortunately, she was transferred before anything could materialize. Eventually, Mr. Sikri took over the same desk and instructed the admin team to invite quotes from us as well.

Within four years, our company gained a solid reputation. Officers began using our services with confidence and trust, making us the preferred agent for all Ministry-related shipments.

Kind help of Mr. K Natwar Singh

At the time, I was outsourcing customs clearance to another company, but I wanted to obtain my own customs license. One day, we handled a shipment for Mr. Natwar Singh, who was highly satisfied with our services and continued to use us regularly. Leveraging his influential position as Secretary, I approached him for help obtaining a custom license. His office directed me to meet the Customs Commissioner.

The Commissioner asked, "Have you applied for the license?"

"Yes, sir. I've already passed the written exam, and I have an interview next week," I replied.

During the interview, the committee asked me several questions:

- **Committee Member:** "Do you have any experience in customs clearance?" **Me:** "Yes, sir. I've personally been involved in clearances, although I've been using another CHA for official filings. I am familiar with all the procedures."
- **Committee Member:** "What does CHA stand for?" **Me:** "Sir, it stands for Custom House Agent."
- **Committee Member:** "What is CIF?" **Me:** "Sir, CIF means cost, insurance, and freight."
- **Committee Member:** "How is duty calculated on CIF?" **Me:** "Sir, in addition to CIF, 1% landing charges are also added."
- **Committee Member:** "Do you know anything about the export-import policy?" **Me:** "Yes, sir. All the procedures, rules, and regulations are documented in the Handbook of Export-Import Procedures. These are governed by the Director General of Foreign Trade, under the Ministry of Commerce. The handbook contains lists of free and restricted goods in its appendices."

Key Milestones:

1. **Obtaining the CHA License**: Successfully passed the exam and earned the CHA license, receiving the prestigious "Card F" for managing customs clearance operations.
2. **Building a Skilled Team**:
   - Trained staff to pass the customs-written examination, enabling them to earn "G Cards" for executing clearance operations independently.
   - Provided opportunities for others to contribute as "H Card" holders, supporting the customs team.
3. **Operational Excellence:**
   - Established a system where staff managed routine clearances effectively, minimizing the need for your presence at the customs warehouse.
   - Personally intervened only in cases involving technical challenges, ensuring high standards of service.
4. **Focus on Personal and Household Goods**: Specialized in handling personal and household goods, including managing "transfer of residence" clearances with a strong understanding of regulations.
5. **Effective Leadership:**
   - Maintained a well-organized team, ensuring smooth operations and compliance with customs regulations.
   - Empowered your team to excel, reducing dependency on your direct involvement.

First speed breaker in my life.

Karma sometimes goes against you, and this episode is something I cannot forget. It still haunts me, leaving a lasting nightmare in my life.

One day, I visited the customs warehouse to meet a customs officer for the renewal of my customs license. Afterward, I went to the customs examination area just to check on the staff and ensure that everything was functioning properly, as it was necessary to keep an eye on them from time to time. While I was there, a gentleman approached me and said, "I am the brother of a woman whose baggage is being cleared by customs. She has asked me to give you Rs.1000 less from the Rs.6000 bill." I remember clearly that our bill was for Rs.6000. I asked him, "Who is the inspector allowing you to reduce our handling charges?" He told me to keep the Rs.1000 and that he would pay me later.

Just then, a group of people gathered around me, and they started questioning why I had taken the money. I explained, "These are my charges." They insisted that I pay the Rs.5000 to the customs inspector. I refused to comply, but the situation escalated. They forcibly took me outside and put me into a tempo traveller, demanding that I give the money to the inspector. I continued to refuse, but they didn't let up. The case was consigned to records at the first stage as no case can be made without customs officers. They took permission to prosecute the custom inspector but the High court dismissed their pleas, and I had to fight for 28 years.

Legal Struggles:

1. **Unjust Detention and Stress:** After being wrongfully detained, the stress of the situation was overwhelming, not only affecting your well-being but also creating deep frustrations within your family.
2. **The Protracted Legal Process:** The case dragged on for **28 years,** causing an immense amount of uncertainty and

difficulty. The legal system seemed to prioritize delays over swift justice, leaving you to endure financial strain and constant anxiety.

3. **Financial Strain:**

   - I faced significant financial challenges during this period, including paying exorbitant legal fees.
   - At one point, I was forced to sell my wife's jewellery to afford the lawyer's fees, illustrating the immense sacrifices you made.

4. **Mental Health Impact:**

   - The constant delays in the case, coupled with the financial burdens, led to **stress and depression**.
   - Managing your emotions and mental health during this prolonged period was an immense challenge, but with the support of your wife and uncle **S.K. Gambhir**, Senior Advocate, was able to push forward.

5. **Final Relief and Justice:**

   - After enduring decades of uncertainty, you finally received justice when the case was dismissed in my Favor.
   - This long journey showed resilience, but also highlighted the flaws in a system that failed to act swiftly and fairly.

6. **Support from Family:**

   - The emotional and financial support from my wife and my uncle, Mr. S K Gambhir Senior Advocate, during this difficult period was pivotal in helping you manage the immense challenges I faced.

- **Refined Commentary on the Legal System**
- A lawyer, before any hearing, often warns clients not to expect miracles from the court—reminding them that *law is law*, with the same definitions and principles applying in every courtroom. However, one court might grant a fair hearing and offer relief, while another might refuse to entertain a case and direct it back to a lower court.
- There is a common perception that the law seems to work more efficiently for politicians or celebrities, leaving the ordinary individual feeling overlooked. This perception arises from high-profile cases garnering extensive media attention and often experiencing faster outcomes, while countless cases involving everyday people move slowly through the judicial process. In reality, the law's framework is designed to serve everyone equally; yet disparities in resources, influence, and public interest can create the impression that not all are treated the same.
- Ultimately, the legal system strives for impartiality, but complexities, procedural delays, and varying judicial interpretations can lead to inconsistent experiences for different litigants. It highlights the need for continuous reforms, transparency, and an unwavering commitment to justice for all—regardless of one's background.

Stress treatment

I remember that I had to go to Dr. Anjali Nagpal, a psychiatrist, for treatment. She gave me a page with the following questions to answer for the next checkup:

1. How long have you been feeling low?
2. Do you still feel hopeless or helpless?

3. Are you feeling weak?
4. Are you losing interest in things?
5. Have you had any fights or arguments?
6. Are you finding it difficult to make decisions?
7. Do you feel guilty or worthless?
8. Have you noticed any changes in your appetite?
9. Is your sleep disturbed?
10. Do you have suicidal thoughts?

I experienced panic attacks during this time and had to take medication for four years. I still take a very mild dose to avoid panic attacks and depression. Overthinking also disturbed my sleep, and after some tests, it was found that I had sleep apnea. This was treated by the well-known Dr. Neeru Bhatia, who advised me to use a CPAP machine at night and gave me the following advice:

- Sleep is essential for forming new memories, consolidating old ones, and removing unnecessary ones.
- Sleep helps maintain and balance our mood, behaviour, and emotions.
- Sleep helps fight infections.
- Sleep is essential for bodybuilding, growth, and rejuvenation.
- Sleep helps us discover novel solutions to complex problems.
- During sleep, all metabolic processes are involved in building organs and tissues, and new molecules are formed.

Dr. Bhatia explained that sleep deprivation in individuals with existing mental health disorders can lead to the worsening of these conditions. Sleep debt, whether short-term or long-term, can result in serious health problems like diabetes, obesity, stroke, heart attacks, immune changes, and high blood pressure. It can also cause mood changes, leading to conditions like depression and bipolar disorder.

The fact is, sleep is a basic necessity of life, as important to our health and well-being as air, food, and water. When we sleep well, we wake up feeling refreshed, alert, and ready to face the day's challenges.

It is often said that the face is the mirror of a person's health, and it would be accurate to add that health is also reflected in a person's sleeping pattern, and vice versa.

Dr. Bhatia also recommended the following foods to aid sleep:

- Yogurt, milk, cheese, oats, bananas, poultry, eggs, peanuts, tuna, tofu, miso, carrots, goya, and kombu. These foods contain the amino acid tryptophan, which, when combined with calcium and magnesium, helps the brain produce the sleep-inducing substance melatonin.

She also advised avoiding coffee and tea after 4 PM, as caffeine has an awakening effect on the body. It tightens muscles to prepare for action and causes the liver to release sugar into the bloodstream for extra energy.

Alcohol affects REM sleep and often leads to waking up throughout the night. Studies show that white tea and chamomile tea, which have high concentrations of polyphenols, are more effective in combating aging and promoting better sleep. A cup of white tea is much better than drinking orange juice. White tea also helps control cholesterol, blood sugar levels, and improves circulation. People who drank alcohol took longer to fall asleep.

As a sleep specialist, Dr. Bhatia advised me not to ignore sleep problems and to seek medical advice early on to prevent minor issues from becoming major sleep disturbances that could affect creativity and overall quality of life. She emphasized that solutions to sleep problems can significantly improve your overall well-being.

Tips for Better Sleep:

- Sleep in darkness.
- Avoid excessive use of stimulants, like gadgets, as they suppress melatonin production.
- Foods like bananas, ginger, garlic, tomatoes, radishes, and red wine are natural sources of melatonin.
- Foods that contain tryptophan can also be consumed in the evening. Tryptophan helps produce serotonin, which is needed to make melatonin. Dairy products, soy, seafood, and nuts are high in tryptophan.
- Chamomile tea is also recommended for better sleep.
- The blue light emitted from laptops and cell phones interferes with melatonin production, leading to insomnia. Gadgets should be turned off at least an hour before bed and kept at a distance while sleeping.

Additional Useful Tips:

- Get a new pillow if needed.
- Open your blinds or curtains when you wake up.
- Only go to bed when you're feeling sleepy.
- Get some exercise during the day.

Additional Tips for Better Sleep:

- Spend some time outdoors in sunlight or natural light.

- Make your bedroom as restful as possible.
- Develop a calming routine before bed, such as brushing your teeth, drinking warm milk, light reading, or practicing relaxation and breathing exercises.
- Use your bedroom for sleep only.
- Yoga can also help improve sleep. Some yoga poses can be done in bed, but it's recommended to start under the supervision of a qualified yoga teacher.

Simple Yoga Poses for Beginners:

- Head-to-toe knee pose (Janu Sirsasana)
- Thread the Needle (Urdhva Mukha Pasasana)
- Reclined Twist
- Nighttime Goddess Stretch
- Child's Pose
- Cat and Cow Pose
- Twist Pose
- Rock-a-bye Roll
- Viparita Karani Yoga (Leg up the Wall Pose)
- Vajrasana

Other Techniques:

- Meditation
- Chanting
- Yoga Nidra (Shavasana)

I would like to express my gratitude to Dr. Manvir Bhatia for her valuable information, advice, and guidance, especially through her book, *The Sleep Solution: Secrets for a Good Night's Sleep*, which has been extremely helpful.

While I've listed a few bedtime yoga poses, detailed instructions can be found through various videos available online, including on YouTube.

My personal favourite is Yoga Nidra, and it has helped me immensely.

Yoga Nidra Practice for Relaxation:

- Lie down in **Corpse Pose** with your arms at your sides, palms facing upward, and your feet gently about two feet apart.
- Close your eyes gently and take three deep breaths.
- As you inhale deeply, chant "OM" three times, feeling each vibration in your body.
- Feel your body relax and mentally scan your body with gratitude, thanking the divine for its proper functioning.

Mantra for Gratitude and Peace:

- "Thank you, God. I am a hundred times better than others."
- "God, bless me with peace, so I can meditate, chant, and experience ecstasy."
- "I am going for Yoga Nidra. I will awaken; I will not sleep. I will remain alert."

Body Awareness:

- Focus on your right foot, right knee, right thigh and right hip.
- Now focus on your left foot, left knee, left thigh and left hip.
- Bring awareness to your right hand, right fingers, right elbow, and right shoulder.
- Move your awareness to your left hand, left fingers, left elbow, and left shoulder.
- Let the awareness flow through your whole body: relax your backbone, head, ears, nose, left side of the face, right side of the face, abdomen, stomach, chest, throat, upper lip, lower lip, teeth (upper and lower).

Deep Breathing and Relaxation:

- Take deep breaths, counting to 15 with each inhale and exhale, and become fully aware of your entire body.
- If you are not yet feeling sleepy, extend the practice further.

Visualization for Deep Relaxation:

- Imagine yourself lying on a comfortable bed, in a spacious room with plenty of space on both sides, and in front of you.
- There is a bed table on the left and right, and a mirror nearby.
- Visualize a window with a beautiful view of a green park.

- See people sitting on benches, observing the lush green trees and colorful flowers. Feel the fragrance of the flowers in the air.
- Visualize a fountain nearby, with water gently falling and flowing, creating a peaceful, calming sound.

Feeling light and at peace, I begin to notice people strolling and jogging nearby. Children are joyfully playing, their laughter filling the air.

- Yoga mats are laid out on the ground, with people practicing yoga, performing pranayama, and deep breathing exercises. A **yoga guru** is guiding them with calm wisdom.
- There is **gym equipment** scattered around, all in use, as people engage in various physical activities, enjoying the lively atmosphere.
- I watch as the **sun rises**, a big red bulb emerging from the horizon, casting beautiful, shifting colours across the clouds–an ever-changing and captivating scene.
- The **sound of harmonium and drum music** fills the air, a melody of bhajans praising **Shiva**. I see a stunning **photo of Shiva**, radiating peace and strength. The candlelight flickers gently, and the air is filled with the soothing fragrance of **agarbatti** (incense).
- I sit back, deeply enjoying the melody of the bhajans. It's a moment of serenity, one that can only be felt in the sacred atmosphere of **India**–a **wonderful experience of Shiva** and divine presence.

Connection with Nature:

- Now, I imagine myself sitting at the **shore of the sea**, watching the activities in the water. I see **fishing boats**, people **swimming**, and others enjoying the gentle **current of the ocean**. The scene is full of life and joy.
- Outside, the world is full of activities: people **strolling, playing basketball, enjoying a picnic**, and **reading books**. The sun begins to set, filling the sky with vibrant **colours**, the clouds painted in beautiful shades. The view of the sky is mesmerizing–what a **lucky moment** to witness nature's splendour.

Journey in Nature:

- I begin to roam in the **jungle**, inhaling the fragrances of burning **incense**–a peaceful, sacred atmosphere. As I walk along a **narrow pathway**, I feel calm and serene.
- I come across a **little hut** and step through the gate, greeted again by the fragrant scent of **haven material.**
- Inside, there is a **large picture of a saint**, his smile radiant and his eyes full of light. I feel a deep sense of peace as I gaze at his face.
- **I bow my head in reverence**, overcome by the grace of this divine presence. I feel humbled and blessed, my heart full of gratitude.

A Moment of Reflection and Gratitude:

I asked the Divine to be kind to me and share some of its divinity, to help me find peace and strength. I rubbed my palms, gently touched my eyes, and took a few deep breaths, allowing myself to relax and drift into a peaceful state of mind.

Often in life, we feel hopeless, helpless, or overwhelmed by the challenges we face. But it's important not to run away from these problems. We must face them with strength, trust in the Almighty, and give our best efforts. With time, our hard work and perseverance will lead us to success, and the results will touch our feet, guiding us to overcome any obstacle in our path.

A Visit to Neeraj's Family:

Today, I received a call from Neeraj. He invited me to a get-together to mark the **first death anniversary (Barsi)** of his mother. It had been a long time since we had met, and he warmly asked me to come. I told him that I would definitely attend and expressed my desire to meet everyone. He shared the address and time with me, and I made my way there as per the itinerary.

I arrived around 3 PM and was greeted by Neeraj's father, who looked visibly weak. Concerned, I asked, "Uncle, you've lost a lot of weight. Are you feeling all right?" He replied, "Yes, since her departure, I've been feeling very alone. It's hard to pass the time, and all the constant thinking has led to depression and hypertension."

I comforted him, saying, "Uncle, you are too strong for this. You need to take care of yourself. Why not consider joining a senior citizen's group? They meet often, celebrate birthdays, organize social gatherings, and even travel together. It keeps them busy and happy, even if they are alone. You have Grandpa, Neeraj, and your sister around. You can stay active, meet new people, and share your feelings and laughter. Don't let these things weigh too heavily on your heart. Stay connected, and it will help you feel better." He promised to think about it.

The Ceremony:

The ceremony began with a **Havan (Yajna)**, followed by heartfelt words from Neeraj. He stood before everyone and spoke, his voice full of emotion:

"Thank you all for being here today. Your presence means a lot to us as we remember my mother. We can never forget her memory and all that she did for us. Mom, you are in heaven, and I'm so grateful for the love and guidance you always gave me. I still remember your gentle care–reminding us to eat well, travel safely, and always giving advice. I owe everything I am today to you, including my Chartered Accountant degree. You taught us how to live as a family, how to love, and how to stay graceful through life's challenges. I cherish every moment we shared."

A Message of Love and Strength:

Today, on this difficult day, I can only send love and strength to all who are grieving. My school friend Ashok, who is here with me, often writes beautiful poems and stories. I asked him to share something with us,

"Hello everyone, recently I had the chance to listen to many speakers, including the pandit ji (preacher), who shared his thoughts about life. One thing he said stuck with me–no one can escape the inevitability of leaving this world. Some leave early, some later, but we all have to go one day.

We all wish for our loved ones, especially our guardians, to always stay with us. As long as their hand is over our head, we never feel the passage of time; we still feel like their children. But, as the Creator designed it, we must all leave one day after playing our part in the grand play of life. We are but actors in this world.

This made me think of a poem about life, which I would like to share:

Life Is a Circle:

Life is a circle, expanding and contracting, Shaped by age and the flow of time.

Look back at my childhood, so close to my mother, A small circle, yet filled with warmth and wonder.

As I grew, the circle expanded, Filled with friends, play, and study. Then came youth, and my eyes, too, expanded, Looking at the world through a new lens, Noticing the opposite sex.

We tasted the sweetness of weddings, But life soon filled us with responsibility. The weight of money and work, I remember my wife once said, "If you wish, I'll take a job." "Why not," I said, "If it'll raise our standard of living."

And so, twenty-five years passed in the blink of an eye. Last night, I was suddenly woken up by my wife, She said, "Today is your 75th birthday, the Golden Jubilee. Look, the kids and grandkids are carefree, But they've forgotten your special day."

I smiled and told her, "Don't think negatively, always think positively." Just then, the doorbell rang. The kids and grandkids were at the door, With cake and gifts in their hands, Ready to celebrate.

And so, my 75th birthday was celebrated, With laughter, joy, and love all around.

Just a few moments ago, my circle was so small—just me and my wife.

Then, in the blink of an eye, my circle expanded at full swing, and that was the happiest moment of my life. It felt like everything was complete, everyone gathered to share in the joy of the occasion.

The praises and greetings for the poem I had shared in life were overwhelming.

Neeraj's sister, Reeta, also spoke about their mother, and her emotions overcame her. She started weeping and sobbing uncontrollably. Her father and Neeraj rushed to console her, showing compassion and care, trying to ease her sadness. Eventually, she calmed down, and the house quieted as everyone began to leave after the prayer event.

As I prepared to leave, I told Neeraj, “Please give me permission to leave now. "He held my hand firmly and said, “I will not let you go, Ashok. We haven’t met in five years. You must stay and have dinner with us.” I replied, “I really must go; I have some urgent work tomorrow.” But Neeraj’s grandfather, who overheard our conversation, immediately called my father and asked for permission for me to stay. Feeling helpless, I agreed, realizing I had no choice but to remain there for the evening.

Neeraj and I were gossiping in his room on the first floor when Reeta came in. She asked, “What’s going on here? What are you two talking about?” I stayed silent, but Neeraj responded, “We’re just reminiscing about life after school.” Then, Reeta said something that caught me off guard, “Ashok, why are you so quiet? What’s on your mind?” I was surprised by her directness, and in my panic, I stumbled over my words, “Nothing, we’re just talking about life.” Reeta’s smile softened, and she said, “If it’s something secret, I can leave, you know.” Neeraj quickly reassured her, “No, sister, there’s nothing to hide. You can stay, and we can talk openly.”

Reeta said, "Ashok, I hope you have a girlfriend."

I was surprised by her question, and without thinking, I replied, "Not so far, but I do like someone. I'm rather attracted to her, though I haven't had the courage to talk to her yet."

Reeta raised her eyebrows, clearly intrigued. "Why haven’t you proposed to her?" she asked.

"Actually," I began hesitantly, "my cousin was in the same competition classes as me, and there were four girls in their friend circle, including her. Unfortunately, my cousin never introduced me to her, and I never found her alone to gather the courage to speak to her."

Reeta looked at me with a mischievous smile and said, "Can I help you?"

I laughed nervously, unsure of what she meant. "How could you possibly help?" I asked, curious but sceptical.

Reeta smiled and said, “Don’t worry, Ashok. Leave it to me. I’ll ask my friend and try to find out about her. If she’s in Moti Lal Nehru College and active in the union, it shouldn’t be too difficult.”

Her confidence gave me a sense of relief and excitement, but I was also nervous. What if Lata didn’t remember me? What if she wasn’t interested? A mix of hope and doubt swirled in my mind.

“When will you talk to your friend?” I asked hesitantly.

“I’ll call her tomorrow,” Reeta replied. “Give me a day or two. I’ll let you know whatever I find out.”

“Thank you, Reeta,” I said sincerely. “You have no idea how much this means to me.”

Reeta smiled warmly. “Don’t worry, Ashok. Sometimes life gives us little opportunities to pursue our happiness. Don’t let fear hold you back.”

Her words stayed with me, echoing a sense of encouragement and optimism. That night, as I lay in bed, I couldn’t help but imagine what might happen if things worked out. Would I finally get a chance to talk to Lata? Would she feel the same way?

The following morning, Reeta approached me with a determined look. “I’ll call my friend today. Just give me some time, and I’ll update you by the evening.”

I nodded eagerly. “Sure, Reeta. I’ll be waiting.”

As the day went on, I felt a mix of anticipation and nervousness. Every time my phone buzzed, my heart skipped a beat, wondering if it was

Reeta with news. By evening, she called me into the living room with a knowing smile.

“Well, Ashok,” she began, “I talked to my friend. She does know a Lata in MotiLal Nehru College, and she’s pretty sure it’s the same person. She said she’ll confirm and arrange an introduction if everything checks out.”

I couldn’t believe what I was hearing. “Really? She’ll arrange a meeting?”

“Yes,” Reeta replied. “But don’t get too excited yet. Let her confirm first. Patience is key.”

I nodded, though it was hard to contain my excitement. For the first time, it felt like my dream might actually come true.

I asked Reeta, how is your life going on?

Reeta replied, her voice heavy with a mix of frustration and sadness. "He doesn't fight with me, but his indifference is worse than any argument. His absences and unwillingness to communicate make me feel invisible. I’ve tried to talk to him, to make him understand, but it’s like he’s in his own world, and I’m just... there.”

Neeraj clenched his fists, his anger barely contained. “This is unacceptable! Didi, you deserve so much better than this. I don’t understand why you didn’t share all this earlier. We’re your family! How can we help if we don’t know what’s going on?”

Reeta sighed, her eyes brimming with unshed tears. “Neeraj, it’s not that simple. I didn’t want to burden anyone, especially when Mom was already unwell. And now, I feel trapped. What will people say? How will society judge me? I don’t even know if I have the strength to make a drastic decision like leaving him.”

Neeraj stood up abruptly, pacing the room. “Forget society, Didi! You need to think about your happiness and well-being. If he doesn’t value you or care for you, why should you suffer in silence? We'll support you in whatever decision you make. But please, don't live like this."

I decided to intervene, trying to diffuse the growing tension. "Neeraj, I understand your frustration, but we need to approach this with calm and clarity. Reeta Didi, you've been incredibly strong to endure all this. But maybe it's time to consider what you truly want and deserve in life. Let's involve the elders and talk it out. Perhaps there's a way to resolve this without escalating things immediately."

Reeta nodded weakly; her gaze fixed on the floor. "Maybe you're right, Ashok. But I feel so lost. I don't even know where to start."

Neeraj knelt beside her; his voice soft but firm. "Start by trusting us, Didi. We're here for you. You're not alone in this. We'll figure it out together."

At that moment, I realized the depth of their sibling bond. Despite the pain and anger, there was an unwavering determination in Neeraj to protect his sister. I silently prayed that their efforts would lead to a resolution that brought Reeta the peace and happiness she deserved.

No, never. The only issue is that he is always on tour and does not provide money so that I can do something here.

There are kitty parties, and it is a beautiful and clean city. Without money, I cannot do anything.

"Neeraj, why don't you take up a job there?" "He is against the idea of me doing any job," she replied. "Thank God I don't have a baby; otherwise, things would have been worse."

Neeraj's blood pressure seemed to rise as he exclaimed, "Sister, this is all your fault! You should have told us at least."

"That's why that bastard hasn't come here even today, even in this mourning hour. Disgusting."

"You don't need to go back to that hell, my sister. We will take care of you—we're still alive. It means you don't consider us your own family. We share blood relations. It is my moral duty to help you. I am willing to help you; just let me know what I can do."

I was too upset by their conversation and sat quietly, unsure of what to say. Finally, I suggested, "Neeraj, don't panic. Stay calm and involve the elders. Act accordingly. Haste makes waste. I wish and pray to the Almighty from the core of my heart that everything is settled amicably and joyfully. I'm sure God is great and will make a way for betterment."

At that moment, the servant came in, and we all went quiet for a moment. He said, "Please come to the dining table; the food is ready, and everyone is waiting."

We proceeded to the ground floor, where a buffet was laid out. Paper plates were arranged, and everyone picked up their plates, served themselves, and walked toward the chairs to sit. Some people were eating on the floor as well.

The three of us started eating half-heartedly. I noticed that Neeraj and Reeta were eating very slowly. Their faces showed their pain, and they left their plates half-finished before retreating to their respective rooms.

I went to his grandfather's room and said, "Please excuse me; I'm going to my house."

He replied, "But I heard from Neeraj that you were staying here tonight."

"I agreed earlier," I explained, "but I need to leave for some urgent work. I do want to meet you again, though, to discuss your and my grandfather's life in Pakistan."

"No issue," he said. "This is your home—you can come anytime. Whatever I remember, I will definitely share with you."

As I was leaving through the gate, Neeraj saw me from the balcony and called out, "Ashok, where are you going?"

Please excuse me, I want to go,

Nothing doing; you promised to stay, come in, Neeraj said,

I had no option but to return and sleep in the Neeraj Room. In the morning, I heard noise and saw Reeta was being taken to Hospital in Ambulance and I too rushed and boarded the van.

The ambulance ride was tense, filled with silent prayers and the occasional beep of the medical equipment monitoring Reeta. Neeraj sat beside her, holding her hand tightly, his face pale with worry. I couldn't help but think about everything she had shared the previous night—the pain, the isolation, and the emotional toll her circumstances had taken on her. It all seemed to culminate in this moment, her body crying out for help those words hadn't been able to express.

At the hospital, the medical staff acted swiftly, taking Reeta into the emergency room. Neeraj and I were left in the waiting area, pacing anxiously. I tried to console him. "She's strong, Neeraj. She'll pull through. The doctors are doing their best."

He nodded but said nothing, his worry etched deep into his face. After what felt like an eternity, a doctor came out. "She's stable now. It was a mild heart attack, but she's lucky she received immediate care. She'll need to stay under observation for a few days, and we'll run some tests to determine the underlying cause."

Neeraj exhaled sharply, relief washing over him. "Thank you, doctor. Can we see her?"

"She's still resting, but one person can visit briefly," the doctor replied.

Neeraj looked at me, his eyes silently asking for support. "You go first," I said. "She needs to see you."

He nodded and went inside. I sat down, my mind racing. Reeta's situation was a stark reminder of how emotional stress and unresolved issues could manifest physically. I felt a surge of responsibility to help her and Neeraj navigate these turbulent waters.

When Neeraj returned, he seemed a little calmer. "She's awake but weak. She asked about you, Ashok."

I got up and went inside. Reeta was lying on the bed, her face pale but her eyes open. She gave me a faint smile.

I said gently, "You scared us all. How are you feeling now?"

"I'm okay," she whispered, her voice barely audible. "Thank you for coming with Neeraj. It means a lot."

I sat beside her, trying to be as comforting as possible. "You need to focus on getting better now. Everything else can wait. We're all here for you.

Tears welled up in her eyes. "I don't want to go back to that house, Ashok. I can't take it anymore."

"You won't have to," I said firmly. "We'll figure everything out once you're better. For now, rest and let the doctors take care of you."

She nodded weakly, and I stayed with her until the nurse came in to check on her. As I walked back to the waiting area, I knew that this was just the beginning of a long journey for Reeta and her family. But one thing was certain: she wasn't alone anymore.

Neeraj immediately called his brother-in-law and informed him about Reeta's condition. "You need to come to Max Hospital," he said urgently. "Didi isn't well."

"What happened?" His brother-in-law asked, alarmed.

Neeraj quickly briefed him about the situation. "Oh my god," came the reply. "Let me check the flight schedule. Don't worry; I'll get there as soon as possible."

Meanwhile, Reeta was moved to the ICU for further treatment, as she remained unconscious. I placed a reassuring hand on Neeraj's shoulder. "Don't panic or get upset. My intuition tells me she'll be alright."

A while later, the doctor came out and motioned for us to follow him to his office. Once seated, he asked, "Was she experiencing any of the following symptoms recently?

- Irrational fears
- Difficulty falling asleep
- Tense muscles
- Restlessness
- Agitation
- Fatigue
- Inability to concentrate"

Neeraj hesitated before answering, "Sir, she only mentioned yesterday that she's been feeling anxious, stressed, and worried because she's struggling to adjust to her life with her husband."

The doctor nodded thoughtfully. "These symptoms are common signs of anxiety."

Neeraj's voice quivered slightly as he asked, "Is it serious, doctor?"

The doctor reassured him, "There's no need to worry. We'll conduct a thorough physical examination and run a few tests, such as blood and urine analysis, to rule out any underlying health issues. Once she stabilizes, we'll ask her a few targeted questions to better understand her mental health. This will help us diagnose her condition accurately."

He continued, “Based on the diagnosis, we’ll create a treatment plan tailored to her needs. This may involve a combination of medication and psychotherapy, also known as talk therapy.”

The next day, Reeta looked more stable, and the doctor came to examine her. He began with a few questions.

“How is your sleep?” he asked.

Reeta replied softly, “I am not getting sound sleep

Then you should consult your doctor in case you have trouble falling asleep.

Start practicing yoga and meditation, this may help you rest and recover. Visualization techniques also help in relaxation.

Have a healthy **diet rich in whole grains, fresh vegetables and fruits, nut** tofu, Miso, Carrot, Goya, Kombu etc. **this also reduces anxiety.**

You must avoid alcohol, nicotine, caffeine and other recreational drugs as they worsen the symptoms and overall health condition.

Regular physical activity and exercise is effective stress busters and mood elevators.

Doctors, how many members are in your family and how are your relations with them?

Reeta looked at her brother and me and replied, Doctor sahib, I am mostly alone at home And my husband mostly remains outstation in India or abroad. Out of 365 days he is out of station

For 265 days. Here also he goes early and comes late from the office. Very difficult to pass the time.

Doctor; I can advise you to avoid isolating yourself with your worries. Social interaction and sharing your thoughts can help reduce anxiety. Get proper treatment, it is curable, if ignored it can be serious like phobia, mental health, depression, PTSD, diabetes, thyroid, cardiac/respiratory disorders, rare tumours etc. Apart from these, certain medications are all known to elevate anxiety as a side effect.

When the doctor left, Neeraj saw Jija jee, brother-in-law who had not yet come. I feel you should Ignore him, divorce him and stay with us. You are well educated MBA; you will have a lot of opportunities here in Delhi.

At this hour, I got the following feeling:

Tough times are like physical exercise – you may not like it while you are doing it, but tomorrow you will be stronger because of it. Just like muscles ache and feel sore when you push them beyond their comfort zone, life's challenges often bring discomfort and struggle. But over time, as you endure and persist, you develop resilience, patience, and a deeper understanding of yourself. The hardships you face today shape you into a more capable and confident person, ready to take on whatever life throws your way. Every difficult situation you overcome is like adding strength to your character, just as every workout adds strength to your body. In hindsight, you realize that the pain and effort were essential for your growth and success.

Just to change the topic.

I told Neeraj that his mother was alright, and how and why she passed away so soon.

He said, you remember when one teacher came to our school to lecture on psychology?

Yes, yes, I said.

Her taxi was delayed, and I discussed and consulted a lot with her about Anxiety and Depression.

She had a remarkable knowledge of this subject. Whatever the doctor had explained, she also conveyed the same to me. "I lost my mother due to anxiety and depression," he said tearfully, "and I will never let her leave us." He began to cry.

I placed my arm on his shoulder, hugged him, and reassured him, "Don't worry. Everything will be alright."

Reeta re-united with Mukesh

Reeta had been staying at her father's house for over a year, undergoing treatment. She had recovered significantly and had begun applying for jobs. During this time, a vacancy opened up in Neeraj's office. Neeraj spoke to his new boss, who had recently moved from the USA, and handed him Reeta's bio-data. After reviewing it, the boss remarked, "I know her! We were friends. It will be wonderful if she works here, but don't reveal anything about me. Let's surprise her."

Neeraj called his sister to Mumbai and then dialled the intercom. "Reeta is here," he told his boss. "Can I send her in?"

"Yes, send her in," came the reply.

Reeta entered the office, and to her astonishment, she saw Mukesh—her old boyfriend. She froze, tears welling in her eyes. Stunned, her throat went dry, and she was unable to speak. Just as she was about to faint, Mukesh extended his hand, steadied her, and guided her to the sofa. He handed her a glass of water, and after a while, she regained her composure.

"Mukesh," she whispered, "what a life... we meet again. You're here, and now I'm working with you. But..." Her voice broke as she added bitterly, "You deceived me. I'm married now. You ruined my life. My partner is rude, and he never accepted me. He's always away on official tours. You know I had panic attacks and suffered from depression and anxiety. I've been undergoing treatment for over a year. I'm only now beginning to recover."

Mukesh, visibly pained, said, "Reeta, I apologize for all the suffering you've endured. I never intended to hurt you. I'm still willing to accept you."

Reeta broke down, clung to him tightly, and sobbed bitterly. Mukesh gently guided her to sit down and said, "Relax. Let me call your brother."

He called Neeraj and explained, "Your sister and I were close friends in college. Circumstances took me abroad for my studies, and I feel responsible for the pain she has endured. I've told her I'm ready to accept her now, but the decision is hers—to divorce him or not."

Neeraj intervened, "Sister, go ahead. Take the divorce and start fresh. Mukesh is a wonderful person."

Three months passed. Reeta, now working with Mukesh and enjoying her time with both him and Neeraj, had found happiness. Her health improved dramatically, and she stopped taking her medications.

Reeta eventually filed for divorce, and after a year, the judge granted the separation. She began living unofficially with Mukesh, and her father soon fixed the date for their marriage.

Neeraj called me and briefed me about everything.

He also briefed me about his affairs with the Maharashtrian girl working in the same office.

I was anxious to know more about her and he praised a lot about her nature, her beauty and other things but she is not a good organizer, her things are a mess in the office as well as at her house. I have to train her, rather I am training her but habits are hardly changed. I cannot be hard on her otherwise she will mind and I don't want to disturb her as she is quite sensitive. This is the only bad habit she has.

I asked Neeraj, "Didn't you attend a workshop on handling bad habits and coping with them in a systematic, professional manner?"

Neeraj sighed and replied, “Yes, I did, but there’s a huge difference between theoretical knowledge and practical application.”

He continued, “The real issue is, we keep accumulating things in our cupboards and never take the time to sort them out. We should make it a habit to regularly review and remove what we no longer use. Sure, some items have sentimental value because they were gifted by someone special—those can be kept separately. But most of the other unused items? They just add to the mess.

“When you need something, you waste time searching through a pile of clutter. Worse, in the process, you create more mess. Prioritization is key: organize daily-use items separately from partywear or occasional items.

“If we can’t bring ourselves to throw away unused things, why not donate them? There are so many NGOs that accept clothing, belts, socks, bedding, books, paintings, and even undergarments for free distribution to the poor. What might be insignificant to us could be a blessing to someone else. Not only will you feel lighter, but you’ll also experience gratitude, and your cupboards will be cleaner, with everything visible and easy to find.

“At the office, I’ve trained my assistant a bit. I taught her how to keep files organized so that they can be found immediately when needed. It’s not rocket science—it’s just a matter of overcoming laziness. If you put things back in their place right away and avoid piling them up, you’ll feel more confident. You’ll know exactly where everything is, and assignments can be completed without delays.

“And let’s be honest, how many times have we apologized to a guest, saying, ‘Sorry, my room’s a mess’? If we follow a simple system, we won’t have to feel regretful or guilty anymore.”

Neeraj's practical wisdom left a lasting impression, emphasizing the importance of decluttering not just our spaces, but also our minds and lives.

Further discussion on Reeta's wedding

I told "Neeraj, I'm so happy for her. She's had a really tough time. Thank God things are looking better. I pray that God never lets such bad days come even for our enemies. I'm really looking forward to your invitation for Reeta's wedding. Please convey my best wishes to her."

Neeraj responded, "Sure, you're truly my best friend."

Ashok continued, "I'm still playing cricket. Whenever you come to Delhi next, let's play together."

Neeraj laughed, "I'm a bit out of touch, but sure, I'd love to play."

That day, Neeraj's grandfather came over with his son (Neeraj's father) to invite us to the wedding. I thought the invitation must be for Reeta's wedding, so I asked for permission to open the card. To my surprise, the wedding card was for both Reeta and Neeraj. I jumped up in excitement and said, "Wow, both weddings together! What great news! Congratulations, Uncle. This is really wonderful. I'm so happy, and we will definitely come to Mumbai for the wedding."

Uncle smiled and said, "Now, it's your turn. When will you be getting married?" He then asked, "I hope you must have a girlfriend by now."

Shyly, I replied, "No, Uncle, I don't have one yet. I haven't thought about it. I'm still struggling to settle down. Once I do, then I'll think about it."

Uncle added, "But Neeraj was saying you liked a girl in college. Did you get her address?"

My face went pale as my father was with me, and I was caught off guard. It felt like I couldn't even draw blood if I cut my finger. I was stunned and didn't know how to respond. My father, hearing this, said, "I'm sorry, I'm just hearing about this college girl from you. He never mentioned her to me."

I quickly explained, “Dad, you know, at this age, all girls seem attractive. That doesn’t mean we’re involved. I don’t know anything about her.”

Neeraj’s father apologized, “I’m sorry for putting you in this awkward position. I didn’t mean to. It just slipped out.” He added, “I’m not sure about the whole story—it might just be a rumour.”

My dad took it lightly and said, “We’re in a modern society, and I have no objection if you choose your own partner.”

After a while, they left the house, saying they had more places to visit to distribute cards.

My father looked at me and smiled. “I didn’t realize my son had grown up. Tell me more about this girl. Don’t be shy. Treat me as a friend. I’d be happy to help.”

I hesitated, but then replied, “To be honest, I don’t really know much about her. I just found out she’s in Moti Lal College.”

Dad, sensing my reluctance, asked, “Are you serious about this girl? If you are, I can inquire with some friends who are professors there.”

I quickly said, “No, Dad, please don’t get involved. It’ll be embarrassing for her.”

"Approaching through a professor wouldn't be a good idea," I said. Dad replied, "Alright, as you wish," and went to his room. Before leaving, he appreciated my decision to say that I wasn’t settled yet and needed time to settle first.

Visit at Neeraj’s house

Today, I had some work in Noida, and I decided to visit Neeraj’s house to meet his grandfather and learn more about their life in Pakistan before the partition. I wasn’t sure why I was so curious to know, but I felt the need to understand.

I reached their house, and Reeta opened the door. She smiled and said, “Oh, Ashok! What brings you here during working hours?”

I replied, “Well, I had some work here and also wanted to learn more about Pakistan from your grandfather, as I’m planning to write some chapters in my forthcoming book.”

She exclaimed, “Wow, you’re a writer too? I didn’t know that. Be sure to give me a copy when it’s ready!”

I added, “Sure, I will.”

She seemed surprised and I said, “I thought you were in Mumbai.”

She smiled and said, “Yes, I am, but I’m here for some shopping related to my wedding.” She continued, “Grandfather is in that room. Should I bring you tea or something cold?”

I said, “No, thank you. I just had some.”

I went to his room and asked if he could share details about his and my grandfather’s life in Pakistan.

He looked at me thoughtfully and said, “Son, why do you want to reopen those old wounds?”

He paused for a moment before continuing,

Life was going well there, we were established. I had a big house, about 4,000 yards. We constructed houses at the back, and the front area was open, where we used to sit in groups, playing cards, and drinking. Some landowners would come over and have hookah (hubble-bubble). We would chant bhajans and poets would recite shayari. Poetry, It was a great time. Hindus and Muslims lived like brothers and sisters. We used to visit each other during festivals and weddings.

"What about law and order at that time?" I asked.

He replied, "It was almost the same as here, but theft and murder happened there as well."

"I remember once my cousin's husband was away on a tour, and a neighbour entered her house. She noticed him in advance and asked her daughter to hide under the bed. She should have stayed quiet, but instead, she said, 'Suhail Bhai, brother, do you only have my house to steal jewellery from?'"

"He said, 'Oh, you have recognized me.' Then he stabbed her several times, and she died. The next day, her daughter came to us and revealed the incident. The man was arrested, but we lost her. I was shattered, and it took me months to recover. After this, I started looking at them with doubt and misgiving. I stopped attending any of their functions, and we all decided not to invite them to any of our occasions."

"Once, my cousin, who lived three blocks away, went to Delhi for a wedding. While he was away, someone occupied his house and tied up an elephant there. The man was involved in politics and was a crook, so nobody could do anything."

Having the guts to ask him to vacate the house was impossible. My cousin stayed with me for six months, and no government authorities did anything because nobody complained about the situation. Unofficially, we knew some police officers, and we informed them, but they advised us to remain silent for the moment. They said they would guide us on what to do. There's a saying, 'If God is kind, everything goes well.'

One day, the elephant crushed the goon, and the police took both the elephant and the goon away. The same police then told us to go quickly and take possession of our house. Luckily, we were able to reclaim the house; otherwise, there was no chance.

We then heard that the partition of India was happening. We were all blank and stunned because our hometown, Gujranwala, would be on the Pakistan side. All the Hindus got together and decided to leave the area, marching towards Amritsar. People were looting houses and shops, killing people openly, and the police had disappeared. We had no other option but to take the train to Amritsar. But we were scared as the riots had spread on a large scale. On the train, we kept praying to Waheguru, asking God to help us reach Amritsar safely.

We travelled as a group, and along the way, many Sikhs and Hindu Sabha volunteers helped us a lot. I can honestly say that we reached safely because of the help from Sikhs and Hindu Sabha groups. In Amritsar, things were also out of control; there was chaos. Disturbances were at their peak, and rumours spread that houses were being burned and shops looted here as well. We stayed for about a week. We were very lucky to be on the first train, and in the second train, there was a lot of bloodshed. Many people lost their lives—so many that you couldn't even count the casualties. It was horrible. The partition led to mass violence, including massacres at the border regions. Millions of people were killed, and millions became refugees. We were one of them.

At the refugee camps, I remember we couldn't sleep for a week due to fear. We didn't know if the person next to us was Hindu or Muslim. If we sent anyone for food, we couldn't relax until they returned safely. It was a daily occurrence to hear that houses were on fire and shops were being looted. I remember there was a girl on our train who was so beautiful. One of her shoulders was covered, while the other side was exposed. Someone might have torn her clothes in an attempt to overpower her or might have tried to rape her. I showed some courage and went near her, saying, 'Beta, son, you must be feeling cold. Take this bedsheet to cover yourself.' Her eyes showed thanks, but she couldn't speak a word. I continued, 'Do you need food? We have a little bit.' She pointed to her mouth and gave me a thumbs-up. I understood that she wanted food, so I gave her some. She folded her hands and thanked me. Later, I found out that she had lost her entire family and was now alone and homeless. I couldn't do much for her because we, too, were homeless, but I placed my hand on her head and blessed her. There was no governance, no law and order. In such an atmosphere, how could we eat? How could we sleep?

One of our cousins was sent to Delhi to look into the situation further."

Some accommodation was arranged, and later, we all reached Delhi. Some settled in Lajpat Nagar, some in Kalkaji, Mehrauli, etc. Again, we started our lives from zero, and slowly we worked hard. I will tell you about your grandfather. He started a general store here, but the clients were not coming. He began selling rice and pulses at cost price, and everybody said, "What are you doing? How will you feed such a big family?" His management strategy started to work, and his sales reached their peak. We were curious about his thinking and management style.

He said, "I sell 50 bags of foodstuff per day and sell jute bags for Rs. 10 each, making Rs. 500 daily, which is enough for my family." He was a great entrepreneur. Later, his business expanded to 20 villages near Mehrauli. I was truly his big admirer. I further told Neeraj, "Yes, he was a very nice person. Whenever I went to his shop, he either offered me toffee or gave me money to buy ice cream."

He continued, "These rulers and their generations are still in power," and he got unconscious while sobbing. I shook him but got no response. I put my hand near his nostrils—he was still breathing. I rushed to the kitchen, grabbed a glass of water, and sprinkled it on his face. He regained consciousness, and I thanked God.

I was sitting beside him when I realized he was better now, but I was upset to hear his story. I thought that not only he but also lakhs of people must have suffered. I thought of my grandfather; he must have faced a lot of issues and problems. See, time is never the same; it brings so many ups and downs, and finally, you thank God when everything gets back to normal.

I tried several times to hear sad stories like this from my grandfather, but he never shared them with me. Once, I asked my father to tell me something about Pakistan and our family. He simply said, "I was only 7 years old, and I don't remember anything." Perhaps he didn't want to tell me sad stories and make me upset by remembering those painful moments.

Today, I received a courier from Neeraj, which contained an invitation card, sweets, my air ticket, and hotel booking vouchers. I was happy to attend both weddings, and I immediately called him to thank him for the invitation and the sweets, which were very good and special. But I asked, "Why did you send air tickets and hotel vouchers? I would have arranged them myself."

He replied, "Don't discuss this; just come, and I will give you some great news."

"What news?" I asked.

He said, "I'm not going to tell you over the phone. I'm eagerly waiting for you to arrive."

I had planned to go, but I could not sleep that night, wondering what news he wanted to give me personally.

Social, spiritual gathering

Today, my father called me and said that some saints are coming. They are our Guru and have spiritual power. He and his pupils will do Bhajans and Satsang. Sit still and listen carefully. He used to come to our house in Pakistan as well. He is very knowledgeable. Your duty is to offer tea and water to all the devotees.

They came, and first, they sang Bhajans on Ram and Krishna with musical instruments. The atmosphere was quite spiritual. Everybody was clapping, repeating, and chanting the words. It seemed like everyone was immersed in devotion. The chief saint began preaching the moral of life with quotes:

The Secret to Living Longer and Better: Eat Half, Walk Twice, Laugh Triple, and Love Without Measure

Eat Half: In a world where abundance often leads to overindulgence, eating half is a call for moderation. It's not about deprivation but about mindfulness. When we eat half, we learn to listen to our bodies, distinguishing between true hunger and emotional cravings. Science supports the idea that a balanced, light diet can prevent lifestyle diseases like obesity, diabetes, and heart problems. Eating in moderation also improves digestion, enhances energy levels, and promotes longevity. Traditional wisdom across cultures advocates for simple, measured meals – not just for physical health but also for clarity of mind.

Walk Twice: Movement is life. Walking twice as much doesn't only mean physical exercise but also an active approach to life. Walking improves cardiovascular health, strengthens muscles, and boosts mental well-being. Beyond the physical benefits, walking often brings opportunities for reflection and connection with nature. It allows us to slow down and appreciate the world around us. Whether it's a brisk morning walk or a leisurely evening stroll, the simple act of walking rejuvenates both body and soul.

Laugh Triple: Laughter truly is the best medicine. It reduces stress, strengthens the immune system, and improves mood. A life filled with laughter is a life of resilience and joy. When we laugh, we create connections, spread positivity, and lighten our burdens. Cultivating humour and finding joy in everyday moments keeps our spirits young and our hearts light.

Love Without Measure: Love is the most profound and limitless force we possess. To love without measure means to give without expecting, to care without conditions, and to embrace life and people wholeheartedly. Unconditional love nourishes relationships and fosters kindness and empathy. It transforms not only those we love but also ourselves, making us more compassionate and fulfilled. Love, in its truest form, transcends boundaries and brings peace and purpose.

Together, these four principles form a holistic approach to well-being. Moderation in eating keeps the body healthy, movement keeps it strong, laughter keeps the spirit joyful, and love keeps the heart open. By embracing this wisdom, we don't just add years to our life – we add life to our years.

His Holiness quotes

- "If you keep walking, you will definitely reach the shore."
- "Keep fighting the darkness. The morning will definitely dawn."
- "When you decide to reach your destination, you will definitely find the way."
- "Oh traveller, don't get tired, keep walking. One day, the time will definitely change..."

Saint continued his message.

I believe that there are many obstacles in life and many speed bumps too, but these ups and downs do not last forever. If we make up our mind that this problem has come and will go away, then why should we worry unnecessarily? They leave us with some new learning and experience.

There are two branches of life: one is material, and the other is spirituality. The person who lives his material life with all his heart and also gives some time to spirituality, his life blossoms well, remains peaceful, and progresses. We have a lot of power within us, but we get so busy achieving the things of this life that we forget the spiritual power within us. To balance our life, we should take care of both branches, and when one becomes mature by practicing continuously, he becomes like a master, a saint.

Keep the following idioms in mind, as they will be useful to you, and your life will improve:

- "No matter how much you hold on, you will surely slip."
- "This is the time, It will definitely change."
- Only birds need wings to rise high in life. The more a man bows humbly, the higher he rises.
- This is an unbreakable truth: Evil can never be destroyed by evil. Hatred can only be destroyed by love.

Holding on to anger is like holding hot coal with the intention of throwing it at someone else. You will only get burned by it.

A person who has lost in the field can win again,

A person who has lost morale, cannot win again.

The most expensive thing in life is your present. Once it is gone, we cannot buy it even with the wealth of the whole world.

Sacrifice is the only power that can win over the heart. Only a person who has a sense of service can have an impact on people. The world around you are beautiful only when you are at peace within yourself

- The sun is a daily reminder that we too can rise again. We do not have to agree with each other, but it is important that we learn to respect each other.
- A beautiful face grows old; a strong body fades one day. Position and power may also end one day. But a good person always remains a good person.

Karma said: Sometimes you have to suffer in life not because you were bad, But because you did not realize when and where to stop being good.

No mirror can show a person as good a picture. As his attitude and way of speaking reflect.

Being strong in spirituality I cannot control anyone else, but I can control:

- My thoughts
- My words
- My will
- My actions
- My reactions
- My future

How mature are you?

Once, someone asked Adi Shankaracharya the meaning of "maturity." Acharya Shankar gave some definitions of "maturity," and he answered:

Maturity is when you stop trying to change others and instead focus on changing yourself.

Maturity is when you accept others as they are.

Maturity is when you understand that every person is right according to his own thinking.

Maturity is when you learn the principle of "letting go."

Maturity is when you remove the expectations of taking from relationships and think only of giving.

Reflections on Maturity and Spiritual Growth

- Maturity is understanding that whatever you do is ultimately for your own peace.
- Maturity is letting go of the need to prove your intelligence to the world.
- Maturity is when you stop seeking approval from others.
- Maturity is when you stop comparing yourself to others.
- Maturity is being at peace with yourself.
- Maturity is the ability to differentiate between needs and wants and the willingness to let go of your wants.
- Maturity is when you stop linking your happiness to worldly things.

Spiritual Purity and Meditation. Reflection

These principles will improve your personality and deepen your connection with the Creator. Meditation, practiced in various ways, can strengthen your inner power, helping to overcome the burden of bad habits. With inner purity, a new glow will naturally emerge within you, and you will feel this transformation yourself.

Reflection: Just as God keeps account of our good and bad deeds, a teacher in class knows everything about their pupils – who excels, who needs improvement, and who has the potential to do better. A teacher evaluates students by the knowledge and effort they display and gives marks according to their ability and understanding. During exams, the teacher watches closely, sometimes staying near the students to observe their work – whether right or wrong – yet remains silent. Only later does the teacher settle the account based on the knowledge and effort reflected in the answer sheet. Similarly, God is always watching us, silently observing our actions and decisions. In the end, He will decide our rewards or punishments based on the karmas we accumulate throughout our lives. This serves as a reminder to always strive for goodness, honesty, and humanity in everything we do.

Wisdom from Sufi Poetry

Sufi poet Bulleh Shah beautifully captures the essence of detachment and surrender:

Going to Makkah is not the ultimate, even if hundreds of prayers are offered. Going to the River Ganges is not the ultimate, even if hundreds of dips are taken. Going to Gaya is not the ultimate, even if hundreds of worships are done. The ultimate, says Bulleh Shah, is when the "I" is removed from the heart.

The Teachings of Saint Tukaram

Once, Tukaram's disciple asked, "Guruji, can we go on a pilgrimage?" The saint replied, "Forgive me this time; I promise to join next time. For now, take this bundle and carry it on the pilgrimage."

When the disciples returned, they handed back the bundle. As they were leaving, Tukaram asked, "Did you understand what was in this bundle?"

- This is a lesson to you all through a simple but profound act. He handed them a bitter bottle gourd (Lauaki) and said, "Make a vegetable out of this and feed everyone."

The disciples cooked the vegetable and served it. However, as everyone took a bite, they immediately spat it out, exclaiming, "Guruji, it is very bitter!"

The saint then explained: "This bottle gourd remained bitter even after bathing in the holy Ganges and visiting all the pilgrimages. If it did not change, how do you think people can transform simply by external rituals alone?"

Hearing this, the disciples were deeply embarrassed and introspective.

Connecting Within Yourself

To connect with your inner self, here are some insights and practices:

In life, sooner or later, we all face difficult and challenging moments. A well-trained mind, body, emotions, and feelings can help confront these ups and downs with grace. Today, let's focus on **Vipassana**, a meditation technique that promotes self-awareness and purification.

Introduction to Vipassana Meditation

Vipassana is one of India's most ancient meditation techniques. Rediscovered by Gotama the Buddha over 2,500 years ago, the term *Vipassana* means "seeing things as they truly are."

It is a process of self-purification through self-observation. Here's how it works:

1. **Start by Observing the Breath**
    - Sit straight on a yoga mat or chair.
    - Close your eyes and your mouth.
2. **Focus on Your Breathing**
    - Concentrate on your natural breath as it flows in and out.
    - Do not worry about whether the breath is passing through your right or left nostril.
    - Simply observe your breath—whether it is short or long, slow or fast.
3. **Be Present in the Moment**
    - Be fully aware of the breath entering your body and leaving it.

- Do not try to control or change it; just observe.

By practicing Vipassana, you cultivate sharpened awareness. This awareness helps you observe the changing nature of your body and mind, leading to the realization of universal truths like impermanence, suffering, and timelessness.

4. **Breathing Awareness: A Path to Inner Transformation**
    - Keep your attention focused on your breathing–when it flows in and when it flows out.
    - Feel the gentle sound of your breath as it enters and leaves your body.
    - Maintain full awareness and vigilance, observing each breath as it goes in and comes out.
    - Be a witness to your breathing, staying fully present in the moment.

Your mind may wander, and that's natural. When it does, gently bring your focus back to your breath, flowing in and out.

The Breath: A Highway to Purity

- Each inhalation brings purity into your being.
- Each exhalation cleanses your inner self, releasing impurities.

The more you purify yourself through this practice, the more active and powerful your soul will become.

Awakening the Soul

- The soul is powerful, angelic, and a source of positivity.
- It inspires us to do good deeds and meaningful work.

- As you practice, you'll begin to notice positive changes within yourself.

Sit quietly and observe your breath for as long as you can—at least **10 minutes a day** is recommended.

Benefits of Vipassana

This simple practice has profound effects:

Overcoming Harmful Habits: You may naturally forget cravings like intoxication, which harm the body and mind.

Mental Wellness: It helps dissolve ego, anxiety, depression, and other illnesses.

Ecstasy and Fulfilment:

- Vipassana brings a state of ecstasy—a supreme joy.
- Once you experience this, worldly desires lose their appeal and become meaningless.
- True ecstasy transcends everything, offering a sweetness and fulfilment beyond worldly pleasures.

A Simple Mantra: "So Hum"

You can enhance this meditation by silently repeating the mantra:

- Say "**So**" as you inhale.
- Say "**Hum**" as you exhale.

This technique deepens the meditative experience, creating a blissful intoxication that lasts longer. It is a joy even gods and goddesses crave.

When you feel the effects of this spirituality, it will seem sweeter than any worldly pleasure.

Now, a True Story to Reflect On:

A Funeral and a Reflection

Yong Juhi accompanied his father to a funeral at the college. The son of the deceased walked ahead of the casket, tears streaming down his face as he cried out in grief for his beloved father.

"My darling father, where are they taking you? Are they going to bury your body in a grave and cover it with heaps of earth? Are they leading you to a dark, narrow house—with no carpets on the floors, not even a straw mat? Will they lay you down in a place where no light ever shines, where no bread is baked, and no aroma of cooking ever rises? A house with no proper door at its entrance, no neighbour to knock and ask after you? How could you, who were so widely revered, ever tolerate such a dark and harsh home?"

Listening to this lament, Yong Juhi whispered to his father, "Don't you think all the details he's describing point to our house? Listen carefully, and you'll see what I mean. He says the house has no light, no food is cooked there, its door is broken, and it has no garden or even a rooftop. That is exactly what our house is like."

But Yong Juhi's words were met with silence, as his father remained lost in thought, oblivious to his son's observation.

Social gathering concluded

The saint presiding over the funeral concluded, announcing, "It is over for today. Please enjoy the offerings—tea and sweets are being served outside."

Journey to Mumbai to meet Neeraj

The following day, I flew to Mumbai to attend the wedding of Neeraj and his sister. Upon exiting the airport, I saw Neeraj waiting outside.

We exchanged handshakes and hugs before heading to the parking area to retrieve the car.

The parking lot was massive, and Neeraj had forgotten where the car was parked. He pressed the car key button repeatedly, hoping the lights or buzzer would guide us. After a long search, the car's lights finally flashed, and we located it.

As we settled into the car, I asked, "When did you buy this?"

Neeraj replied, "Oh, this isn't mine–it belongs to my brother-in-law. It's the latest model, and he got it for ₹2 crore."

"Wow!" I said, admiring the luxurious interior. "It's a fantastic car, so comfortable and elegant."

A Late-Night Drive

It was 11 p.m., and the car cruised along at 100 km/h, though it felt as smooth as 50 km/h. As we neared Dadar, a patrolling police officer stopped us and issued a challan for over speeding, demanding ₹2,000.

Neeraj protested, "Sir, even at night, you don't let us enjoy a car ride? At 50 km/h, it feels like we're driving a scooter!"

The policeman, unfazed, responded, "No arguments–rules are rules. How would you like to pay, cash or in court?"

I intervened, "Sir, I'm from Delhi. Neeraj came to pick me up, as tomorrow is his wedding."

The policeman smiled and said, "Promise me you'll follow the speed limit and drive safely tonight. I'll let this go as a wedding gift."

Neeraj nodded sincerely, and we drove away, laughing at the unexpected turn of events.

I said to Neeraj, "Your Mumbai police are really good."

Neeraj replied, "Ashok, police across India are the same, but some officers are genuinely nice–like this one. A good guy."

Smiling, I teased him, "Don't tell your brother-in-law about the speeding, or he might stop giving you the car!"

Neeraj laughed nervously. "I usually don't drive fast, but we were talking, and I didn't notice the speedometer in the flow of our conversation."

Arriving at the House

When we reached his house, I was struck by the dazzling decorations. The place was lit up with electric bulbs, and there was light everywhere.

"Neeraj, your house is beautifully decorated! Did you hire professionals?" I asked.

Neeraj smiled. "Yes, this is all part of the plan organized by the wedding planner. We had so many meetings with my family, Reeta's family, and our fiancées to finalize everything–live music at the groom's reception, the cuisine at the bride's place, the budget, and the number of events to include.

"We had to cut some events due to budget and logistical constraints. Both families are sharing the costs of the reception and cuisine. We also discussed the total number of guests from both sides and went through a long process to finalize the venue.

"After checking numerous locations, we chose the Hotel Taj Land sandnd. It was perfect for accommodating everyone, including senior citizens, with easy access to all areas. We've even booked your room there!"

Wedding Planning Insights

Neeraj continued, "The planner briefed us in detail about everything. We had discussions about whether the venue should be indoors or outdoors, and they showed us many YouTube videos on decorations, caterers, mandaps, linens, fabrics, florists, photographers, videographers, makeup artists, beauticians, DJs, mehndi, and more.

"The priest was a critical element—forgetting the priest would make everything else meaningless!" Neeraj joked, and we both burst into laughter.

Checking Into the Hotel

Neeraj dropped me off at the Hotel Taj Lands End, where I checked in. My room was already allotted, and it was spacious and beautifully decorated. A platter of snacks awaited me on the table.

Feeling peckish, I grabbed a sandwich and a beer from the bar fridge. Exhausted from the day's journey, I quickly fell asleep.

A Late-Night Call

I was startled awake by the ringing of the telephone. Groggily, I walked over to the phone and picked it up.

“Hello?”

Neeraj's voice boomed from the other end. “I came to your room twice! Where were you?”

I chuckled. “I was here! I had a beer, ate a sandwich, and then fell asleep. Must have been more tired than I thought!”

An Unexpected Reunion

“Neeraj, you missed the lunch and Mehndi ceremony,” I teased over the phone. “Now, in the evening, we're meeting in the bar at 8. Don't forget! And this time, don't go to sleep after selling the horse.”

I laughed and replied, “Neeraj, I'm sorry, but which bar, and where is it?”

"Stupid! The bar is on the ground floor of the same hotel," he said with a chuckle.

"It's 5 now," I said. "I'm heading to the spa for a sauna and steam session. Don't worry, I'll be there at 8 sharp."

After a quick cup of tea, I made my way to the spa. The desk attendant greeted me warmly.

"Your room number, please?"

"209," I said, and she handed me a towel, directing me to the spa area.

A Surprise Encounter

On my way, I spotted someone familiar. It was Lata, a classmate from my competition classes for UPSC

"What a surprise!" I exclaimed. "How are you here?"

She smiled. "I'm here for Mukesh's wedding."

"You mean Reeta's fiancé?" I asked, surprised.

"Yes," she replied, laughing.

"Nice meeting you here!" I spoke. "See you at the wedding. We have a program at 8 in the bar, and I thought I'd have a sauna and steam session in the meantime."

She said, "I just came from the spa. The steam was great, but the sauna wasn't working."

"Good to know. See you at the function!" I said, heading to the spa.

When I informed the attendant that the sauna wasn't working, she assured me, "It's operational, sir. You can start with the steam, and I'll adjust the sauna temperature so it's perfect by the time you're ready."

Relaxation and Rush

After enjoying the steam, I took a chilled shower and entered the sauna. The temperature was perfect, and I felt my heartbeat quicken with the heat. To relax, I reclined on a chair and accidentally fell asleep.

When I woke up, it was exactly 8 p.m.! In a rush, I changed quickly and headed straight to the bar. It was 8:30 by the time I arrived. Though there were several people there, Neeraj was nowhere to be seen.

I stepped outside and sat on a sofa, feeling a bit out of place. Soon, I saw Mukesh and Reeta entering the bar.

Meeting the Couple

I approached them and greeted them warmly.

"Ashok, why are you standing outside?" Reeta asked. "Come in!"

She introduced me to Mukesh. "He's Ashok, a classmate and good friend of Neeraj."

Mukesh extended his hand. "Nice to meet you, Ashok! What would you like–beer or whisky?"

"Anything," I replied, smiling.

He called over a friend. "Tony, this is Ashok, a good friend of Neeraj's. Please make sure he feels comfortable and has a good time."

Tony nodded, and I joined him with a glass of beer. I noticed Mukesh and Reeta enjoying wine.

Tony poured another whisky and offered it to his friend, who quickly waved it off. "No more, please. I've already had four!"

Tony chuckled, raising his glass. "I always drink a glass of water after every whisky," he said proudly. "It prevents dehydration and hangovers. You should try it."

His friend shook his head, looking a bit uneasy. "Sorry, Tony, I know my limit. I've already gone way beyond my capacity tonight."

Tony wasn't one to give up so easily. "Hey, buddy, this is a wedding! If you don't drink here, then where else will you?"

Before Tony could push the glass towards him again, his friend quickly got up, muttered something about needing a break, and darted off to the washroom, leaving Tony laughing at the table.

Tony drank a little too much and said friends listen to a song on this alcohol

Ode to Whiskey

Oh, golden spirit in a glass, with warmth that makes the moments pass, you dance with fire, smooth and bold, A story in amber, timeless and old.

Born of barley, rye, or corn, through years in barrels, you've been reborn, aged in oak, kissed by time, your essence is crafted, sublime and fine.

You whisper tales of hills and streams, of craftsmen's toil and dreamer's dreams, A sip, a taste, a gentle burn, in your embrace, life takes a turn.

You join in laughter, soothe the pain, A companion in joy, a friend in rain, but whiskey dear, let's tread with care, for too many of you is a dangerous affair.

So, here's to the spirit, warm and neat, A toast to life, both bitter and sweet, raise your glass, let's clink and cheer, For whiskey's magic, sincere and clear.

All clapped and laughed and cheers

Another guy here, another one from me.

Delicate as a rose, brighter than a spark,

Every sip hides a magic secret.

A gathering of friends, or a night of solitude,

It burns hearts, or speaks.

Take the glass, but don't lose your senses,

Never drown your sorrows in its juice.

This companion is for a moment, a game of feelings,

If you do it too much, it will create trouble.

An old story flows in every sip,

It passes away with time.

But walk carefully, these roads are sharp,

Don't be a slave of whiskey in life.

Tony, what a wonderful thing my Jumru Talia,

very nice and he stands up and hugs him and kisses him

Tonny to Mukesh sir anything from your side, poem, jokes

Reeta, Ashok, please say something of your choice.

Well, I remember one joke which I hope you all will enjoy;

A man walks into a bar and orders a whiskey

When the barman serves it up, he takes it out to the bench in front of the bar to drink it.

As he's enjoying his drink, a nun walks by, and glares at him sourly. "How can you pollute your soul with the Devil's drink like that?" she asks.

The man shrugs. "It's not the Devil, it's just whiskey."

"But it's sinful and wicked!"

"How do you know it's so bad, then? Have you ever tasted whiskey?"

"Of course not! My sisters and mother superior told me how evil the drink is."

"But how do they know? Have they ever had a drink?"

They go back and forth like this for a while, before at last, the nun relents. "Well, I suppose that if I were to try a sip of whiskey, I would better understand how it corrupts the soul. But it wouldn't do for any of my sisters to come by here and see me drinking. Could you order me one in a teacup?"

The man agrees this is fair, and walks inside to the barman.

"Two whiskeys, but put one in a teacup, please."

The barman slams his hand down on the bar and shouts, "Is that damn nun here again!?"

Feeling Out of Place

Despite the lively atmosphere with over 20 people, I felt alone and out of place. It seemed as though I was being forced to sit there, and I grew restless.

After finishing my beer, I told Tony, “Excuse me, I’m just going to the washroom.”

He nodded, and I headed toward the lift.

A Chance Meeting

As the lift doors opened, Neeraj and his fiancée stepped out.

“Neeraj, what happened? Where are you going?” he asked.

"I was heading back to my room," I said, feeling slightly frustrated.

Neeraj Palak is my best school friend and our family also knew each other.

Palak, Ashok, let us go to Bar to meet our friends.

Neeraj. Ashok sorry we are late due to delay in functions as you know in India it happened.

Don't worry, I am fine. I spoke

Neeraj took me again to the Bar and ordered three beers. We three sat near the table of tony, Tony saw me and raised his hand for cheers, I too raised my hand with a glass of beer and touched beer glasses with Neeraj and Palak and said cheers. Mukesh and Reeta were dancing with wine glasses in hand and their steps were moving like professional dancers. I was enjoying their steps and saw amazing happiness on their faces. Reeta saw that I was looking at her and I raised my Thumbs up.

Rita gestured with her hand to come here and I stood first and asked the question, I, she said yes Ashok come here. I went there and she took my hand in her hand and started dancing, I did not know what was happening and how to dance. I was nervous, she just said keep both hands at my waist, when I go back you come ahead and when I go ahead, you go back. After some time, I was enjoying and feeling good, she called Neeraj and his finance and we were just dancing and dancing for two hours. I got tired and said excuse me let me go I am tired. Neeraj said, right you go but I will come in your room to give you the good news. I said I know the news; He stand still and He stood up in surprise and asked, do you know the news,

I said, are you talking about Lata, Neeraj, my dear friend, how did you find out? Well, I saw her upstairs in the spa and we exchanged hello also.

Neeraj, it's okay, I am not in my senses right now, let's talk openly tomorrow

I took my breakfast and decided to go to the golf course for a game as the ladies sangeet and cocktail is in the evening and hardly any programmes during the day.

I entered a golf course named Bombay, Presidency golf club. I entered and went to the pro shop for green fees, the cashier said are you a member here, No I replied. Sorry sir, you can play only with any member of this club. Well, I have come from Delhi and I remember once I played a tournament here

Organized by Standard chartered Bank and I was the runner up. I liked this course, well maintained. It was short but reasonably challenging, with many trees, nice fairways, and an unduly green link course. He said nice to know that but our club rules are like that, you can play only with the members.

A Round of Golf and Unexpected Generosity

As I stood by the golf course entrance, a gentleman approached me and said, "We're a group of three, and you can join us. I'll speak to the cashier to allow you as our guest."

I thanked him sincerely, and when I reached for my wallet to pay, the gentleman intervened.

"No need," he insisted. "Put his charges on my account. He's from Delhi and is my guest."

I tried to pay, but he remained firm. Ultimately, I thanked him for his generosity.

Meeting the Group

We proceeded to the first tee-off, where the gentleman introduced me to his friends.

"Ashok, meet Naresh, Suresh, and I'm Vaswani," he said warmly.

I shook hands with them, and Vaswani asked, "Would you like to play with some stakes? The ceiling is ₹ 2,000. Otherwise, the three of us will play four-two-zero."

I replied, "I'm fine with stakes. Let's play!"

The Game

The game turned out to be delightful. By the end, I had won ₹ 1,000, and my partner, Suresh, had also earned the same.

Naresh complimented me, "Well played! It seems you're familiar with this course."

"I played here four years ago during a tournament," I said, smiling. "I'm happy with my game today."

Afterward, they took me to the bar, where we enjoyed two glasses of beer each.

I told them another game story of mine.

The Unexpected Swing

I was a young and ambitious golfer, having trained for months to participate in the prestigious Golden Trophy golf tournament. When I arrived at the lush Qutab Golf Course, I was eager to showcase my skills. As I began to play, I noticed a group of experienced golfers, including the defending champion, Vikram. Though I felt intimidated, I was determined to give my best.

The game remained neck and neck until the 17th hole. It was there that I hit an unexpected, brilliant shot, landing the ball just inches from the hole. Vikram, taken aback by the incredible shot, stumbled on his next swing, sending his ball into the bunker. Seizing the opportunity, I sank my putt and took the lead.

The final hole was a nail-biter, but I held my nerve and won the tournament by a single stroke. As I lifted the Trophy, the crowd roared in jubilation. Vikram, gracious in defeat, approached me and said, "I underestimated you, young man. Your determination and skill are truly inspiring." I beamed with pride, savouring the sweet taste of victory.

Vaswani commented wow this story gives good lesson and moral.

- Humility can lead to unexpected successes.
- Jubilation is sweeter when earned through hard work and determination.
- Never underestimate others, as they may surprise you with their hidden talents.
- Stay humble and grounded, even in the face of success.
- Hard work and determination can lead to triumph over adversity.
- Treat others with respect and kindness, regardless of their background or skills.

Suresh Jokes

That makes total sense! Bad golfers (or at least, not-too-serious ones) usually bring a more relaxed vibe to the course. No stressing over handicaps, no obsessing over the perfect swing—just enjoying the game for what it is. Good company, fresh air, a few drinks, and plenty of laughs? That sounds like the ideal round of golf.

Sharing a Joke

I shared a joke with them:

“You know, once four players met at a golf course.

The first introduced himself, 'Hi, I'm a Major, settled in London. I have three children, all doctors.'

The second exclaimed, 'That's surprising! I'm also a Major, settled in London, with three children—all engineers.'

The third said, 'What a coincidence! I'm also a Major, settled in London, with three children—all IT experts.'

They turned to the fourth player and asked about him.

He replied, 'Oh, I'm not a Major, not settled in London, unmarried—but I have three children. And guess what? All are Majors!'"

They laughed heartily, and the joke lightened the mood.

Conversations Over Drinks

Vaswani asked, "Ashok, what do you do?"

"I'm into logistics, freight forwarding, relocations, and warehousing," I said.

Suresh chimed in, "I handle a lot of import-export. Do you have an office in Mumbai?"

"My Mumbai counterpart only handles relocations, not commercial operations," I replied.

I turned to Naresh and Vaswani, asking, "What about you both?"

Vaswani said, "I help finance startups."

"Under Modi's program?" I asked.

"Yes," he confirmed, smiling. "And Naresh assists with the government's skill development

programs."

I shared an incident with them from my time at the Delhi Golf Course about 20 years back.

One day, while playing golf, I met an NRI from the USA. During our conversation, he praised Mr. Modi, recalling an experience from when Modi was the Chief Minister of Gujarat. He had presented a proposal for setting up an industry, and to his surprise, he received land within a month, along with all necessary assistance. His factory was operational within a year.

However, he expressed disappointment with the Haryana Government, stating that despite two years passing, he had yet to receive land for his project. Frustrated by the delay and inefficiency, he decided to drop his plan of setting up a factory in Haryana.

His remarks reflected public perception of how different governments function.

Back at the Hotel

I said, excuse me "I'd love to stay longer, but I must leave to attend a wedding event. I missed the Mehendi ceremony yesterday, and I don't want to miss another function."

I thanked everyone, especially Mr. Vaswani, for covering my green fees and beer.

Naresh said, "You had a good day–great game, great jokes, and great company. Let's exchange numbers so we can connect when you're in Mumbai or when we visit Delhi."

We laughed, exchanged numbers, and I headed back to the Taj Hotel.

It was 5 PM when I reached my room. I noticed the phone's red-light blinking, indicating missed calls. I picked it up and found a message from Neeraj, asking me to call him back.

Before doing so, I decided to shower and refresh myself. The golf game had left me exhausted, and the humid weather had drained my energy.

Feeling rejuvenated, I called Neeraj.

"Where have you been?" he asked immediately.

"I just got back to my room after a round of golf. It was a great game, and I even earned Rs. 1,000!" I replied cheerfully.

Neeraj laughed. "Good for you! But listen, don't disappear again. Be at the poolside for the Ladies' Sangeet and cocktail party by 8 PM. No excuses this time."

"I promise I'll be there," I assured him.

Ladies' Sangeet and Cocktail Party

I dressed in a kurta-pyjama with a jacket and a colourful scarf, feeling festive for the occasion. When I arrived at the poolside venue, it was beautifully decorated. The women, mostly in lehengas and sarees, were gathered on one side, while the men and boys stayed on the other.

A temporary bar counter showcased a wide variety of liquor.

Neeraj greeted me warmly. "What will you have–beer or whisky?"

"I'll take a single malt," I said.

He brought me a glass, raised his own for a toast, and downed it in one go. "Let me get another one," he said, heading back to the bar.

I chuckled, "I'll take my time with this one."

A Chat with Reeta

Reeta approached me, smiling. "How do I look, Ashok?"

"You look gorgeous," I replied sincerely. "I saw you in your Mehendi lehenga too–it was stunning."

She beamed. “Thank you! I remember you weren’t at the Mehendi ceremony, though.”

“I arrived late,” I admitted, “but I did catch a glimpse of you as you were heading to your room.”

“So, this lehenga is specially for the Ladies’ Sangeet?” I asked.

She nodded enthusiastically. “Yes, it’s custom-made for tonight. I wanted it to be perfect!”

“It absolutely is,” I said, and she smiled brightly before returning to the group.

Reeta smiled warmly and said, “Ashok, you know this *Sangeet Sandhya* is the most joyous celebration before the wedding. It’s all about music, dance, and vibrant energy. To truly enjoy the night, one needs a stylish yet comfortable outfit to dance freely and light up the stage. That’s why I chose lightweight fabrics like net and organza, adorned with dazzling embellishments. My designer even suggested sequins or other eye-catching details that would sparkle under the lights. But I declined—I liked this lehenga better.”

I smiled and replied, “In my eyes, this lehenga is just as eye-catching, and you’re shining like a star.”

She twisted her lips into a playful smile. “Thanks for the compliment. Now enjoy your drink!” With a graceful wave, she walked back to join the others.

The Festivities Begin

Neeraj returned with another drink. “Come on, Ashok, you’re so slow! Finish that first glass already.”

“I’m savouring it,” I replied.

He grinned. “Fine, but don’t take forever.”

Waiters passed by with trays of snacks. I grabbed a chicken tikka–it was delicious.

The *Ladies' Sangeet* began with a burst of energy. A woman played the *dholak* with a spoon, creating a rhythmic, familiar beat. The lively tunes of Punjabi folk songs filled the air, accompanied by laughter, clapping, and dancing.

The women sang popular wedding songs like:

- Kala Doriya
- Lathe di Chadar
- Mera Long Gawacha
- Kala Sha Kala
- Amritsar de Papad
- Ichak Dana Beechak Dana
- Bajre di Roti

The atmosphere was infectious, and soon everyone was tapping their feet or breaking into impromptu dances.

Words from the Couple

The anchor took the mic and called Mukesh, Reeta, Neeraj, and Piya onto the stage.

Mukesh began, "Hello, everyone! First, I want to thank all our guests for being here and making this evening unforgettable. I hope you're all having a great time!"

The crowd responded with cheers of "Yes! Absolutely!"

Mukesh continued, "Life is like a grand play, and we're all actors performing the roles assigned by the Creator. Many of you know that I went to the USA, and Reeta and I have known each other since our school days. We drifted apart over time, and I never imagined we'd meet again. But here we are, reunited. It feels like destiny, a script written by the divine."

He paused; his voice filled with emotion. "I can't describe how happy I am to have Reeta back in my life."

Reeta stepped forward and took the mic. "And I'm so happy to have you back in mine. It feels like the universe conspired to bring us together again."

Reeta's Backflash: A Journey from Sadness to Joy

Reeta stood there, glowing with happiness, but as she glanced at Mukesh, memories of her past swept through her like a flood. She had been through a rough time, struggling with her own fears and doubts. There had been moments when she doubted love, when life felt like an endless path of challenges. The pain of being apart from the people she loved, the loneliness she felt despite the bustling world around her—it all seemed so far away now.

This was her new life; one she had never dreamed would be so beautiful. She looked at Mukesh, her fiancé, and felt a deep sense of peace. She could never have imagined that this would be her fate, but now, as she stood with him, surrounded by friends and family, she realized that everything had led her to this moment of pure bliss. She was no longer that sad woman she once was. She was the happiest she had ever been.

Neeraj's Emotional Words

Neeraj approached the microphone, his face glowing with love for Piya. "I agree with my brother-in-law, Mukesh. Life is like a script written by Almighty. I never thought my boss would become my brother-in-law, and that my colleague would turn out to be the love of my life. Her Hindi might not be great, and my Marathi is almost in a coma, but I feel truly blessed to have her as my life partner. Piya, I love you."

Piya smiled and blew him a flying kiss, her eyes shining with affection.

Ashok's Poem

Neeraj then turned to me. "Now, I'd like to request my school friend Ashok to recite one of his poems. He writes beautifully."

I hesitated, slightly embarrassed by the attention. "Neeraj, I can't," I protested. "I'm drunk, and all the guests are forcing me to come to the stage."

I scanned the room, hoping for a familiar face to ground me, but my eyes searched in vain. I was disappointed when I couldn't spot Lata, the first crush who had lingered in my heart for so long. My thoughts wandered, and I felt a strange mixture of loss and nostalgia.

Neeraj noticed my hesitation and reassured me, "Don't worry, Ashok. Just say whatever comes to your mind."

With a deep breath, I gave in and walked to the stage, my voice shaky at first, but slowly gaining confidence as I began to recite my poem.

The Poem

"Hello, everyone. I'm not a professional poet, but sometimes I do write. Here's my first poem. I hope you'll like it."

Tired of the hustle and bustle of the world, I went to my village, slept well at night, lost in dreams. Opened my eyes in the morning, went for a walk, walking on the *pagadandee*, the trail, the flowing water felt good. The swaying of the mustard plants, the mild breeze felt good.

Meanwhile, the *panaghat*, the well arrived, the drawing of water, the filling of the pitcher, The herd was going, the catwalk felt good.

Meanwhile, a voice came, "Hey, Babu, sir, lift the pitcher," The lifting of the pitcher, it's going, turned back and looked at me.

I liked the tinkling of the anklets. My eyes opened, oh, this was a dream. Okay, whatever it was, it felt good.

Neeraj shouted, Ashok one more

I looked at the gathering and all said yes one more.

By the Blue Sea

I stood by the blue sea one day, where people often come to celebrate their holidays.

Its waves were ferocious–so strong That I struggled to keep my balance.

Yet many frolicked in the surf, Laughing, rowing boats, fishing, swimming, Simply enjoying life.

On the shore, footprints in the sand Bore silent witness to countless arrivals and departures. Some waited patiently, eager to watch the sunset, Where the vast sea seemed to meet the distant sky. What a spectacle– The sun dipping below the horizon, the sky, the clouds, the water, all painted in shifting hues. Everyone gazed in awe, trying to capture that fleeting moment.

Suddenly a thought crossed my mind: The sea is restless, its water salty, Enduring the sun's heat, yet from that very heat come the clouds and rain, Bringing life to this world. Salt, fish, water–countless ways the sea helps all of us.

Waves churn in my heart too, stirring commotion. Am I contributing anything to this world, or merely drifting aimlessly? Perhaps my mind should be calm and steady, Like the endless sky– Only then might I truly Savor All this world has to offer.

The Standing Ovation

As I finished the poem, there was a moment of silence, followed by loud applause. The guests rose to their feet and gave me a standing ovation. The applause and kind words of appreciation filled me with warmth. I was overwhelmed, not just by their kindness, but by the realization that this evening was turning into something truly special.

The recognition, the joy, and the connections I was making with these wonderful people–it all felt surreal. I had no idea I would be here, reciting poems and receiving such warmth. This was a memory I would cherish forever.

Back to Delhi

The plane journey was a quiet one, despite my co-passenger being a friendly person. We had talked briefly about our lives, but when he started reading his book, I decided to let him be. I couldn't help but notice the book title–*Ikigai*. Something about it intrigued me, so when he asked for a bit of space to head to the toilet, I took the opportunity to glance at the pages.

As I flipped through, the content was enlightening–focused on longevity, a concept from Japan that seemed deeply connected to peace of mind and a balanced life. I made a note of some of the key ideas in my diary, fascinated by the simplicity and beauty of the philosophy:

The Secret to Long Life:

- **Don't Worry** – Keep your heart young and open. Let it stay fresh, no matter how old you get. The key is to greet life with a smile and an open heart, which invites positivity and a sense of connection.
- **Say Hello to Strangers** – Step outside your comfort zone. The best way to avoid anxiety and stress is to smile and

greet people. It's a simple act, but one that can change your day and yours—and others'—outlook on life.

- **Spend Time with Loved Ones** – Building relationships, being kind, and enjoying each other's company is what truly matters. Avoid conflicts, and focus on making happy memories.
- **Gardening Brings Joy** – A simple life, where you can enjoy nature and nurture something you grow with your own hands, brings unparalleled peace. Whether it's tomatoes, mandarin oranges, or anything else, the connection with the earth and its rhythm grounds you.
- **Start Your Day Early** – There's joy in waking up early, observing nature, tending to your garden, and making your own breakfast. The small acts of daily life, like caring for vegetables, can fill your day with satisfaction.

After reading, I couldn't help but reflect on how these simple principles could have such a profound impact on how we live. The connection between small joys, like tending to a garden, and living a long, healthy life made so much sense to me. As I sat there, I thought to myself, I would try to live in such a way—focusing on the present and nurturing the things that truly matter. The wisdom in that book stayed with me, even after the plane landed and I stepped out into the hustle and bustle of the airport.

On my way to Delhi, I felt a renewed sense of clarity. The hangover from last night's party still lingered, but the lessons from *Ikigai* were much clearer now.

Conversation with Dad on return

"I went for a few days, Dad. Just for the wedding," I replied casually, though in my mind, I was still reflecting on the deeper lessons I'd learned about living a long and fulfilling life. The concept of *Ikigai* had stayed with me, its wisdom slowly weaving into my thoughts as I navigated back to my daily routine.

He nodded; his expression thoughtful. "You've been away for a while, but you look good. Did you enjoy the wedding?"

I paused, then said, "Yes, I did. The wedding was beautiful, but what struck me the most was the conversations I had with some people. They really made me think about life differently." I didn't go into details about the book I had read or the advice it offered about longevity, but I felt a quiet conviction building inside me.

"You know, Dad," I continued, "there's a lot more to life than we realize. Simple things like taking care of your health, eating well, staying active, and just being around people who make you smile... Those things really matter. It's about living each day with purpose, like the old people in Japan."

He raised an eyebrow, intrigued. "Tell me more about this. I know you read a lot, but what did you learn from all these people?"

I took a moment to gather my thoughts, thinking about the wisdom I'd gained. "It's about balance. Not just physically, but emotionally. It's the little things we do daily, like staying active, eating well, laughing, and connecting with others. We take so much for granted, but the most important thing is to keep your heart open, stay positive, and live fully."

He smiled, clearly pleased to hear me speak with such conviction. "I'm glad you learned something valuable during your trip. Sometimes it takes a journey to realize what's important."

That conversation with my father stayed with me. It was like a gentle reminder that, despite all the noise of life, the most profound lessons are often the simplest ones. Keep moving, keep smiling, and always cherish the people who bring joy into your life. And that, I realized, was my own *Ikigai*.

I plant my own vegetables and cook them myself. That is ikigai

The key to staying sharp in old age is in your fingers. Your fingers to your brain, and back again. If you keep your fingers busy, you will live to see one hundred.

I get up at 4 every day, I set my alarm for that time, I take a cup of coffee, and do a little exercise, lifting my arms. It gives me energy for the rest of the day.

If you don't work, your body breaks down,

I go to friends once in a week, we chat and to dancing

Eating vegetables helps you live longer.

To live a long time, you need to do three things: exercise to stay healthy, eat well, and spend time with people.

Optimistically, every day I say to myself, Today will be full of health and energy/ Live it to the fullest.

I am Ninety-eight, but consider myself young. I still have so much to do.

Laughter is the most important thing. I laugh wherever I go.

I am going to live to be hundred, of course I am, it is huge motivation for me.

Dancing and singing with your grandchildren are the best things in life.

I feel very fortunate to have been born here. I give thanks for it every day.

The most important thing in life is to keep smiling.

I do volunteer work. For example, I use my car to help friends get to Hospital.

These are good tips for a happy and long life.

In Japan, generally people take the following diet for longevity

Cabbage, seaweed, Onion, soy sprouts, cucumber, soybeans, sweet potato, peppers. Jasmine tea, Tofu, Carrots, Tuna, Sea kelp, Goya, Misco. These are rich in Antioxidants and are eaten every day.

In today lifestyles, we read so many articles in the newspaper, magazine which highlight

the same but questions are how many of us follow strictly.

My father also follows the same diet and he just turned 94. He recently shared a post on Facebook while driving a cycle in thc gym.

Relation moved towards Lata

I reached home, and my father questioned me, "You went to Mumbai for how many days?" "Dad, I went for two days, but there were so many functions, and Neeraj did not allow me to go. I really enjoyed all the functions."

"You've started a new business, you should be serious... either you go to play or for a stroll, how long will this go on? Tomorrow, you have to get married. Where will you feed her?"

I flared up and went inside quietly. He also got angry. He was about to slap me, but my grandmother saved me. All my fun disappeared, and under this atmosphere, I could not ask him about the girl I liked. I dared to reveal it to my grandmother. At first, she was shocked, then smiled, and said, "Keep quiet for the time being."

One day she came to me and said, "Let us go one day to her house, and later I will tell your parents if I like the girl." We both visited her house without any appointment. She was alone at her house.

My grandmother looked at her. She made a cup of tea, and my grandmother asked for more sugar, as she was taking three spoons in a cup of tea. I could not even talk to her, and we left. My grandmother told me on the way that her teeth were good. I laughed and said, "What are you talking about? You've seen only her teeth and not her."

She replied, "She is good-looking, from an educated family, but when she smiled, I liked her white teeth."

One day, she passed on the news to my parents that she went there with Ashok and that I liked the girl.

My father called me and said, "Are you not serious about standing on your feet? Why are you in a hurry to get married? I said, "No, I am not in a hurry. Liking a girl doesn't mean I'm in a hurry to get married."

"I'm going there to see the girl because your mother is more interested. Tell them that we are coming next weekend."

I was excited but didn't know how to inform them, as I didn't have their phone number. I boldly decided to go myself and convey the message. I went to her house, and there were some relatives. Her mother told me, "You came with your grandmother, but unfortunately, we were not here. We were planning to come to your place, and please tell your parents that we will come there next weekend."

I wanted to talk to her, but there were too many people, so I could not talk to her. She simply asked, "Why are you coming to our house?" I was frozen, fixed in a moment, and simply spoke, "I liked you."

They came to our house, and after discussing things, the engagement was fixed. We kept going on dates, but I was not keen on marriage until I was well-settled. I was the happiest person in my life and invited Neeraj to the engagement. Not only Neeraj, but his wife, his sister, and his brother-in-law all came. The function started, the ring was exchanged, and we had refreshments together. Neeraj told my fiancé...

Let us go out for a party. Her mother was listening and gave permission, saying, "Yes, she can go. I give permission."

We went to a bar. It was quite big and full of youngsters, with no place to sit or even stand. We decided to go to another bar. The same situation was here too. One of the bar staff told us to go upstairs, where there was a meeting room we could use. "I will send a service boy," he said.

The crowd was so agitated that it was difficult to even walk. Many times, we had to walk sideways. A Sardar ji was carrying a 5-liter jug of beer to his table, struggling to save the jug. However, he collided with someone, and the beer and jug fell to the floor, breaking into pieces. The beer and glass pieces scattered on the floor. Everyone was looking at the poor Sardar ji and the mess on the floor. Anyway, we reached the meeting room upstairs with great difficulty.

Neeraj ordered 6 beers to start. We finished the first round quickly, then he ordered whisky, but all the ladies raised their hands and said, "Sorry, no more. We will not take anything for the time being." We were sipping whisky slowly and enjoying snacks. At that time, I realized I didn't have enough credit, and I was worried. I may not have enough cash with me, and it would be a big insult.

Mukesh and Neeraj ordered whisky again, but I refused to take more because of my tension regarding the payment. I took Neeraj aside and told him, "I haven't brought much cash. Please order sensibly."

He replied, "Who is asking you to pay? We brought you here, and we will pay."

"Thanks for that, but it doesn't look good if it's my engagement and you're paying. How can you pay?" I replied.

"Don't worry, this party is from our side, meaning from us. Now, please, no further discussion."

Mukesh said, "Ashok, your poem was very good at our ladies' sangeet. Please say something."

I made this while driving a car. Here it is:

"Clouds covered the sky, my heart stretched, your picture came into my eyes. I wish she would come down personally from my eyes, and we both enjoy this weather."

Here's one more:

"No matter how much I drink, her image does not disappear from my sight."

She is near and perhaps far. Is this the intoxication of youth or madness?

Neeraj: "No comments, this is between you both," and he laughed.

Mukesh: "Last, please, one more."

"Believe me, I have nothing to tell you today. Yes, there was a time when the storehouses of letters were full. The alphabet used to be made of letters just like that. It so happened that I was just singing praises. The poem that was made by singing praises, maybe that was the way I was complimented a lot when I sang the song to strangers, but oh, my fate, she did not like my humming. For whom I was making it? Sharp arrows against them, who is she for whom you are making? Praise is being sung. The truth struck me, and I stopped writing. And today, to be frank, I have nothing to tell you."

Mukesh praised, and Reeta said, "Ashok, what depth you go into! Amazing, unbelievable." I said, "Don't stop writing, keep writing. I wish to listen more and more from you in the future."

I bowed my head and thanked everyone, then came out of the bar. It was 2 AM, And still, the crowd was there, dancing and drinking. Many were dancing like madmen in intoxication.

Neeraj: "I understand there is a very famous paan, betel shop where film stars also come. I want to have paan."

I took them to the opposite Sangam theatre, took paan, and ate it. It was really very tasty and aromatic.

Some personality always leaves good vibes, impacts.

I have experienced that more than 99% of people and clients are very good. However, some clients can be really challenging to handle. Life is not easy, and these incidents have provided me with great experience. I hold no grudge against anyone. Every moment teaches us something, and even bad experiences come with valuable lessons.

I came across so many wonderful people in person and business and found them thoroughly gentle people though they reached at the top. I cannot write all the names, it will be in thousands but would like to mention some who left a nice impact on me.

Mr. AB Patwardhan, M K Rasgotra, H S Puri, Vijay Gokhale, Ajay Bisaria, J N Dixit, S S Menon, Rajinder Khanna, Chander Shaker, Bombaywala, Ramesh Bhandari, Brijesh Mishra, AB Vajpayee, H V Shringla, V M Kawatra, Arun Chatterjee, K Raghunath, Lalit man Singh, K Sibal, Shyam saran, Ranjan Mathai, S Jaishankar, Vikram Misri, Pardesi, P Kumaran, Tri Murty, Shashank, G Balasubramaniam, Viraj Singh, Sujata Mehta, , Amar Sinha, R K Srivastava, Piyush Srivastava, Navtej Sarna, S Suri, N Suri, Aseem Mahajan, Dr. Aman Puri, B Reddy, S. Reddy, Kumar Tuhin , P Verma, Arun Singh, Charanjeet Singh,

I got a lot of exposure, experience under these officers and also feel proud connected to them. Also got the opportunity to handle big conferences, events like NAM CHOGAM, G 20, etc.

How Connections Form and Fade

I have already mentioned my 28 years of experience dealing with court cases, which taught me many things. It made me bolder and more pious. Life is full of speed breakers; you have to face the jerks, but the beautiful thing is that life keeps moving forward.

Desi man is desi don't understand gimmicks.

Not long ago, a potential business partner visited my office to propose a collaboration with his Chennai branch. We agreed to cooperate on a few shipments and began exchanging business. When I planned a trip to Pondicherry to oversee the shipment of donated goods by sea, I flew into Chennai first. This same person arranged a taxi for me, and despite my offer to pay, he insisted the ride was complimentary. I appreciated his generosity, and after my work in Pondicherry, we met for dinner before I returned home.

Sometime later, he visited my office again to say he was heading to the United States to launch the same moving business and asked if I could introduce him to the Indian Embassy and consulates. He suggested we continue our reciprocal arrangement there as well. Excited by the opportunity to expand into the U.S. market, I agreed wholeheartedly.

Over the following year, I travelled to the U.S. four or five times—spending considerably on airfare, accommodation, and transportation—to help us get listed on the Indian Embassy's panel of approved service providers. Eventually, we were successful, and he began sending me shipments. When **Mr. Jaishankar** was appointed as Foreign Secretary, I sent a message to his office, offering our services. He graciously used them in the U.S., which seemed like a significant step forward.

However, when I inquired about how the shipment was progressing, I discovered it had already been cleared and delivered by a woman who was apparently working directly with my associate. Shocked, I immediately called my friend in the U.S. He offered an explanation, saying his sister wanted to start her own business in Delhi and he couldn't stop her. Before long, not only did his sister's venture compete with me, but his own company also entered the Delhi market, leveraging their Foreign Ministry connections in ways that impacted my business. I'm not concerned about losing business; what pains me more is losing the connection with valued customers like Shri Jaishankar.

I was stunned that a seemingly strong partnership could unravel so quickly. On a spiritual level, I understand these things can happen to anyone–friendships and partnerships can dissolve as unexpectedly as they form. Recently, I ran into him at the airport in New York, where he had come to pick up his daughter. Initially, I hesitated to greet him, but he approached and we exchanged hellos. I learned he had undergone heart surgery and experienced a serious lorry accident in the U.S. I said oh sorry, I was not knowing about your surgery and accident. I am very happy that all went well at last and wish you all the best in future. I realized that sometimes people feel compelled to act when family or other internal circumstances dictate their next steps, even if it hurts or undermines a prior arrangement.

Trapped for the Second Time

I remember visiting a leading packer and movers' company in London to establish a reciprocal business partnership. During our discussion, we nearly finalized the collaboration, and they informed me that their president was currently in the USA. He would be attending an upcoming conference, where we could meet and finalize the agreement.

After this meeting, I visited another moving company that was on the panel of the Indian High Commission in London. It was a small firm, and its owner invited me to dinner the next evening. I politely declined, explaining that I was leaving for the USA to attend a conference. Curious, he asked for details about the event–its nature, location, and schedule. Since I had no competition or conflicts with him, I freely shared the information.

As planned, I later met with the president of the first company in the USA. However, during our discussion, he abruptly told me, "I'm sorry, but we cannot proceed with the partnership. One of your representatives from London has already approached us, and we cannot tie up with competitors."

I was stunned. I clarified, "Sir, I am the sole representative from India, and we do not have any operations in London." He then introduced me to the so-called "representative" from London–none other than the person I had met at the small moving company. He was wearing a badge with the name "Ashoka International," my company's name, but with "New Delhi" removed and "London" overwritten.

Frustrated, I confronted the conference organizers about how they had issued a badge in my company's name without my authorization. However, they were more interested in collecting fees than maintaining integrity, allowing him to register under "Ashoka International" simply because he had paid.

As a result, I lost a golden opportunity to collaborate with a major international group.

Sometimes, no matter how hard you try, fate has other plans. If something isn't meant to be, it simply won't happen.

Reflecting on this experience, I see that life is unpredictable. One day, someone can be your steadfast ally; the next, you're practically strangers. Yet even these challenges offer lessons in resilience, understanding, and the delicate balance of trust in the business world–and beyond.

HAPPINESS

1. Have Faith, Dismiss Fear

Placing your trust in a higher power—be it God, the universe, or simply the goodness in life—empowers you to face challenges with courage. Faith lightens the weight of uncertainty because it reminds you that there is guidance and support beyond your own efforts. When you genuinely believe that the universe is working in your Favor, your life outlook shifts from fear and doubt to opportunity and hope.

Additionally, every obstacle you encounter contains a hidden lesson. Embracing these lessons—rather than avoiding them—unlocks your potential. True growth stems from confronting hurdles, gleaning insights, and moving forward stronger than before. With an unshakable belief in life's benevolent nature, your confidence in overcoming difficulties expands, ultimately transforming an ordinary life into something extraordinary.

2. Be Wary of Negativity

Negative energy—whether it comes from acquaintances, colleagues, or even family members—can stifle your sense of peace and happiness. Trust your instincts: if someone's pessimism, criticism, or constant drama leaves you feeling drained, it's wise to maintain some emotional or physical distance.

Creating boundaries is not about shutting people out; it's about preserving your own well-being. Give yourself permission to say "no" to negativity and "yes" to positivity. Seek out those who uplift and inspire you, helping you stay focused on your goals. The more you surround yourself with encouragement, the more resilient you become in maintaining your own happiness and peace of mind.

3. Avoid Comparisons

A major source of unhappiness is the habit of comparing yourself to others. Social media and modern culture can exacerbate this, making it easy to envy another's success, appearance, or possessions. Yet constantly looking over your shoulder at what others have diminishes your own sense of worth and joy.

Instead, adopt an attitude of gratitude. Celebrate your small victories, appreciate your unique path, and love without conditions—starting with yourself. When you practice unconditional acceptance, you discover that happiness arises naturally, without forcing or striving. Your self-esteem remains intact, and you can truly connect with others, supporting them without feeling threatened.

4. Money as a Tool

Money is a powerful resource: it can bring comfort, support dreams, or even transform lives. At the same time, it can become a source of stress, greed, and conflict if mishandled. By treating money as a positive force—a form of energy—you remain in control of your finances, instead of letting them control you.

Spend intentionally: direct your funds toward endeavours that align with your values and create good vibrations. It may be helping someone in need, investing in your education, or simply enjoying a well-deserved treat now and then. By seeing money as a friend rather than an enemy, you shift your mindset to abundance and gratitude—creating a virtuous cycle that fosters more contentment.

5. Manage Your Desires

Desires can motivate us to pursue goals and enrich our lives. However, when they spiral into unchecked greed, they can disrupt our peace and strain our relationships. The key lies in recognizing when healthy ambition crosses the line into obsession.

Practice self-awareness: periodically ask yourself why you want certain things, and whether the longing stems from genuine need, joy, or societal pressure. If you find yourself chasing more and more without feeling satisfied, consider simplifying. By keeping your wishes balanced and grounded, you create space for true happiness—contentment that doesn't vanish the moment you obtain the next "must-have" item.

Bringing It All Together

Happiness isn't a single event or purchase; it's a state of being cultivated through mindful choices and daily practices. Faith in a guiding force frees you from fear, while healthy boundaries preserve your mental space. Living without constant comparisons fosters authenticity, and viewing money as a helpful resource keeps you focused on what really matters. Finally, keeping desires in check ensures that your joy remains rooted in genuine fulfilment rather than fleeting cravings.

By weaving these principles into your life, you not only nurture your own happiness but also positively influence the people around you, creating a ripple effect of contentment and well-being.

LIFE

I believe that there are many obstacles in life, and there are many speed breakers too. But these ups and downs do not last forever. If we make up our minds that problems come and go, then why should we worry unnecessarily? Thinking like this makes the problems feel much smaller. They eventually leave, but not without giving us some new learning or experience.

Life has two branches: one is material, and the other is spiritual. A person who embraces material life wholeheartedly and also dedicates some time to spirituality Finds their life blossoming well, remaining peaceful, and progressing steadily.

We have a lot of power inside us, but we get so busy chasing material things That we forget the spiritual power within. To create balance in our lives, we should nurture both branches. When one becomes mature through continuous practice, they become like a master, a saint, or someone carefree and fulfilled.

Social gathering

I was called by my dad today and said that Guru Ji is coming this weekend to take care of the devotees. Last time you were gossiping with friends and numbers of guests left without Prasad, offering. This time, it should not have happened. Serving saints is also a form of charity and it also gives rewards. One should serve saints and devotees with body, mind and money. It gives peace to the mind, I said yes, I will definitely do it.

Big pandal was made and about 200 people came and guruji, the teacher came and started his lecture.

Namaskar and Jai Shri Ram,

Some people worry unnecessarily, and they are the ones who spoil their future. This constant state of anxiety clouds their judgment and prevents them from making sound decisions. They become so entangled in their fears and negative thoughts that they miss opportunities for growth and happiness. On the other hand, those who are ready to face and solve new problems in life, without running away from them, are the ones who rise in society. They embrace challenges with courage and patience, knowing that every problem carries the seed of a solution and an opportunity to evolve.

This ability to rise above adversity is possible only when the mind is clean—free from jealousy, hatred, fear, and unnecessary desires. A clean mind fosters clarity, creativity, and wisdom. It helps individuals stay focused on their goals without being distracted by negative emotions. When the mind is burdened with dirt—such as grudges, doubts, and insecurities—even thinking about development becomes difficult. A clouded mind cannot see the path ahead clearly, and indecisiveness takes over.

It is said that when the mind is pure, the flow of thoughts is like the sacred Ganga–clear, powerful, and nourishing. Just as the Ganga nurtures life along its banks, a pure mind nurtures positive actions, compassionate behaviour, and wise decisions. A pure mind brings balance, strength, and the ability to stay calm in the face of challenges. It allows individuals to find joy in simple things, maintain healthy relationships, and contribute meaningfully to society. Ultimately, the journey of personal and spiritual growth begins with cleansing the mind and nurturing positive thoughts.

You're reflecting on some deep and profound ideas about freedom, happiness, and detachment. It sounds like you're contemplating the nature of reality, the self, and how external attachments–like money, power, and prestige–can pull us away from inner peace.

- **Sanity is in self-contentment**–true happiness comes from within, not from external validation.
- **Interference disturbs peace**–when you're happy, there's no need to control others or let them control you.
- **Spiritual places radiate good energy**–but ultimately, the real journey is within.
- **Problems are unreal**–they exist as long as we give them importance. When we detach from them, they vanish.
- **Bondage is compulsion and obsession**–true freedom is breaking free from mental chains, not just physical ones.
- **Inner chatter causes conflict**–and that leads to a crowded, restless mind. Oneness comes when we silence that noise.
- **Freedom is an internal state**–even if the body is trapped, the soul can soar beyond limitations.
- You're diving into the paradox of human nature–the contrast between the purity of the heart and the restless

greed of the mind. Your thoughts seem to reflect the idea that:

- **The Heart is a Mirror** – It reflects the truth, but few look deep enough to see it.
- **No One is Parallel to Him** – Every individual is unique, yet lost in the illusion of comparison.
- **Human Greed is Endless** – Satisfaction is rare; desires keep growing.
- **The Brain is Another Mirror** – But unlike the heart, it remains unnoticed, left unchecked.
- **Even in Play, the Heart is in Control** – Whether we realize it or not, emotions and deeper truths influence all actions.
- I am reflecting on the hidden depths of human nature, the contrast between mind and heart, and how people often remain unaware of their own reflections.

This kind of wisdom is timeless, resonating with teachings from spiritual traditions like Zen, Vedanta, and Sufism.

In our scriptures, in the words of saints, we find a storehouse of knowledge and saints have been uplifting human life for centuries. If we keep in mind that nothing is mine in me, whatever is there is all is yours oh lord, then half or total problem is solved. This competition or dilemma that this should become mine, to get it, we have left ourselves somewhere. What are you, why have you come here, you just have to think a little about this and when you get the right and true knowledge of life, then a lot of changes come in life. Few lines are below from a saint.

I have now learnt how to live

I am happy, I am pleased, I am blissful

Because I have stopped running after desires

I and the jewels inside me are priceless

Any comparison with external things is meaningless

The soul inside is pure, God is also pure

If there is impurity and evil, it is me, my life

It has to be purified in this life

But we are walking on the wrong path

Keep walking, you will not achieve anything

If you will achieve only disappointment,

If there is a drop of hope, nectar, it is only inside

When the inner strength increases,

then there will be an increase in inner satisfaction and happiness

The feeling of fear and insecurity inside will also decrease

If we have to awaken the energy of spirituality inside us

Then we have to awaken the feeling inside us

You're expressing a profound understanding of karma, universal balance, and divine reciprocity. Your words carry deep spiritual insight, reflecting the belief that every good action leaves an imprint on the universe and is eventually acknowledged or rewarded.

Key Takeaways from Your Reflection:

- **No Good Deed Goes Unnoticed** – Even if the world does not recognize it, the universe registers our actions, and they come back to us in due time.
- **Timing of Rewards** – Some kindness is repaid instantly, while others take time, but nothing is ever lost.

- **Divine Acknowledgment** – Acts of goodness resonate with a higher power, earning silent blessings.
- **Emotional Value Over Materialism** – True gifts are those carried in the heart, not just physical possessions.
- **Universal Reflection** – When we feel isolated, God sends us people (mirror images) who help us find comfort and understanding.

He sang a bhajan which was as under;

Lord, I remember you and calling you Sahib Sahib, master

Temples, mosques, Gurudwaras, I have searched everywhere

Ram, Allah, Waheguru, I cannot see them here

I made the structure of bricks and mud

And what's more, Thakur, I too settled you here

I am not your true devotee

Why would I fight and die in the name of your and house

God made the structure of flesh and bones

Lord, you reside in this temple of my heart

After eating meat and fish inside me, I made it a graveyard

I am not your true devotee

Why should I search for Sahib here and there

Sahib is within me so near; I was only one away from Sahib

When my heart got attached to you Lord

This bond of attachment and love

got connected in such a way that it became unbreakable

Now this meditation, remembrance has become a way of life

This is the key to success

Whether it is the path of the world or of God

Only these devotions, commitment is required

Om is a very powerful mantra. When you chant Om, its vibrations work miracles within you. It can cure depression, anxiety, and purify negative emotions such as ego, jealousy, greed, and hatred. You should chant Om at least thirteen times daily and gradually increase the count. It also helps improve your sleep.

Advice to Control Bad Habits Bad habits are the root cause of unhappiness. Here are some suggestions to improve your life:

- Eat only 80% of your hunger; avoid snacking in between meals.
- Limit intake of toxic foods, sweets, and fried items. You can indulge once a week and celebrate it as a cheat day.
- Reduce time spent on TV, mobile phones, and social media. Shut these down two hours before bedtime and avoid them for two hours after waking up.

Resilience in Life We must cultivate resilience in life. Setbacks and adversities are part of our journey; they give us opportunities to improve. Developing an antifragile attitude ensures that we can find solutions and grow stronger with every challenge.

Staying Active After retirement or during vacations, don't sit idle–stay active.

- **Students:** Create a timetable for studying. Read any subject slowly and carefully, as haste always leads to waste.
- **Daily Practices:** Incorporate yoga, exercise, and time in nature into your routine. Watch greenery, birds, and their nests–it's therapeutic.

Fostering Happiness

- Make good friends and engage in creative activities such as gardening, pottery, painting, or helping the less fortunate.
- Spend time on social gatherings, play games, and read books. You will notice significant changes in your life.
- Take inspiration from babies—they cry only when hungry but otherwise remain calm and happy. They live in the present moment, unlike us, who regret the past and worry about the future.

A Disciple's Poem One of my disciples once narrated this poem. I hope you'll like it:

I was driving; the destination was far away, I kept moving forward. I didn't know where my heart and mind were— And yet, on reaching the destination, I was simply surprised.

I am deeply thankful to God for bringing me to this point in life.

Many people more capable than us often lose their way.

Some are blessed with luck and keep climbing the ladders of success.

Unfortunately, instead of thanking God, they start believing they are invincible,

even thinking of themselves as God.

The lesson is simple: always thank God if you achieve something, and if not, don't worry—He might have something better in store for you. Never let success inflate your ego; remember that everything we have is because of His kindness.

We reap the results of our deeds. The Master gives and takes away as He sees fit. You must have noticed that sometimes a warehouse burns down, or a business suffers a loss. In such times, always remember to be thankful to God. Life is full of highs and lows—people rise from the ground to the skies and fall back down again.

Life's Fragile Nature Life depends on a single thread—our breath. Your value here lasts only as long as you are breathing. The moment your breath stops, you become a lifeless body. Will your loved ones keep your body at home? No. You will be taken to the graveyard, and that will be your ultimate journey.

We all know this truth, yet our attachment to material things persists.

Happiness and Sadness Happiness and problems are interconnected in life. A wise person views happiness and sadness as two sides of the same coin. However, an ignorant person clings to sadness, leading to a disturbed mental state. Such individuals trouble themselves, spread negativity, and harm their relationships with loved ones.

Why do we face this dilemma? Who is it for? We just need to understand that we are more than mere human beings—we are spiritual beings, saints at heart.

Finding Inner Peace I am not saying you should abandon everything. Instead, embrace life fully:

- Practice meditation.
- Express gratitude.
- Strive to remain happy from both inside and outside.

When you achieve this balance, life becomes meaningful and fulfilling.

Only the Body Knows (Bhajan) Only the body that is touched feels the pain, Who else can understand my sorrow? The jeweller knows how to test gold, Just as only the devotee knows the value of God's name.

The Guru has revealed a sacred truth to me, I am ready to sacrifice myself for you, oh Master. The sweetness of the sacred name now delights my soul, While the worldly pleasures taste bland.

If the Guru blesses me, I shall always remember God's name, and in this devotion, I will find eternal bliss. This happiness surpasses all, making worldly pleasures seem trivial and empty.

The Guru, a Treasure of Nectar the Guru is a treasure of nectar, which is why countless devotees follow. Here, one experiences a divine transformation, but only a rare soul attains it– The one who has earned it through great deeds.

In the end I will say

This reflects a deep understanding of mindfulness and the essence of living in the present moment.

- Dwelling on the past brings sorrow - Regret and nostalgia can weigh us down.
- Worrying about the future causes fear - Anxiety stems from uncertainty.
- Living in the present brings joy - A simple smile can transform the moment into something meaningful.
- The Math of Life: Addition, Subtraction, Multiplication, Division – and the Balance of It All
- Life, in many ways, can be seen as a form of mathematics. The choices we make and the way we interact with others often reflect the basic operations of math – addition, subtraction, multiplication, and division. Each of these reflects a different philosophy, a different approach to life.
- Addition: The Builders Some people believe in doing "plus" – adding value wherever they go. They add kindness, love, knowledge, and support. These are the builders and nurturers, the ones who uplift others and enrich lives. Their presence brings growth, joy, and positivity. They believe life becomes meaningful when you

contribute and add to the happiness and well-being of others.

- Subtraction: The Simplifiers Some live by the philosophy of "minus" – they focus on reducing negativity, cutting away unnecessary burdens, and simplifying life. These people seek peace by letting go of anger, ego, and materialism. They remove toxicity from their lives and help others shed their fears and insecurities. Subtraction isn't about loss – it's about clarity and making space for what truly matters.
- Multiplication: The Expanders There are those who believe in "into" – multiplying their efforts, dreams, and love. They don't just add goodness; they amplify it. They inspire others, spread ideas, and create waves of change. Multipliers think big and help others grow exponentially. Their vision and energy create abundance in life.
- Division: The Sharers Some practice "divide" – sharing what they have, whether it's knowledge, resources, time, or love. They believe life's joy multiplies when it's divided. By dividing their blessings, they build communities and foster unity. They teach the value of generosity and the importance of giving.
- The Final Balance: God's Equation But when the time comes, God balances it all. In the end, the plus, minus, into, and divide even out. Life's joys and sorrows, gains and losses, successes and failures – everything finds equilibrium. This divine balance reminds us that no matter our approach, we are all part of a greater equation.
- Understanding the math of life helps us appreciate different perspectives and embrace balance. Whether we

add, subtract, multiply, or divide, what matters most is how we contribute to the harmony of the whole equation.

This wisdom aligns with many spiritual teachings—whether it's Buddhism's focus on the "now" or Stoicism's lesson on embracing the present.

That Is All for Today "I bless you all with a happy life," the Guru concluded.

After the Satsang, my duty called me outside the auditorium. I ensured the tables, chairs, snacks, and tea were arranged. I instructed the vendor to prepare everything, As the audience was about to leave.

As devotees began to exit, I invited them, "Please have the prasad, offerings." Gradually, everyone moved to the tables for snacks and tea.

My father arrived and saw me diligently managing the arrangements.

Serving Devotees and a Sacred Blessing As I continued serving and requesting the devotees, "Please do not leave without having the snacks," my father approached me. He placed his hand on my shoulder and guided me toward Guruji, the spiritual master. He introduced me to the master, who blessed me warmly.

My father then requested Guruji to bestow upon me the *Naam Daan*—the sacred word. Guruji leaned close to my ear, imparted the sacred name, and instructed me to meditate on it daily, repeating it as long as I could. I bowed before him, touching his feet in reverence. He placed his hand on my head again and blessed me, saying, "Be happy, and may the Almighty grant you prosperity."

A Troubled Friend The next day, Neeraj called me, saying he was in Noida and wanted to meet at a coffee shop. He mentioned needing my advice on something. I laughed, saying, "We're the same age. How can I advise you?" But sensing urgency in his voice, I agreed to meet him the following day at a mall in Noida.

On my way, I encountered a massive traffic jam caused by a farmers' procession. It took a while for the police to clear the road, and we were diverted to an alternate route. By the time I reached the coffee shop, I was two hours late.

Neeraj was waiting patiently, but his face was pale and tired. "Neeraj, I hope everything is okay. You don't look well," I said.

He sighed heavily. "Yaar, I'm in trouble," he confessed.

"Tell me what's wrong," I urged.

He explained, "Piya had an abortion three months ago. Since then, she's been staying at her mother's house and refuses to return. I've tried everything to console her, and so has her mother. We've explained that such things happen and that she has her whole life ahead of her. But she blames the miscarriage on our house being on the fourth floor. She insists I move to a ground-floor apartment, or she won't come back."

After listening carefully, I replied, "Neeraj, I understand how difficult this is for both of you. If moving to a ground-floor house will help Piya heal emotionally and physically, then I suggest you cooperate and make the change. A peaceful and supportive environment is essential for her recovery."

.I am searching but either not getting or it is too expensive to afford. A little away, Andheri sides, a house is available, and there also she is saying it is too far and she cannot go in such a crowded local train.

I said jokingly, "Then become a son-in-law of their house." Neeraj looked at me. I had never seen him so sad. Neeraj said, "It is not possible as their house is only one bedroom. No chance; it cannot be adjusted."

I said, "Neeraj, see, some people, when shocked due to any reason, and they are not coming to normal, I will advise you to consult some psychologist."

Neeraj and I together visited a psychologist and narrated the whole story.

Doctor: "Where is she?" Neeraj: "Madam, she is at her house in Mumbai." Doctor: "Let us have a video call, I can talk to her. I do video consultancy."

Neeraj connected to Piya. Doctor: "Hello Piya, this is a psychologist. Neeraj is our family friend, and if you don't mind, can we start the consultation? Neeraj has already briefed me." Piya: "Where is Neeraj?" Doctor moved the camera towards Neeraj. Neeraj: "Hello Piya, I discussed this with you yesterday. Please listen to the doctor and don't worry, all will be fine."

Doctor: "See, Piya, in this life, so many things happen. That does not mean we should break. We should fight with the situation. You are educated, mature, and you are not alone. Many women have had abortions. Healing takes time. Be patient and kind to yourself. You should not feel any kind of guilt, shame, or anxiety.

If you are facing difficulty in daily activities or managing emotions, it's important to give yourself time to heal and recover. What you're feeling is normal after such an experience, but remember, this is not the end. Life has its way of offering new beginnings."

The doctor continued: "Here are some steps that might help:

- **Acknowledge Your Emotions**: It's okay to feel sadness, anger, or guilt. Don't suppress your feelings; instead, share them with someone you trust, like Neeraj or a close family member.

- **Engage in Mindfulness**: Practices such as meditation, yoga, or even simple breathing exercises can help calm your mind and reduce anxiety.

- **Routine and Structure**: Create a daily routine that includes small, manageable tasks. Accomplishing even one task can give you a sense of progress and control.
- **Physical Activity**: Regular exercise, such as walking or light yoga, can be a great way to release pent-up emotions and feel rejuvenated.
- **Social Interaction**: Spend time with friends or family, even if it's virtual. Positive interactions can lift your spirits.
- **Seek Joy in Small Things:** Watch a movie, read a book, or pursue a hobby you love. These small joys can act as stepping stones to a brighter mood."

Piya listened attentively, nodding occasionally. The doctor added: "You're not alone in this, Piya. Many women go through similar challenges, and they emerge stronger. Your strength and resilience will guide you through this time."

Neeraj reassured her, "I'm here for you, Piya. We'll get through this together."

After the call, the doctor said to Neeraj, "She seems willing to listen and work on herself, which is a great sign. Be patient with her, and keep encouraging her to follow these steps. You can call me if any additional support is needed."

Two months later, Neeraj shared an update. Piya had started practicing yoga and mindfulness and had reconnected with her family and friends. She was gradually regaining her confidence and was even considering moving forward with plans for a new home.

When I spoke to Neeraj, he said, "She's getting better, and I can see the positivity returning to her life. Thank you for your support and for suggesting professional help. It made all the difference."

I replied, "I'm glad to hear that. Always remember, challenges are temporary, and with love and patience, everything falls into place. Keep supporting each other and be thankful for the journey ahead."

It was truly heartening to see how compassion, understanding, and the right guidance could transform a challenging situation into a hopeful and healing journey.

Counter with Vaswani at Golf course

Today, I went to play golf at DLF. It was a great surprise to see Vaswani there, whom I had met in Mumbai, and we had played golf together. He was with another group initially but requested me to join them since they were three players.

I agreed, and we played a good round. I even made a hole-in-one, which meant I had to treat them at the pavilion restaurant. While we were dining, I asked him how he happened to be here.

"Well, I've come here for a conference related to a skills program. Today I was free, and these guys brought me here. It seems it was fate for us to meet and play again," Vaswani said with a smile. "It was wonderful, and again, congrats on the hole-in-one."

Curious about the skills conference, I asked more about their role and activities. Vaswani handed me a catalogue on the subject, which was highly informative. Here's a general outline from the catalogue about a skills program:

Program Structure

- **Needs Assessment:** Identify skill gaps and areas for improvement.
- **Goal Setting:** Establish clear, measurable objectives.

- **Curriculum Development**: Design training modules and materials.
- **Training Delivery**: Implement training sessions (in-person or online).
- **Evaluation and Feedback**: Assess progress and provide feedback.

Core Skills Categories

- **Communication**: Enhance verbal, written, and interpersonal communication.
- **Leadership**: Foster the ability to inspire and guide others effectively.
- **Problem-Solving**: Develop strategies to analyze and resolve challenges.
- **Time Management**: Learn techniques to prioritize tasks and manage time efficiently.
- **Teamwork and Collaboration**: Build skills to work harmoniously in a team setting.
- **Adaptability and Flexibility**: Cultivate resilience and the ability to adjust to changes.
- **Critical Thinking**: Strengthen logical reasoning and decision-making skills.
- **Emotional Intelligence**: Improve self-awareness and empathy for better relationships.
- **Conflict Resolution**: Learn techniques to address and resolve disputes effectively.
- **Digital Literacy**: Acquire knowledge of essential digital tools and technologies.

Additional Training Methods

- **Self-Paced E-Learning Modules:** Flexible learning options tailored to individual schedules.
- **Mentorship Programs:** Guidance from experienced professionals to foster growth.
- **On-the-Job Training:** Hands-on experience to apply skills in real-world settings.
- **Coaching and Feedback Sessions:** Personalized support to enhance performance.

Evaluation and Assessment Methods

- **Quizzes and Assessments:** Measure understanding and retention of concepts.
- **Project-Based Evaluations:** Assess application of skills in practical scenarios.
- **Peer Feedback and Reviews:** Gain insights from colleagues for improvement.
- **Self-Assessment and Reflection:** Encourage introspection to identify strengths and areas for growth.
- **Certification or Badge Programs:** Recognize achievement and skill mastery.

Program Benefits

- **Enhanced Skills and Knowledge:** Gain expertise in targeted areas.
- **Improved Job Performance:** Increase efficiency and productivity.

- **Increased Confidence:** Build self-assurance through competence.
- **Better Career Prospects:** Open doors to advanced roles and opportunities.
- **Enhanced Adaptability and Resilience:** Equip participants to navigate challenges effectively.
- **Stronger Team Dynamics:** Promote collaboration and harmony within teams.
- **Competitive Advantage in the Market:** Stay ahead in a fast-paced professional landscape.

Tailor your skills program to meet specific needs and goals. Ensure continuous evaluation and refinement to achieve optimal impact and long-lasting benefits.

The program seemed quite structured and comprehensive. Vaswani shared that the conference was focused on discussing best practices and strategies to implement such programs effectively.

It was a delightful day, both on and off the golf course, and the serendipitous meeting with Vaswani turned out to be as enlightening as it was enjoyable.

Self-training

Initially, I relied on my father to handle correspondence, especially when dealing with serious issues from valued customers. However, I realized this arrangement couldn't last forever. To improve myself, I began reading children's books and gradually progressed to more advanced material. Over time, I noticed significant improvement and started managing correspondence independently. and today I am writing my third book in a row.

Morning walk

Our routine often included dropping the kids off at school and then heading to the Rose Garden near IIT Gate for a walk. I vividly recall one amusing incident during one of our walks.

A group ahead of us noticed a foreign couple holding hands while walking. One of them remarked, "Look at how lovely this couple is, walking hand in hand. And look at our wives–they're trailing two hundred meters behind us!"

Another replied with a laugh, "Yes, but we don't know when this foreign couple might separate or divorce. Meanwhile, no matter how far behind our wives are, they will never leave us!"

They all burst into laughter, and we couldn't help but join in.

Travel Mishap That Remains in My Mind Forever

Some interesting incidents are worth sharing:

I was traveling from Rome to Geneva by train when the warden came to me and said, "You are alone in the cabin, please take care of your goods and lock the cabin from inside." I locked the cabin and went to sleep. At 4 AM, I woke up and saw that everything seemed fine. I opened the door to check and saw no one around. I rushed to the washroom and came back within two minutes. After locking the cabin again, I noticed my bag was missing.

I immediately went to the warden and told him that someone had taken my bag. He replied, "I told you to be careful." I explained that I had only gone to the washroom for a couple of minutes, and when I returned, my bag was gone. The warden apologized but said there was nothing he could do.

I decided to take matters into my own hands and threatened to pull the chain to stop the train. The warden said, "You go that way, and I'll go the other way." I ran like a marathoner, crossing five wagons. In the sixth wagon, I saw a man coming out of the toilet. I thought he might have stolen my bag, so I decided to check the washroom.

To my surprise, my bag was there! I grabbed it and confronted the man, asking him to return whatever he had taken. He nervously responded, "Don't make a scene," and pulled money out of his shoes, handing it back to me. I took my bag and money and returned to my cabin, feeling a huge sense of relief. I took a deep breath and thanked God.

The warden congratulated me and said, "You're lucky to have found your lost items."

Incident at Johnsburg Airport

Once, I was at Johnsburg Airport, waiting to catch my flight to Cape Town. I met Mr. R. P. Singh, an Indian diplomat, and we shook hands. He was surprised to see me there. I told Mr. Singh, "I need some money, where is the ATM here?" He kindly took me to the ATM machine, but when I put my card in, it wasn't working.

Just then, another person came over to help me. Before I could fully understand what was happening, the Embassy driver, who was with Mr. R. P. Singh appeared. He shouted, "Sir, he has swapped your card!" and caught the thief red-handed. The thief quickly threw the card on the ground and ran away.

I thanked God and Mr. R. P. Singh. It felt like God had sent him to ensure my safety.

Incident in Madrid

I was holding two shopping bags in Madrid, walking towards my hotel, while my wife, who had knee problems, was coming behind me. I noticed some teenage boys playing on the road. They had different-coloured hair, which I had never seen before, particularly on boys. I was watching them when, as I got closer, one of the boys threw some coins between my legs and started moving through them.

Before I could understand what was happening, my wallet was stolen. My wife shouted, "That guy has taken your purse!" I immediately ran towards him, but he threw my purse and ran away. He was about to get hit by a car but, luckily, he managed to cross to the other side of the road.

Once again, I was lucky. God was truly kind to me. I'm thankful to Him.

Incident in Kathmandu, Singapore and USA

Once, I was traveling to Kathmandu and was detained by immigration officials in India. They informed me that there was a pending case against someone with the same name as mine and the same father's name, though their address was different. They suspected that I was linked to a criminal who was absconding. I provided my ration card as identification, and after verifying it, they allowed me to proceed, apologizing for the delay and the inconvenience. I told them, "No regrets, you are doing your duty."

Once I landed in Singapore, where the immigration staff called her supervisor and took me to a room, locking it from the outside. They took my wife to the luggage belt and examined all the suitcases. She was understandably worried about me and requested to meet me. I knocked on the door, and a lady opened it, starting her inquiry: "Why have you come? What is the purpose of your visit here? Do you know anyone in Singapore?"

I recalled that we had recently moved the baggage of our Ambassador, T.C. Raghavan. I mentioned that I could provide a reference from our Indian Ambassador, Mr. Raghavan. After about two hours, I was allowed to go, and I thanked God once again for His help.

Incident at New York Immigration

After a long 24-hour journey to New York, USA, I landed with my wife and daughter. Once again, the immigration officer told me to sit on the sofa and not move. After an hour, I approached the officer and asked, "Sir, why are you not allowing me to go? I have a valid visa. If you need any reference, I can provide one from our Embassy or Consulate." He shouted loudly, "I told you not to move. Why have you come here?" I was scared and returned to the sofa.

My wife, daughter, and our one-year-old baby were all upset and quietly sat, at the mercy of the officer. My daughter said, "I will write to the authorities about this harassment." I told her, "They don't spare film stars like Shah Rukh Khan, and who am I?"

Thank God, after some time, they finally allowed us to go.

Such things happen occasionally, but after Mr. Modi's tenure, I never faced any issues regarding immigration worldwide. Later, my daughter received a reply from U.S. Immigration, apologizing for the harassment and advising us that in the future, we should show this letter if we face any problems. I framed that letter to show it in the future.

The next time I stood at the immigration window, I submitted my passport and that framed letter. The officer saw the letter and smiled. He said, "No need for this letter, I am satisfied. You can go and enjoy it." I don't know how correct this is. Our passport value has increased since the Modi Government was in power and so far, I have not faced any obstacle/harassment at any airport worldwide in the last 10 years.

Meeting Naresh at the Air Cargo Exhibition

Again, I visited Mumbai for the Air Cargo Exhibition at the Jio World Convention Centre. After meeting some exhibitors, I spent about three hours there before coming out. I saw a gentleman who also looked at me. As we approached each other, he said, "I think we have met somewhere before."

I thought for a moment and recognized him. "You are Naresh, if I'm not wrong," I said.

"Yes, I'm Naresh," he replied, but he couldn't recall where we had met.

I said, "We met at the golf course with Vaswani and Suresh. We played golf together and had a beer afterward."

Naresh hugged me and said, "Yes, Vaswani told me you played together at DLF in Gurugram. How are you here?"

I replied, "I'm here for the Air Cargo Exhibition."

"We're also having a conference here related to startups. Let's have coffee," he said. He took me to the exhibition hall, where we had coffee. I picked up a catalogue from the counter on the startup subject.

It was quite interesting, and the contents were as follows:

Startup Idea

- **Identify your passion**: What problem do you want to solve?
- **Research your market**: Understand your target audience and competition.
- **Refine your idea**: Validate your concept and create a unique value proposition.

Business Planning

- **Develop a business plan**: Outline your mission, goals, and strategies.
- **Create a financial plan**: Establish a budget, funding requirements, and revenue projections.

- **Define your team structure:** Determine the roles and responsibilities needed to execute your plan.

Funding and Finance

- **Explore funding options:** Consider bootstrapping, crowdfunding, angel investors, or venture capital.
- **Establish a financial management system:** Set up accounting, invoicing, and expense tracking processes.
- **Manage cash flow:** Monitor your startup's financial health and make adjustments as needed.

Marketing and Sales

- **Develop a marketing strategy:** Create a plan for branding, advertising, and promoting your product or service.
- **Establish a sales process:** Define your sales funnel, pricing, and customer acquisition strategies.
- **Build a sales team:** Hire and train sales professionals to execute your sales strategy.

Operations and Management

- **Set up business operations:** Establish processes for customer support, supply chain management, and logistics.
- **Develop a management structure:** Define roles, responsibilities, and decision-making processes.
- **Foster a company culture:** Encourage collaboration, innovation, and continuous learning.

Launch and Growth

- **Launch your product or service:** Execute your go-to-market strategy and promote your offering.
- **Monitor and analyse performance:** Track key metrics, identify areas for improvement, and adjust your strategy accordingly.
- **Scale your business:** Expand your team, operations, and marketing efforts to drive growth and increase revenue.

Starting a successful startup requires careful planning, execution, and adaptability. Stay focused, be resilient, and continually learn from your experiences.

Additional Resources:

- **Startup accelerators and incubators:** Explore programs like Y Combinator, 500 Startups, or Techstars.
- **Online courses and tutorials:** Utilize resources like Coursera, Udemy, or edX to develop new skills.
- **Startup communities and networks:** Join organizations like Startup Grind, Startup Weekend, or the Entrepreneurs' Organization.

Best of luck with your startup journey!

After that, I saw a desk for MSME (Micro, Small, and Medium Enterprises) and asked Suresh about it. He took me there, spoke in Marathi, and gave me an article by Shivani Rangra, which I also found quite informative. The contents of the article are as follows:

MSME Overview

MSME stands for **Micro, Small, and Medium Enterprises**. The definition of MSMEs has been revised by the Ministry to ensure that benefits extend to more companies, encouraging growth. Previously, benefits were limited to entities with smaller turnovers or investments, which often discouraged businesses from expanding to avoid losing benefits. Under the new definition, companies with a turnover of up to Rs. 100 crores are now eligible, enabling enterprises to scale their operations with government support.

MSME Types

Under the revised guidelines, MSMEs are classified into three categories based on investment and turnover:

1. **Micro Enterprises**
    - Investment: Up to Rs. 1 crore
    - Turnover: Up to Rs. 5 crores
2. **Small Enterprises**
    - Investment: Up to Rs. 10 crores
    - Turnover: Up to Rs. 50 crores
3. **Medium Enterprises**
    - Investment: Up to Rs. 20 crores
    - Turnover: Up to Rs. 100 crores

Eligibility for MSME Registration

Any of the following business entities can register as an MSME:

- Proprietorships
- Partnership Firms
- Private Limited Companies
- Public Limited Companies

- Limited Liability Partnerships (LLPs)
- Hindu Undivided Families (HUFs)
- Self-Help Groups
- Societies / Cooperative Societies
- Trusts

MSME Loans

MSME loans are provided to enterprises by financial institutions like banks and NBFCs (Non-Banking Financial Companies). Additionally, several government schemes facilitate MSME loans to support business development.

MSME Loans and Schemes

MSME loans aim to provide financial aid and funding for new and existing entrepreneurs in the country. Key schemes include:

- CGTMSE (Credit Guarantee Fund Trust for Micro and Small Enterprises)
- Mudra Loan
- PMEGP (Prime Minister's Employment Generation Programme)

These schemes ensure that entrepreneurs can secure the necessary financial resources to grow and sustain their businesses.

MSME Registration Process

The MSME registration can be done online via the official website. Any entrepreneur with a valid Aadhaar Number is eligible to apply. The steps to register are as follows:

- **Enter Aadhaar Details**: Provide the Aadhaar number and personal information.
- **Fill the Application Form**: Enter business details such as name, type, and financials.
- **Make Online Payment**: Pay the applicable fee for processing the application.
- **Executive Processing**: The application is verified and processed by an authorized executive.
- **Receive MSME Certificate**: Once approved, the certificate is emailed to the applicant.

How to Get an MSME Certificate Online?

To obtain the MSME certificate, follow these steps:

- Fill out the online application form with accurate details.
- Make the required payment through the portal.
- Wait for the executive to process your application.
- The MSME certificate will be sent to your registered email address.

Emergency Financial Support for MSMEs

During the COVID-19 pandemic, the government introduced **Rs. 3 lakh crores Collateral-free Automatic Loans for Businesses**, including MSMEs, to help businesses overcome financial challenges.

Key Features of the Scheme

1. **Emergency Credit Line**: Businesses/MSMEs could access up to 20% of their entire outstanding credit as of February 29, 2020.

2. **Eligibility**:

    - Borrowers with up to Rs. 25 crore outstanding credit.
    - Turnover of up to Rs. 100 crores.

3. **Loan Terms:**

    - Tenor of 4 years with a 12-month moratorium on principal repayment.
    - Interest capped to make loans affordable.

4. **Credit Guarantee**: 100% credit guarantee cover provided to Banks and NBFCs on both principal and interest.

5. **Availability**: The scheme was available until **October 31, 2020**.

This initiative was a lifeline for businesses struggling due to the pandemic, enabling them to address operational liabilities, purchase raw materials, and restart operations.

Additional Benefits of the MSME Loan Scheme

- No Guarantee Fee & No Fresh Collateral: MSME loans under this scheme do not require a guarantee fee or any fresh collateral, significantly reducing the financial burden on small business owners.
- Safeguarding Employment: The initiative aims to help 45 lakh MSME units resume business operations, thus protecting jobs and ensuring economic stability for millions of workers.

Naresh offered me to play golf tomorrow. "No, I am leaving tomorrow and having dinner with Neeraj and his family," Mukesh, I replied.

"Please call them all to the club; we can have dinner together."

"Sorry, Naresh, this time, please excuse me. Next time for sure, we'll sit together."

Naresh handed me his card. "I won't insist, but here's my card. If there's any hope, just call me."

I was about to leave when Neeraj called to inform me that the restaurant he had booked was full, and they needed to choose another place. I mentioned Naresh's proposal. Neeraj thought it was a wonderful idea and suggested booking the table at the club.

Naresh was sitting in his car when I knocked on his window. He stopped and rolled it down. I told him, "Sorry for the back-and-forth, but we all can join you today at 8 PM at the club because Neeraj

couldn't book the table."

Naresh stepped out of the car, visibly delighted. "Fine! See you at 8. Vaswani will also join us. We usually meet here on Wednesdays for drinks."

At 8 PM, we arrived at the club. Our table for ten was ready, but Suresh, Naresh and Vishwani were not there yet. I called him at 8:30 PM. "Where are you?"

"Sorry, I'm stuck in traffic, but I'll be there in ten minutes. You can go ahead and place the order for snacks and beer," Suresh replied.

I called the waiter and ordered four beers, chicken tikka, and fish tikka.

Reeta, my wife, said, "I won't drink. Who will drive the car otherwise?"

Neeraj assured her, "By the time we're ready to leave, it will be fine. Have one." She smiled, and I asked the waiter to bring four beers.

I was happy to see Neeraj's wife with us, especially since she was expecting. Naturally, we couldn't ask her to drink. I turned to her and asked, "Bhabhi Ji, what would you like to drink or have as snacks?"

"Fish tikka is fine for snacks, and I'll take a soda with lemon, no ice," she said.

As our first round was finishing, Suresh and his group were still missing. I called him again.

"Suresh, where are you? We're all waiting!"

He replied apologetically, "Ashok Bhai, I'm really sorry. Actually, I'm..." at the police station. This inspector is being very fussy. He isn't listening or settling the matter

and I'm trying to get things sorted. I've already informed his seniors, and I hope to be free soon."

Confused, I asked, "Suresh, what have you done? Which police station are you at? Do you need any help?"

Suresh replied, "No, you enjoy, Ashok. Don't worry about us. We were just drinking in the car when the inspector spotted us and brought us to the station."

I narrated the story to the group. Everyone had a different opinion. Someone said, "Just pay the bill and leave."

But the waiter informed us, "Neither cash nor cards are accepted here. The club bills members monthly."

We asked to speak to the manager. When he arrived, we explained the situation and mentioned that Naresh, who had invited us, was stuck at the police station.

We requested to settle the bill in cash.

The manager pointed to another club member sitting nearby. "You can give him the cash, and we'll bill him directly," he suggested.

When we asked the total, he replied, "Just one thousand rupees."

Fortunately, the member agreed to help. We handed him the cash, settled the matter, and decided to leave immediately. Everyone was visibly worried, and the incident left a sour note.

We ended up eating dosa and idly at a small restaurant nearby. The whole evening felt surreal.

Late into the night, we speculated about them. One person joked, "What if they're criminals?" Another added, "Maybe they caused an accident while driving drunk." Reeta expressed concern, "I hope they didn't bluff us."

I tried to reassure everyone. "How is that possible? Naresh had booked the table for us."

Despite my efforts, guilt weighed heavily on me. I couldn't sleep, questioning why I had taken them for dinner in the first place.

The next morning, Suresh called and apologized profusely. "Ashok Bhai, I'm so sorry about yesterday. The police inspector was being unreasonable. My entire family and lawyer were there, and we weren't released until 3 AM."

I had no words and finally replied, "No issue, Suresh. Hope to see you soon."

Back to Delhi

Later that day, I returned to Delhi. As I checked my mail, I saw an invitation to register for a conference in Istanbul. Without hesitation, I signed up, even though it was scheduled two months later.

That evening, my grandmother approached me and said, "Guru Ji hasn't visited us in a long time..."

I paused for a moment, thinking about what my grandmother had just said. "Did you receive any letter from him?" she asked again, her tone filled with curiosity.

I replied, "Why would he write to me?"

She looked at me intently, "Perhaps he left his cloak behind."

"It's possible," I said, though I wasn't sure what she meant.

She hesitated before asking, "Will you do one thing for me? Will you take me to Pusa Road Radha Swami Satsang? I've heard the Sant there is a very accomplished soul."

I had immense respect for her, so I immediately agreed. There was a three-day continuous Satsang and social gathering happening at the venue. We decided Sunday would be the best day to attend.

The Satsang was led by Sant Charan Singh, whose soft-spoken demeanour and profound wisdom captivated the entire gathering. His words, though in Punjabi, resonated deeply, as if every syllable was a pearl falling from his lips.

Among his teachings, I vividly recall a few of his messages:

- Accept Destiny and Be Content Whatever God has written in our destiny; we are destined to receive. Be grateful and content with what you have, and remain patient.
- The Eternal Guidance of Saints For thousands of years, saints have graced the earth, showing humanity the path to spirituality, peace, and happiness. From Ram, Krishna, and Nanak Dev Ji to Christ, Mahatma Buddha, and countless others, they all led humanity toward inner peace.
- Life's Dualities The world is a mix of joy and sorrow. Those with good karma experience fewer hardships, while others endure more suffering. True peace, however, lies in distancing oneself from worldly distractions and worshipping the Lord.

- Material Wealth and Inner Peace Riches do not guarantee happiness. While some wealthy individuals sleep only after taking medicines, the poor struggle for survival. True happiness is not found in palatial homes, dry lands, or remote forests–it is found in devotion to the Lord.

He emphasized that true saints guide humanity toward the divine and that life's purpose is to connect with God.

After the Satsang, my grandmother was visibly moved. She clasped her hands and said, "I've never heard anything so profound. Every word was like a blessing."

The atmosphere at the Satsang and the wisdom of Sant Charan Singh lingered with us as we returned home. That evening, I realized how powerful spiritual teachings could be in grounding one's life amidst the chaos of the world.

A Visit to Dera Beas, Punjab

After my mother's demise, I got the opportunity to visit Dera Beas to immerse her ashes in the Beas River. The arrangements for immersing the ashes were very well-organized. First, the sevadar (volunteer servant) conducted prayers, and then the ashes were placed in a large pipe built over the river. Due to the slope, the ashes went straight into the river, ensuring no dust was raised or visible. It was an arrangement worth appreciating for its cleanliness and thoughtfulness.

After completing the ritual, we went inside the Dera. The atmosphere was deeply spiritual and peaceful. The entire system and management of the place were remarkable and amazing. Every aspect, even the smallest detail, was taken care of, and everything ran smoothly, entirely managed by volunteers. The sevadars , volunteers performed their duties selflessly, without any discrimination or greed, offering their services for free.

We hired a mini-bus for a parikrama (circle/orbit) of the entire Beas premises. I paid the driver Rs. 200, and he kindly guided us through the key locations. There were about six people in the bus, and we visited the various ashrams spread across the vast campus. The driver pointed out meditation halls, dining areas where langar (free community meals) is served, and residential accommodations for visiting devotees.

The serenity of the place left a lasting impression. Every corner of the Dera reflected discipline, simplicity, and a sense of purpose. It felt like being part of a perfectly orchestrated symphony, where each individual contributed to creating a harmonious environment.

During the parikrama, the driver shared how thousands of people volunteered daily, performing seva (selfless service) without expecting anything in return. Some cooked meals, others cleaned the premises, and many maintained the gardens and pathways. Their dedication was inspiring, and it was evident that their service came from a place of devotion rather than obligation.

We visited the satsang hall, a massive structure designed to accommodate tens of thousands of devotees. Though empty at the time, its sheer scale and simplicity were awe-inspiring. It was a testament to the collective effort and unwavering faith of the followers.

Next, we visited the langar hall, where free meals were being served to everyone, regardless of religion, caste, or social status. Volunteers served with a smile, and the food, though simple, was delicious and fulfilling. Sharing a meal in such a setting, surrounded by people united in faith and devotion, felt like a blessing.

The visit to Dera Beas was a transformative experience. It wasn't just about immersing my mother's ashes; it was about immersing myself in an atmosphere of spirituality, humility, and service. The teachings of the master seemed to echo in every corner of the Dera, reminding me of the importance of selflessness, gratitude, and faith in the divine.

As we prepared to leave, I felt a deep sense of calm and renewal. The journey had been more than just a ritual; it had been a profound lesson in how simple acts of devotion and service can create peace and harmony.

The driver and guide for our parikrama explained the fascinating transformation of the Dera. What started as a small ashram had gradually expanded into an entire colony. He mentioned that at the langar, 50,000 people could eat simultaneously, and during Maharaj Ji's satsang, the number of attendees could swell to 5 lakhs. To accommodate this massive gathering, numerous rooms were constructed in several blocks. Booking a room required prior reservations–three months in advance for local visitors and six months for international devotees.

Permanent volunteers, who often were educated professionals, also served at the ashram. They contributed financially to the community, but only after their ability to pay was thoroughly verified. The ashram generated its own electricity, some of which was supplied to the Punjab government. All the grains used in the langar were grown on the ashram's farms. Food items were available at remarkably low prices, ranging between Rs 4 and Rs 30, setting an example for efficient management and self-sufficiency that even the government could learn from.

The Satsang hall, accommodating about 4 lakh devotees, was an architectural marvel. It was designed to be adaptable–expandable when required–and ensured seamless operations even with translations for attendees from around the globe.

My Trip to Turkey and got to know about famous Rumi Philosophy

The date for my convention in Istanbul arrived, and I boarded my flight to Turkey. The conference was engaging and offered ample networking opportunities. One of the highlights of my trip was the opportunity to attend a performance showcasing Rumi's philosophy and artistry. This was the *Hodjapasha Whirling Dervishes Ceremony*, a 360-degree spiritual journey. The event was mesmerizing, with the dervishes performing their graceful, whirling meditation, symbolizing their spiritual ascent and union with the divine.

Rumi's quotes and stories resonated deeply. I came across several inspiring lines in a catalog available at the event. One of my favourites was: "*The wound is the place where the light enters you.*" This profound statement encapsulates the essence of finding strength and enlightenment in life's challenges.

At dinner in my hotel, an unexpected yet pleasant encounter occurred. A tall, slim gentleman approached our table with a warm smile. "You're from India, aren't you?" he asked. We nodded in agreement.

"I love India," he exclaimed. "It's a land of rich cultures and traditions. But what I admire most is the divine atmosphere."

We were delighted to hear his admiration. "You must visit India again," we replied. "Here in Turkey, too, you have a great legacy of spirituality, particularly the teachings of Rumi."

"Oh, you know Rumi!" he said, his eyes lighting up.

He mentioned he was from Konya, the very village where Rumi had spent much of his life. "If you ever wish to visit, I have a house there," he offered kindly. "You can stay as my guest. I stopped here to speak with you because I have a special fondness for India."

Although his invitation was warm and generous, we felt cautious and decided to politely decline. "We're leaving the day after tomorrow," we replied, hoping to gently end the conversation.

Undeterred, he said, "If you meet me for breakfast tomorrow, I'll bring you some printed literature about Rumi's works and stories. I'm sure you'll enjoy reading them."

True to his word, he met us the next morning and handed me a collection of Rumi's writings. His unexpected kindness left a lasting impression. It felt as though a divine connection had been made. Months later, I received a call from him. "I just wanted to say hello," he said. "If you visit Turkey again, do meet me."

Reflecting on this encounter, I couldn't help but feel that he had been a tool in God's plan, sent to inspire me and introduce me to Rumi's profound teachings. This serendipitous meeting planted the seed for my desire to delve deeper into Rumi's philosophy and perhaps share it with others.

Rumi's Legacy

Rumi, one of the greatest spiritual masters and poetic geniuses of humanity, was born in 1207 in the city of Balkh, in a region that is now part of modern-day Afghanistan but was deeply intertwined with Turkey's cultural and spiritual heritage. To Rumi, God was the only real and absolute existence. All beings and the universe itself, he believed, were mere reflections of the Divine.

Key teachings from Rumi's philosophy include:

- Unity with God: Everything originates from the spiritual realm, and all life forms, including humans, are reflections of God.
- Human Superiority: Among all creations, humans are unique in their ability to comprehend and strive for a higher spiritual essence.
- Inner Journey: True human dignity and worth can only be realized through the inward journey of the soul—a journey that connects one with the Divine.
- Devotion to Islam: Rumi's teachings were deeply rooted in the principles of Islam. However, his understanding of

spirituality transcended rigid frameworks, emphasizing love and connection over dogma.

- Practical Sufism: Rumi's Sufism was not an abstract philosophical ideal. It was a deeply practical, heart-centered way of living that embraced the evolution of the human soul.

Rumi also taught that human evolution was an ongoing process, far from complete. The journey toward spiritual enlightenment, he believed, was continuous and unending, akin to the revolving movements of the dervishes who seek divine connection through their whirling meditation.

Man was created to evolve into maturity, perfection, and completeness. To achieve this, it is necessary to renounce all known emotions–both positive and negative–along with all beliefs, actions, and habits.

In essence, this journey involves rejecting the limited identity of a human being and accepting an unknown and unknowable consciousness, existence, and essence that is distinct from the ego. This transformation begins when the hidden secret within the heart shines forth–the divine light and fire illuminating the soul. It is a complete metamorphosis, involving a shift in the mind, the brain's cells, and even the very atoms of the body. The individual transforms into a being whose body becomes light, transparent, and free of obstacles. Vision becomes clearer, and one gains the ability to see and understand everything, to be present everywhere. This is known as Fana Falah–dying before dying.

A Poem by Rumi:

If the words come from the heart, they will enter the heart. If they come from the tongue, they will remain no further than the ears.

The power of love entered me, and I became fierce like a lion and gentle like the evening star.

The inspiration you seek is already within you. Be still and listen.

The morning wind has secrets to tell you. Do not fall asleep. To hear this secret, we must be silent, concentrated, and open to receiving it.

Answer every call that excites your soul. Ignore those who make you sad or dear, those who hold you back with sickness and death.

Come near, come near. Since you are me and I am you, there is no longer any separation. We are light upon light; what light flees from such a light?

We are all one complete being. Then, why this duality?

Why do the rich look upon the poor with disdain?

Why does the right hand look upon the left hand with contempt?

Since you are a part of both, what is good is right. What is unpleasant about leftism? We are one essence, one intellect, and one hand, Yet we appear as two due to our misunderstanding.

How long will you carry the burden of five senses and six directions? Come closer to unity. Rise above your selfishness and merge all within yourself. You are but a seed of grain, yet together you are a mine of gold.

Know that the soul is one, though the bodies are innumerable. Just as the oiliness is inherent in almonds, So too is the meaning of a word consistent across languages. When the cup breaks, the water becomes one.

The soul conveys news to all, And for the unity of the heart, the vision is free from the bondage of words.

I found it strange but perfectly balanced, That I need my wounds to heal my faith, And my faith to heal my wounds. I wish for your sun to reach my raindrops, So that your warmth may lift my voice like a cloud.

Where can one find a more generous being than God? He buys the worthless trash that is your wealth, And He gives you the light that illuminates your heart. He accepts these frozen, lifeless bodies of yours,

And He gives you a kingdom beyond your wildest dreams, He takes a few drops of your tears, Eternal life is attained by completely renouncing one's own life.

When God appears to His ardent lover, The lover is absorbed in Him, and not a single hair of the lover is harmed. True lovers are like shadows, may that moment be blissful when we, you and I, sit in the palace.

With two forms and two figures, but with one soul, you and I. The colours of the garden and the sounds of the birds will give immortality The moment we come to the garden, you and I. The stars of heaven will come to look upon us;

When I die, and my coffin is being taken out, you must never think, "I am missing this world." Pray thus and overcome your difficulties: "Give us goodness in the house of our present world, and give us goodness in the house of our next world."

May that moment be blissful when we, you and I, sit in the palace, With two forms and two figures, but with one soul, you and I. The colours of the garden and the voice of the birds will give immortality The moment we come to the garden, you and I.

The stars of heaven will come to look upon us, for we live in the kingdom of joy.

Rumi's poetry here speaks to the unity of lovers with the Divine, the transcendence of the material world, and the hope for spiritual reunion in the afterlife.

His vision of a shared divine existence, beyond individual separation, mirrors the idea of oneness with God and the eternal joy that comes from this union.

The Fly Who Thought She Was a Sailor (story)

A weary donkey had spent the entire day carrying a heavy load, trudging tirelessly along, without a moment's respite. Not even a brief pause to rest. At last, his owner reached their destination, and the donkey was relieved of the mountain of merchandise piled on his back. Finally unburdened, the poor beast let out a contented bray as he emptied his full bladder.

Nearby, a tiny fly rested on a fallen leaf. As the donkey's urine began to stream downhill, the current caught the leaf, and it began to float, taking the unsuspecting fly along with it. Initially startled, the fly struggled to comprehend what was happening.

Before long, however, her confusion turned into delusion. "Ah," she thought, "I am sailing on the great seas! Behold the mighty captain of this ship—me! What a seasoned navigator I am! Who could dare to stop me now?"

Filled with pride, the fly revealed in her imagined grandeur, floating on the stream as if she truly commanded the winds and waves. She believed she was conquering the seven seas, blind to the reality of her situation: she was still the same insignificant fly, swept along by forces far beyond her control.

Unaware and unreflective, the fly failed to see that nothing was as it seemed.

This is a beautiful and heartfelt poem. This captured the essence of seeking peace and divine connection amidst the chaos of life. The use of the two doors - one leading to the worldly distractions and the other to a place of quiet within - is a powerful metaphor. And the simple yet profound chanting of God's name, as a source of solace, is a timeless theme in many spiritual traditions.

A Door to the Divine (Ashok Kumar) Khanna

When morning arrives, I wake up, wrapped in my soft sheet, falling back to sleep, Brother, I know I've wasted precious time.

Two doors exist in our life: One leads to the world's noisy path, The other opens to the heart's quiet space. Oh Lord, don't trap me in the world's noise, Call me to the peaceful place in your heart.

I stand at your door, not just on the floor, hoping to be close to you, waiting for your kindness, oh my Lord, Hoping for your blessing today. I've come to your doorstep with hope; Believing I will see your light.

My mind remembers your simple name, Sing the name of Hari, God, how short and sweet your name sounds, just two letters that mean so much. Chant this name, and watch How troubles melt away, how sorrows start to fade, how my boat crosses life's big ocean, Carried by the power of Hari's name.

Visit at Golden temple

That's a beautiful experience at the Golden Temple, where you observed the spirit of equality and humility among people from all walks of life, coming together under one roof. The idea of everyone, regardless of their status, eating together in the langar is a powerful example of the oneness and universality of humanity in spiritual teachings.

They emphasize the importance of patience, perseverance, and humility in spiritual practice.

Here's a slight refinement of the stories for clarity and flow:

The Guru's Search for a Successor

A Guru was searching for a worthy successor to pass on his responsibility. To test his disciples, he instructed them to build a wall in front of him. They worked hard and built it, and then the Guru asked them to break it down. They repeated this several times. Eventually, most disciples grew bored with the task and began to avoid it. However, one disciple, Chitrabhanu, remained focused on the work.

One day, the Guru approached him and asked, "Why are you still working while the others have left?" Chitrabhanu folded his hands and replied, "How can I step back from the Guru's fire? I will not leave work unless you stop me."

The Guru, moved by his dedication, recognized him as the true successor. He then told the other disciples, "Most people in the world have great aspirations but lack the perseverance to follow through. They try a little and then retreat. To achieve anything significant, not only desire but also courage and patience are required. Chitrabhanu has both, and such a person is my true successor."

Guru Nanak's Lesson on Oneness

Once, Guru Nanak was sent to protect a field from birds. As he sat watching the birds pecking at the grains, he became completely absorbed in observing them. The birds moved freely, with no fear or restraint, taking only what they needed.

At that moment, Guru Nanak had a revelation. He realized that the whole world is pervaded by God, and that all living beings, no matter how small or seemingly insignificant, are connected through the divine. How could the food on Earth belong to just one person? It belongs to everyone, as a gift from God.

Instead of chasing the birds away, Guru Nanak felt an overwhelming sense of joy. He saw the light of God in the birds and in every particle of the field around him. Overcome with happiness, he began to sing a hymn, celebrating the divine presence in all beings:

"Ram's birds, Ram's field, Eat, birds, to your fill."

Through this, Guru Nanak conveyed a powerful message: that we must recognize the divine in all of creation and live in harmony with the world around us. Nothing is truly ours; everything belongs to God, and we are all part of the same divine creation. This story teaches us to let go of attachment, see the light in all things, and share the abundance of the world with all beings.

Guru Gobind Singh's Lesson on Service and Work

Once, Guru Gobind Singh was preaching in a village. During his discourse, he asked a young man to bring him some water. The young man, eager to serve, brought a wet bowl filled with cold water. However, as Guru Gobind Singh took the bowl, he said, "Oh, your hands are very soft."

The young man responded proudly, "I don't have to do any work. There are many servants in my house who do all the work. I simply enjoy myself, and my time passes well."

Guru Gobind Singh, however, refused to drink the water and said, "I cannot drink from hands that have never known service or hard work. Hands that have never been used for helping others or working selflessly are impure, regardless of how clean they appear."

The young man was startled by this response, but Guru Ji continued, "Even though you have heard the sermons of saints, you have yet to understand their true meaning."

This experience deeply affected the young man. He began to reform himself and dedicated himself to serving others. Wherever Guru Gobind Singh went, the young man would arrive first, spreading knowledge and serving the devotees selflessly.

Story 2:
The Wisdom of the Young Boy and Guru Nanak

In the company of Guru Nanak, the devotees often gathered to sing bhajans (devotional songs) and recite shabads (sacred hymns). During these times, a young boy would quietly stand behind Guru Nanak, silently observing.

One day, Guru Nanak asked the boy, "Son, why do you come every morning? Why do you stand here instead of lying down to sleep? What do you gain from listening to the teachings? Does your mind wander and play, or are you truly focused?"

The boy respectfully bowed his head and explained, "Once, my mother asked me to burn wood in the stove. While doing so, I noticed that small, thin sticks caught fire quickly, while large, thick sticks took longer to ignite. It occurred to me that, just like small sticks catch fire quickly, children too can grasp knowledge rapidly. That is why I come to your company every day. I want to learn quickly."

Guru Nanak was impressed with the boy's insight and said, "You may be small in age, but you possess great wisdom. You have understood the value of seeking knowledge and wisdom with devotion."

Guru Nanak and the Magician of Kamrup

Guru Nanak, along with his companions Bala and Mardana, travelled throughout India to spread the message of God's love and oneness. They walked everywhere on foot, relying on their faith and simplicity.

One day, they arrived in the remote region of Kamrup, a place known for its people's strong belief in black magic. As they approached the outskirts of the city, Guru Nanak decided to meditate under a tree. Bala stayed with him, while Mardana ventured into the city to find food and water.

At the city's well, Mardana began filling his containers when a group of girls noticed him. Curious about his appearance and the way he spoke in a different language, one of the girls teased him, saying, "He sounds like a sheep! He's bleating like one!" The girls burst into laughter, and one of them decided to play a trick on Mardana. She tied a magical thread around his neck, and immediately, Mardana was compelled to get down on all fours and began bleating like a sheep, "Baaah, baaah, baaah."

The onlookers laughed at the sight of Mardana, but Guru Nanak, sensing something unusual happening, rose from his meditation. He and Bala began walking towards the well. The girls, seeing them approach, decided to cast a spell on the Guru as well. One of them raised her hand and tried to cast a spell saying, "Bark like a dog!" However, instead of affecting Guru Nanak, the spell reversed, and the girl herself began barking like a dog.

The other girl, alarmed, attempted to cast another spell to defend her companion, but her arm froze in mid-air, unable to move. The girls tried many more spells, but whatever they attempted was reflected back on them, causing confusion and fear.

A woman, witnessing the events unfold, rushed to tell the Queen of Kamrup, who was known as a powerful magician. The Queen arrived at the well and was shocked to see that her sisters' magic had been completely nullified. She tried using her own magic to help them, but it had no effect. Even when she tried to use magic against Guru Nanak, it failed.

Realizing that Guru Nanak possessed a divine power far beyond her own, the Queen surrendered. She said, "You are a great magician! Please free my sisters and teach me your magic!"

Guru Nanak, with his boundless compassion, spoke kindly to the Queen. He said, "The true magic lies not in spells and illusions, but in understanding the oneness of all beings and surrendering to the will of the Divine. The power of love and humility is the greatest magic of all."

The Queen, humbled and enlightened, apologized for her actions and thanked Guru Nanak for showing her the true path. Guru Nanak, with his divine wisdom, freed the girls from their magical trance, and they too, learned to understand the deeper meaning of life and spirituality.

Visit at Sathya Sai BabaIt's wonderful that I had the opportunity to visit the Sathya Sai Baba Ashram at Puttaparthi, especially during Diwali – a time of spiritual celebration and devotion. The experience you described sounds deeply profound, especially the realization about the sacredness of a name being shared openly, something that was previously meant to be kept secret. This reflection speaks to the idea that the spiritual path is not bound by secrecy or restrictions but is meant to be shared with the world for its upliftment.

Soham Soham Dhyan Karo

Sadguru Sai Dhyan Karo [Soham Soham ...]

Soham Brahma Soham Vishnu

Soham Sai Dhyana Karo

Soham Atma Shiva Paramatma

Brahmananda Se Hrudaya Bharo

After some time, the prasad (offering) was served, and it took about ten minutes to serve all forty thousand people. I decided to take a round of the complex. It was a large complex with many canteens, houses, foreigners, sevadhars, and devotees. I took a thali (plate) with three vegetables, curd, water, rice, bread, etc., all for just ₹ 100, and the food was reasonably good.

Acquaintance with foreign devotee

Just beside me at the table, a foreign lady was sitting, so I casually greeted her and asked, "Hello, from which country have you come?" She replied, "Italy." I continued, "What attracts you here?"

She responded, "I love this place; I love Sathya Sai Baba, and I come here every year."

Curious, I asked, "How long do you stay here?"

"I stay every year for three months. Sometimes, I don't get accommodation here, so I stay in a hotel outside," she said.

I was thinking to myself, "What could she do here for three months?"

We both finished our food, and I asked, "Can we talk more?"

She agreed and said, "If you have time, let's walk and see the fireworks near Lakshmi Mandir."

On the way, she shared with me, "Sai knows me very well. I am his big fan, and I have huge faith in him. I observe that he is always with me, taking care of me.

"Once, I fell down in Rome in a lonely place, crying in pain. An Indian man came to me and asked if I needed help. I told him to call an ambulance, and he did. I thanked him with Namaste, and in return, he told me, 'Thank Sathya Sai Baba, I am only the source.' He gave me the reference of this holy place. I have so much trust and faith in him; he has saved my life many times.

"Once, I fell in the bathroom and lost consciousness. My family got worried, took me to the hospital, and miraculously, I didn't have a scratch.

Once, I was traveling in a car when the driver lost control, and the car fell into a 10-foot ditch. The car was badly damaged, but I was completely unharmed. All of this is due to his kindness and mercy."

She continued, "I have two main benefits from coming here: One, I get peace. I do a lot of meditation here."

She smiled and laughed as she added, "And I save money too. Staying here is graceful and economical." She then went to a hawker and bought a plate of idli for just Rs. 20. Proudly, she showed it to me and said, "See how cheap things are here!"

As we spoke, she also shared some quotes from Baba Ji:

- "Life is a challenge, meet it! Life is a dream, realize it! Life is a game, play it! Life is love, enjoy it!"
- "Start the day with love, spend the day with love, fill the day with love, and end the day with love. That is the way to God."
- "There is only one caste... the caste of humanity. There is only one religion... the religion of love. There is only one language... the language of the heart."
- "Always have complete faith in the indwelling God who takes care of everything. True greatness can only come from faith."
- "The secret of perfect health lies in keeping the mind always cheerful–never worried, never hurried, never burdened by fear, thought, or anxiety."
- "Most important, do not ever think that you and God are separate. Think always, 'God is with me; He is inside me; He is around me. All there is is God. I myself am God. I am the Infinite, the Eternal. I am not two; I am one, only one. There is no one else besides me. I and God are one and the same.' To realize this Unity, the first step is to develop self-confidence. It comes when you realize that God is not outside of you."
- "The gift of food to the hungry is the noblest of all gifts."

- "Anger, ego, jealousy are the biggest diseases. Keep yourself aloof from these three diseases."
- "The body is just a water bubble. The mind is like a mad monkey. Do not follow either the body or the mind. Follow the conscience. It is above the mind. It is permanent. It is the voice of God, the voice of unchanging truth inside you."

It was a good experience at the Sathya Sai Ashram/Mandir, and I returned to Delhi via Bangalore.

Visit to Rome

What a wonderful and meaningful encounter! It's interesting how life can bring people together in unexpected ways. Meeting the same nun three times, especially at different places like the Vatican Museum, the Dubai airport, and then Tel Aviv, seems like a sign of a special connection. It's also fascinating how spirituality can create bonds across the world, no matter where we come from. I can see the glow on her face and eyes were shining, a sign of spirituality growth

Her insights into spirituality must have been enriching. Sometimes, when we least expect it, we meet people who help us reflect on our own spiritual path, and these moments can become memorable. The fact that sharing Indian connection and had these conversations highlights the universal nature of spiritual experiences.

It's lovely how small encounters like this, often random, can leave us with a deeper understanding and remind us of the connections that bind us as human beings.

That's wonderful! Meeting insightful people can be such a rich source of learning and growth. Every encounter brings something new to reflect on.

The Vatican City is a small, independent city-state located entirely within Rome, Italy. It serves as the spiritual and administrative centre of the Roman Catholic Church, and it is one of the most significant sites in Christianity. The Vatican is not only a religious centre but also a hub for art, culture, and history.

As the residence of the Pope, the Vatican City is the spiritual and administrative headquarters of the Roman Catholic Church. The Pope, who is elected by the College of Cardinals, holds both a religious and political role. He serves as the Bishop of Rome and is the head of the Church, guiding millions of Catholics worldwide.

Vatican City's cultural and artistic contributions are profound and unparalleled. Among its most famous landmarks are:

- St. Peter's Square: This grand open space in front of St. Peter's Basilica is often the site of papal events and gatherings. It is known for its iconic obelisk and surrounded by a colonnade designed by Gian Lorenzo Bernini.
- St. Peter's Basilica: One of the largest churches in the world, St. Peter's Basilica is a masterpiece of Renaissance architecture, designed by Michelangelo, Donato Bramante, and others. It is also the burial site of St. Peter, one of the apostles of Jesus and the first Pope.
- The Sistine Chapel: Famous for its ceiling painted by Michelangelo, the Sistine Chapel is a stunning work of art and serves as the site for the papal conclave, where a new Pope is elected.
- The Vatican Museums: These museums house one of the most important collections of art and historical artifacts in the world, including works by Raphael, Leonardo da Vinci, and other Renaissance artists.

- The Apostolic Palace: The official residence of the Pope, it includes the Vatican's administrative offices and the Papal apartments.

With its rich history and incredible art, the Vatican City is not only a religious centre but also a symbol of cultural heritage for humanity.

An educational message

What a heartfelt expression of gratitude and reflection! It's clear how much Mr. Uttam Chawla's messages resonate with your journey toward spirituality and self-awareness. His wisdom and the poetic beauty of his thoughts offer profound lessons on perseverance, inner purity, and the power of the soul. which he shared on what's app.

These words, like treasures, remind us of life's deeper truths:

The emphasis on continuing the journey, no matter how hard it gets, reflects an unwavering faith in eventual success and inner peace. "Keep walking, you will definitely reach the shore" is a mantra of hope for anyone feeling lost.

Recognizing the soul as the seat of true transformation—this is a powerful reminder that lasting change starts within, not in external pursuits.

The idea that chasing desires leads to disappointment aligns beautifully with the teachings of spiritual masters who urge us to seek contentment within.

- Inner Treasure: The acknowledgment of inner jewels being priceless is a call to focus on self-discovery, nurturing the soul, and letting go of external comparisons.
- Purification and Redemption: The recognition of our own flaws and the commitment to purify ourselves in this life is a courageous and humbling goal.

The reflection about finding nectar within, growing inner strength, and achieving lasting happiness speaks volumes about the journey of self-realization. It's inspiring to see how you've embraced these lessons to enrich your life and deepen your connection to spirituality.

Key Insights:

1. **Overcoming Fear and Insecurity:**
    - Awakening the energy of spirituality requires nurturing inner feelings and focusing on the self. This is a gentle reminder that inner peace is the antidote to fear and insecurity.
2. **Balance in Life:**
    - "Excess of anything causes harm" is a universal truth. It's a warning against being trapped in dilemmas or overindulging in conveniences, as both can lead to stagnation or peril.
3. **Transformation Through Spirituality:**
    - The metaphor of turning dust to gold or a stone to Kohinoor beautifully illustrates how spirituality can transform even the most ordinary into the extraordinary.
4. **Acts of Service as Devotion:**
    - The notion that being of use to someone or offering solace is also an act of devotion is inspiring. It shifts the perspective of devotion from ritual to action and kindness.
5. **Wholehearted Commitment:**
    - The phrase "With half a heart, you will not be anywhere" emphasizes the importance of total dedication, whether in spiritual practice or worldly pursuits.

6. **Gratitude and Humility:**
   - The narrative about reaching the destination and being thankful to God underlines the importance of acknowledging divine guidance and staying humble, even after achieving success.
7. **The Perils of Hubris:**
   - The cautionary note about people forgetting God after achieving success is a reminder to stay grounded and grateful, recognizing the divine role in our lives.
   - the heart and mind. The simplicity and depth of these words have the power to resonate universally, cutting across boundaries of culture, religion, and personal beliefs. The piece invites us to reflect, grow, and live with intention, making spirituality an integral part of our daily lives.

My expression serves as a beacon for those seeking purpose and peace, encouraging a life of service, gratitude, and humility. It's a reminder that the path to spiritual awakening lies not in grand gestures but in the small, consistent acts of love, kindness, and self-awareness. Truly a timeless and enriching message!

the heart and mind. The simplicity and depth of these words have the power to resonate universally, cutting across boundaries of culture, religion, and personal beliefs. The piece invites us to reflect, grow, and live with intention, making spirituality an integral part of our daily lives.

My expression serves as a beacon for those seeking purpose and peace, encouraging a life of service, gratitude, and humility. It's a reminder that the path to spiritual awakening lies not in grand gestures but in the small, consistent acts of love, kindness, and self-awareness. Truly a timeless and enriching message!

Poem on Life (Ashok Kumar) Khanna There is little, and little is needed. If I had understood this, I would not have grieved. In the hope of getting more and more, I kept building up a pile of gunpowder. I knew it would explode when neither I nor these things would remain. Even before dying, I could not calculate what I lost and what I gained. Behold, this is the last journey of the fire, after everything has turned to ashes.

WhatsApp Messages: Life's Wisdom

Never Blame Anyone in Your Life: Every Person Has a Purpose

Life is a journey filled with people who cross our path for a reason. Each one leaves an impact, shaping who we become and how we see the world. It's easy to blame others when things go wrong, but if we look deeper, we realize that every person—whether good, bad, worse, or best—plays a significant role in our growth. Instead of blame, we should embrace gratitude for the lessons and memories they bring.

Good People Give You Happiness The good people in our lives bring joy, comfort, and positivity. They are the ones who support us, stand by us in tough times, and celebrate our successes. Their presence makes life brighter and easier. Good people remind us of the beauty of kindness, love, and friendship. The happiness they give becomes a source of strength and optimism.

Bad People Give You Experience Not everyone we meet has good intentions, and sometimes we encounter people who hurt, disappoint, or deceive us. While these experiences can be painful, they teach us valuable lessons. Bad people show us the importance of caution, resilience, and self-respect. Through them, we learn to set boundaries, trust our instincts, and become wiser in our choices.

Worse People Give You Lessons The worst experiences often come from the most difficult people. They test our patience, challenge our values, and sometimes break our hearts. Yet, these individuals teach us the most profound lessons. They show us the consequences of negativity and the importance of staying true to our principles. Through their actions, we learn about forgiveness, strength, and the art of letting go.

The Best People Give You Memories The best people leave an imprint on our hearts that lasts a lifetime. They are the ones who love us unconditionally, inspire us, and share our most cherished moments. Their kindness, wisdom, and companionship create memories we treasure forever. Even when they are no longer with us, their influence continues to guide and comfort us.

Embracing Every Experience When we stop blaming others and start understanding the purpose they serve in our lives, we cultivate gratitude and wisdom. Every person we meet adds something valuable to our story–whether it's happiness, experience, lessons, or memories. Together, these encounters shape us into better, stronger, and more compassionate individuals.

Instead of regret or resentment, let's choose appreciation. Thank the good people for their love, the bad ones for their lessons, the worse ones for their challenges, and the best ones for their unforgettable memories. This acceptance brings peace and helps us move forward with an open heart and a wiser mind.

- Happiness is the spiritual experience of living every minute with love, grace, and gratitude.
- Your mercy, your name Nothing is mine. Even my breath is yours, even my feelings are yours. You are my only true Guru.
- Leave the worries of tomorrow. Spend today with a smile. Whatever happens tomorrow, let it happen to you. May the Lord bless you with goodness.

- Everyone has bad days. Don't give up. Pause. Rest. Reset. Restart. But never quit. Always pick yourself up and keep going.
- Life was given to be of use to someone... But time is slipping by to earn pieces of paper. What will you do after earning so much money? There are no pockets in a shroud, nor cupboards in a grave. And the angels of death don't even take bribes...
- All friends meet again in the middle of life. Those who once rode cycles now meet in cars. That childhood blossoms again, when even those who used to drink complaints meet in bars...
- Let the love of friends and the blessings of elders remain indebted to me. This debt is very beautiful; let me remain indebted.
- Wish for such a rain in which ego drowns, the fortresses of differences collapse, Pride shatters, The mountains of anger melt, Hatred is buried forever, and we all transform from "I" to "we"...
- Who can destroy the love of God? If everyone were good, who would commit sin? O God, keep my friends safe, for who else will pray for my safety? And keep my enemies safe too, for who else will pray for me to come to you...
- A loving atmosphere in your home is the foundation of your life.
- If everything could be bought with money, then no one would be in need of blessings.
- Don't be satisfied with stories about how things worked for others. Uncover your own myth.

- When you shift your focus from competition to contribution, life becomes a celebration. Never try to defeat people; instead, win their hearts.
- These games of fate don't end by simply trying to erase them. Keep doing good deeds, and then witness the glory of God.
- When the problem is with your own people, seek a solution, not justice. In justice, one is happy and the other is angry. But in a solution, both find happiness.
- If we fully trust and have faith in the Almighty, He can see what's in our hearts. We must ignite the fire of love in our souls. The soul is an angel, full of positivity; it opens pathways and removes obstacles. True devotion not only banishes unwanted thoughts but also liberates us from the cycle of birth and death. Otherwise, there are more than 8.4 million species in this universe to traverse through.
- The Guru, the Master, gives you the words of God for repetition. God has implanted wisdom in the Master to guide his pupils closer to the Almighty. But we must surrender as guided by Him.
- We listen to the Guru carefully, but after social gatherings, we get reattached to the world, work, and family, forgetting His teachings. To embrace the pleasure of inner transformation taught by the Master, we must sacrifice the fleeting pleasures of the mundane world.
- Any form or name of God that arises from the depths of your heart is always cherished by the Almighty. The deeper your love for Him, the closer He comes to you—until you and He are one.

Now let us come back to the story: Recently, I celebrated my 70th birthday.

I was deeply touched and impressed by the beautiful words my 13-year-old granddaughter, Avina Chawla, wrote for me in a birthday card. Her heartfelt message read:

HAPPY 70TH B'DAY NANU *21st November 2024*

- You are a golf player.
- You are also a cricket player.
- You are an expert in the world of wonders.
- You are an expert in making everyone laugh.
- You are carefree and cool.
- Ask him about the latest news sometimes!
- He is the founder of *Ashoka International*, And the work is still going on.
- He is enthusiastic and knowledgeable.
- He is a winner and a player.

After all, he is our Nanu!

Wishing you a long life, health, laughter, and joy, dear Nanu.

Happy Birthday!

The card was not just a collection of words but a treasure filled with love, pride, and admiration. It made my 70th birthday all the more special and unforgettable.

Life's Challenges and Changes

We all find ourselves caught in the web of responsibilities, and even in retirement, life seems to be racing ahead. After retirement, I stayed in touch with Neeraj, who has been working as a consultant for some multinational companies. He mentioned that he's planning to return to his house in Noida. His father is bedridden, and his grandfather passed away long ago.

After ten years, I met Neeraj again. He looked much older, was bald, and was struggling with knee problems. He expressed his fear of undergoing surgery. I reassured him, saying it's a straightforward procedure, recovery is quick, and delaying it might lead to worse consequences. He promised to consider it.

We chatted about his family. His son is pursuing an MBA in the UK. However, Neeraj didn't mention anything about his wife. Curious, I asked, "Neeraj Bhai, how is Sister-in-law? Where is she?"

He hesitated, looked at me, and then said, "Sorry, I didn't inform you. We separated by mutual understanding."

I was shocked. "Why? What happened?" I asked.

Before he could reply, he suddenly struggled to breathe, likely an asthma attack. The nurse caring for his father quickly provided assistance, giving him water and an inhaler. It took over an hour for him to stabilize and regain his composure. Thankfully, he returned to normal.

Once he was calm, he explained, "My relationship didn't work, Ashok. She was mentally unstable. I did everything I could to adjust and support her, but nothing helped. I took her to countless specialists, but if someone is truly insane, no medicine can cure them. Despite guidance from doctors, myself, and her family, she never changed. I don't even know the cause of her illness.

Eventually, I remarried a woman who was a in my office. But that marriage didn't work either. Her family was greedy and manipulated her into demanding money from me. They filed 14 cases against me, but thankfully, I had the resources to fight back. The judge saw through their ploy and ruled in my favour. I paid a significant amount to free myself from that toxic atmosphere."

He paused, looking defeated, and then continued, "Now my father has been bedridden for six months. I've hired two servants and a nurse to care for him, but the entire family is affected by the sorrowful environment. Whenever we're near him, he apologizes and says, 'I've ruined not only my life but everyone else's in the family. I know you're serving me with your body, mind, and money, but I pray that God never shows such days even to enemies. Oh God, please take me away soon.'

It's a heartbreaking situation. While we're doing our best to care for him, the emotional toll is heavy. Thankfully, my grandfather passed away peacefully and didn't have to endure such suffering."

We stayed with him, talking late into the night, until 11 p.m. The next morning, we found him–still, forever at peace.

Before that moment, I had hugged Neeraj tightly and said, "Don't worry, everything will be fine." Tears welled up in his eyes as he said, "Perhaps I committed grievous deeds in my past life, and I'm now paying the price. I'm broken and no longer wish to live in this world." His voice trembled as he began to cry, loudly lamenting his bad karma.

It seemed he had delved deeply into the concept of karma, for he reached for a book lying nearby and began explaining it to me:

Understanding Karma

Definition: Karma refers to the principle of cause and effect, where a person's actions influence their future. Good deeds bring positive outcomes, while harmful actions result in negative consequences.

Origin and Context:

- A foundational concept in Indian philosophies, particularly Hinduism, Buddhism, and Jainism.
- Derived from the Sanskrit word *Karman*, meaning “act” or “deed.”

Types of Karma:

- Sanchita Karma: Accumulated actions from past lives that shape current experiences.
- Prarabdha Karma: A portion of Sanchita Karma currently being experienced.
- Kriyamana Karma: Present actions that will shape the future.

Philosophical Aspects:

- Karma is not limited to physical actions; even thoughts and intentions contribute.
- It emphasizes moral responsibility and accountability for one’s actions.

Karma and Liberation:

- Hinduism: Liberation (*Moksha*) is achieved by exhausting karmic debts.
- Buddhism: Karma influences the cycle of rebirth (*Samsara*), with freedom attained through enlightenment.
- Jainism: Liberation involves purifying the soul by shedding accumulated karma.

Practical Implications:

- Encourages mindfulness in actions and thoughts.
- Inspires ethical living, compassion, and altruism.
- Promotes self-awareness and accountability for life's trajectory.

Modern Interpretations:

- Often simplified as "what goes around comes around."
- Used to explain personal and collective experiences in life.

As he spoke, I could see he wasn't just reading the words to enlighten me; he was trying to console himself, seeking solace from the pain and hardships he was enduring.

I placed a reassuring hand on his shoulder and said, "I'm your old and best friend. Let me share some tips and a mantra that I believe will help. These steps can guide you toward peace and a path free of distress."

Coping with Pain and Distress

1. **Embrace Mindfulness:**

   - Stay present in the moment and accept your emotions without judgment.

2. **Practice Gratitude:**

   - Shift focus from what's lacking to what you already have. Gratitude nurtures inner peace.

3. **Focus on Positive Actions:**

   - Even small acts of kindness or creativity can foster a sense of purpose.

4. Strengthen Spiritual Connections:

- Meditate, pray, or chant a mantra to reconnect with your inner self and the divine.

5. Seek Support:

- Talk to loved ones, friends, or a counsellor. Sharing your burden eases the weight.

6. Physical Activity:

- Gentle exercise or yoga can help release tension and uplift your mood.

7. Reflect on Karma Positively:

- Think of each challenge as an opportunity to learn and grow, lightening the burden of past deeds.

I concluded, "These small steps might not erase your pain overnight, but they can help you walk the right path with renewed strength and hope. Together, we'll overcome this."

His expression softened, and though his pain lingered, a glimmer of peace began to take root.

Deep Breathing and Relaxation: Slow, deep breaths can help calm the nervous system and reduce physical and emotional pain. Try inhaling for four counts, holding for four counts, and exhaling for six counts.

Sometimes, focusing on a hobby, reading a book, watching a movie, or listening to music can help take your mind off the pain.

Express Your Feelings: Share your feelings with a trusted friend, family member, or therapist. Talking can provide emotional relief and open up new perspectives.

You can also write down three things you're grateful for each day. This simple practice can shift your focus toward the positive aspects of life, even in tough times.

If you feel overwhelmed, try grounding techniques such as naming five things you see, four things you feel, three things you hear, two things you smell, and one thing you taste.

Set Boundaries: Focus only on what's within your control, and give yourself permission to step back from responsibilities when needed.

Consistency in Routine: Maintaining a consistent sleep schedule, regular meals, and daily activities can help stabilize your mood and energy levels.

A balanced diet rich in fruits, vegetables, lean proteins, and whole grains supports both physical and mental health.

Dehydration can worsen pain and fatigue, so it's important to drink plenty of water throughout the day.

Gentle exercises like yoga, swimming, or tai chi can help reduce chronic pain and improve your mental well-being.

Consider using apps like Calm, Headspace, or YouTube videos for guided relaxation practices to reduce stress and enhance focus.

Seek Support: For emotional distress, therapy can help you process your feelings and develop effective coping strategies.

Joining a support group for people facing similar challenges can be both comforting and empowering.

Neeraj, remember that healing takes time. It's okay to feel vulnerable during this process. Celebrate small wins, even if it's just getting out of bed or taking a moment to rest.

Life is full of ups and downs. Time has a way of healing wounds. Nothing is permanent here–clouds come and go, weather changes, and both pain and joy switch places over time.

If you're sick, remember that healing and recovery are part of the cycle of life.

Neeraj responded, "Thanks for the tips, but all these things I've already been taught by my doctors. Once you're in pain, it's hard to focus on anything else. The remedies are there, but it depends on your personality–how bold you are to face it. If the pain persists for a long time, it can shatter you completely, and recovery seems impossible."

I replied, "Have courage. The dark will disappear, and light and happiness will come. Time never stays the same–it keeps bringing both good and bad. The important thing is to keep moving forward, knowing that healing will come eventually."

This is not just about offering advice, but also about providing hope and reassurance during difficult times. It's a beautiful reminder that pain, though intense, is often temporary, and with patience, support, and perspective, recovery is possible.

We must face all that life presents us, and accept it as God's will and desire. This acceptance is the ultimate solution.

In his eyes, I saw solace, and as the night grew late, he himself stood and told me to leave. We all experience sorrow and joy daily, but the real meaning of life often eludes us. True happiness lies in devotion to the Almighty. Once we understand the reality of the Creator and love Him, we conquer the ups and downs of life. You cannot attain His love without letting go of greed, attachment, and the tendency to hurt others. Once God becomes a part of your life, the concerns of gain or loss fade, for He Himself will take care of your desires and needs.

Though I try to live a pious life, it doesn't mean I've been without challenges. Life's obstacles and "speed bumps" are inevitable, but God shapes us to face them, helping us to appreciate both His gifts, whether they seem useful or not.

I too have faced many speeds breaker; some are as under;

We were tasked with packing and shifting the goods of a Minister and quoted about Rs. 5 lakhs as the charges. However, a year passed, and we had not received our payment. We reached out to the concerned officer and requested the payment. He explained that the previous boss had agreed that the Ministry would pay, but he had been transferred. The new officer claimed there were no such provisions and even offered to pay from his pocket the actual cost of the shifting of goods. Eventually, we were paid Rs. 1,50,000 by him. At the time, we didn't realize that if this officer were aggrieved, he could potentially harm our business.

We handled a shipment for a defence officer in Chennai. Since we didn't have our own office there, we used third-party services. The bids for the job were invited, and our bid was the lowest at Rs. 1,70,000, which was awarded to us. Our agent in Chennai, however, made an error while amending the Air Waybill (AWB) due to a miscalculation. By mistake, both the AWBs were included with the batch of papers. Later, we received a letter accusing us of forgery, citing two different amounts written on the AWBs. We explained that there had been no forgery, as we could not charge more than the sanctioned amount. Our actual bill was Rs. 1,20,000, which was less than the sanctioned amount of Rs. 1,70,000. We had reduced the bill honestly since the goods were less than what had been originally entitled.

Even though we acted in good faith, the concerned officer found an opportunity to punish us. He issued an order to debar us for three months. We fought hard against this, but despite the officer admitting he was about to leave for his hometown and agreeing that we couldn't charge more than the sanctioned amount, he still suggested we to appeal. I immediately filed an appeal, but government procedures are slow (This slowness procedure is also a punishment) and by the time the process was completed, the debarment period had ended.

As a spiritual person, I prefer not to engage in lengthy legal battles. I accepted the punishment, even though it was not due to any fault of mine, and chose to bear the consequences with patience.

Another jerk

I built a warehouse in Haryana and successfully completed the project on time. I applied for the completion certificate and began visiting regularly to check on the status, but the process was exhausting. After multiple attempts, I decided to approach a politician, a Minister, for assistance. His Officer on Special Duty (OSD) spoke to the Chief Administrator on my behalf and gave me a letter, advising me to meet with the Administrator.

When I visited the Administrator, he was polite and courteous. He took down my address and told me to come back in 15 days. I sent my manager to follow up, but the Administrator again took note of the address and advised him to return after 15 days. In an attempt to expedite the process, I approached the Minister once more, and his OSD spoke with the Administrator again, urging him to address our grievances.

On my manager's next visit, he was directed to wait in the Administrator's office, where an accountant was present. The accountant immediately demanded Rs. 500,000 for processing the completion certificate. I requested that he first complete the necessary work before any payment. After ten days, the accountant called me and handed me a letter, stating that the waiver period had been sanctioned.

I was surprised by this letter, as I had applied two years earlier, and couldn't understand how time could have elapsed without any action. When I questioned him, the accountant became rude and said, "Now that the job is done, you're questioning me?" I refused to pay and decided to take a different route. I engaged an agent, who took a small amount of money, and successfully obtained the completion certificate.

Another hiccup

One day, there was a function at a temple near our office, and a politician sent the corporation inspector to inspect our premises, claiming that his office was very influential and that we should undergo a check. The inspector visited our office several times, but we didn't pay much attention, as everything was in order.

We got to know the inspector, and he suggested we speak with his counsellor, but even then, we didn't feel the need to act. Eventually, we received an official notice, to which we promptly replied, as everything was compliant. Despite the matter being settled, we still had to make multiple visits, wasting time and energy on an issue that was ultimately unnecessary.

There are numbers of misshaping in life, these can be same or different, Bad news and bad times shake everyone but life keep on going and time heals the wounds

Life is not easy, struggle is there

Recently we handled some shipments and after final packing we found the goods are not even one third of container, we advised professionally to the customer that your goods will damage if we use big 40ft container due to huge empty space in the container, there are full chances of damages. He understood and allowed us to send a 20-ft container and we took a certificate from him as per the format provided by the Organisation. The goods reached safe and sound and there was no complaint and even we were asked to explain and finally we have to approach high authority for relief and happy to say, they listen to our grievances and matter was sorted out,

The Government's Appeal System and How It Helped

The government has a robust mechanism allowing citizens to appeal a decision if they feel it is unjust or insufficiently considered. This system is designed to ensure fairness, offering a pathway to higher authorities who can review the case with fresh eyes.

I experienced the value of this process first-hand when I had an important matter that didn't receive the outcome I'd hoped for at the initial level. Rather than feel helpless, I gathered the necessary documents, made my case in writing, and approached higher officials for an appeal. They reviewed my situation impartially and provided a fair resolution. Without this structured appeals system, it would have been much harder for me to be heard.

Overall, the government's appeals mechanism not only helped me with my specific grievance but also reminded me that a transparent, accessible system can bring much-needed relief during challenging times. This will be helpful only if you are honest and sincere in your work. During this period, my dear friend Neeraj lost his father. It was already a stressful time, and having the option to appeal gave me a sense of control and reassurance. Although the loss of Neeraj's father was a separate, deeply personal event, it underscored how important supportive systems and fair processes can be in difficult moments.

Neeraj's father expires

I received a call from Neeraj informing me that his father had passed away, and the funeral would take place at 3 PM. Without hesitation, I cancelled all my appointments and made my way directly to the cremation ground.

When I arrived, I was the first to reach there. As I looked around, I noticed numerous hoardings, either painted or on walls, each offering profound messages. Some of them read:

- "In life, you can fly high, but remember, the road must always be visible."
- "Why claim ownership? Why say 'mine'? This world is just a shelter for the night. Nothing is truly yours, and nothing is mine."
- "This is just a game of breath—when the breath is active, we feel that everything is ours. But once it stops, nothing belongs to anyone."

- "Everyone knows this, but few truly accept it."
- "You can acquire worldly things and still be happy, but wisdom comes only when you find peace within."
- "Only a strong soul can attain supernatural power. God is closer to us than the beat of our own heart–He is omniscient. He listens to our prayers and fulfils them."
- "Human, why are you afraid of dying? We are but actors here, playing our roles until we leave."
- "Ego, attachment, and wealth exist only up to this point."

It's said that one should 'die while living.' The great individuals who came before us showed the way to connect with our inner selves. Unfortunately, we often fail to follow their path, instead elevating our Guru to a pedestal, chasing after them in a frantic manner. After their departure, we worship their photos, seeking comfort for a brief time. True peace, however, comes when we follow their teachings and live by their guidance.

We are tourists here on Earth, and God is our travel agent. He has already planned our routes, reservations, and destinations. Trust Him, and enjoy the journey called life under His blessings.

By the time other friends and relatives of Neeraj arrived at the cremation ground, the body was being unloaded from the van. The priest was busy explaining the rituals of the cremation. He began to narrate the details, saying:

"In Hinduism, death is seen not as an end, but as a natural transition, an inevitable part of the life cycle. With deep roots in Vedic literature, Hindus believe that death is merely a step into the next journey of the soul."

It was a deeply emotional and sorrowful day when I learned that my dearest school friend, Neeraj, had passed away. His sister, Reeta, called to inform me that while they were on holiday in London, Neeraj collapsed during dinner. They rushed him to the hospital, but he was declared dead. Reeta was in tears, and she shared how Neeraj's loss had left them all in pain. I was at a loss for words, unsure of how to console her or what I could do from such a distance.

She handed the phone to her husband, and I expressed my heartfelt condolences, saying, "I am so sorry to hear of Neeraj's passing. Please take care of Reeta; I know how close she was to him, and I can feel her pain. May God give you all the strength to bear this loss."

I asked about their plans for the cremation and formalities. He informed me that they were considering cremating Neeraj in London as his aunt was there, and traveling to Mumbai was not feasible. They planned to do the prayer ceremony and other rituals the following Monday. He promised to send me the details soon. I assured him, "Please share the details with me, and let me know if there's anything I can do to assist."

He mentioned that their next-door neighbours, Mr. Chopra, would be involved, and asked if I could help with arrangements for the priest and refreshments for the gathering. I said, "Don't worry, I will take care of everything."

Determined to help in the best way possible, I rushed to Mumbai the same day. There, I met Mr. Chopra, and after some consideration, I decided to hire a professional service provider to manage the arrangements. I found a company that specializes in these services through the internet, one that was familiar with handling such tasks and would make the process smooth and dignified.

The company's approach was straightforward, with a clear three-step process that was quick, reliable, and hassle-free. They also provided a detailed write-up, explaining their services:

Last Journey Pre-Planning and Special Services in Mumbai Planning a funeral is an important decision, both financially and emotionally. Their pre-planning services include handling legal formalities, managing finances, selecting the type of service, choosing products and floral arrangements, settling donations, and addressing any other wishes. They also offered services to assist grieving families with their emotional needs, such as:

- Celebration of Life Events
- Counselling Services
- Dog Therapy Services

The service was available 24/7 to support families during this difficult time.

What Makes Last Journey Stand Out?

Their approach to helping grieving families was unique. The team was committed to supporting families from the beginning to the end of the process. What set them apart was that they provided their services directly at the mourning family's doorstep, ensuring comfort and ease for those who were grieving.

I felt confident in their ability to handle the arrangements, and I was reassured knowing that Neeraj's final journey would be planned with care and respect.

The services provided by the funeral company were thorough and caring, giving me immense relief during such a difficult time. They went above and beyond to address the specific needs of the family. Apart from the basic funeral services, they made room for the family's wishes, providing special floral decorations for the funeral vehicles and the gathering space. They also made arrangements for the funeral vehicle and offered the option of setting up donation camps in honour of the departed soul.

Moreover, professional artists and singers were arranged to create a serene and devotional atmosphere, and the team deployed multiple members to supervise the rituals. They took full responsibility for caring for the deceased, ensuring that the family wouldn't face any issues during the cremation. Their transparency and willingness to address any concerns about their services and charges gave me confidence in their professionalism, so I paid the charges in advance without hesitation.

On Monday, I met with Reeta and her family and reassured them that everything was taken care of. Her husband visited the site, confirmed that the preparations were underway, and thanked me for my efforts. I assured him that the arrangements were minor matters and prayed that everything went smoothly, as I had never managed such a task before.

As scheduled, the prayer ceremony began on time, and I was relieved to see how simple yet impactful the arrangements were. The priest began the ceremony, explaining the significance of Hindu funeral rites and how they help guide the departed soul toward moksha (liberation). The gathering participated in the rituals, lighting a ghee lamp and incense sticks to invoke positive energy and the divine presence.

Offerings of rice, flowers, milk, Tulsi leaves, and water were made to honour the departed soul, followed by the recitation of mantras dedicated to the deities of death and protection, such as Yama (the god of death) and Vishnu (the preserver of the universe). The final prayers were offered, with everyone joining in the chant of "Om Shanti Shanti Shanti" for peace.

The priest tied a turban to Neeraj's cousin, and everyone stood in line at the gate, paying their respects and offering condolences to the family with folded hands. Outside, refreshments were served as prasadam to all who attended. Afterward, I took permission from the family and left for Delhi in the evening, feeling relieved that I had been able to help in this difficult time.

The journey back to Delhi was a reflective one. Sitting in the plane, my thoughts were consumed by memories of Neeraj. Despite his cheerful exterior, it seemed he carried the weight of unspoken struggles–trapped in the web of his sentiments and troubles. The realization of his hidden pain brought a deep ache to my heart. It reminded me how life can often be an intricate mix of joy and sorrow, much of which remains unseen to the world.

As I reflected on our friendship and the end of his journey, I couldn't help but ponder the transient nature of life. The teachings of our saints echoed in my mind–life is fleeting, and our actions here are what define us. Many understand this and lead lives of compassion, kindness, and devotion, helping others without expecting anything in return. Such people, I believe, are true devotees of the Lord, sent as His representatives to assist us in our times of need.

As I landed in Delhi and stepped into the familiar streets, I carried with me not just the grief of losing a dear friend but also a renewed sense of gratitude for the bonds and kindness that enrich our lives. Life, with all its ups and downs, becomes more meaningful when we cherish the moments of connection, compassion, and shared humanity.

An example as below

This train of thought reminded me of a personal experience that left a profound impact on me. Once, during a golf game, a sudden downpour caught me off guard. In the chaos, I slipped and broke my right arm. The pain was excruciating, and the swelling began almost instantly. Struggling to manage, I was fortunate to cross paths with a gentleman, Mr. Arjun. Without hesitation, he offered to help, drove me to the hospital, and stayed with me for over two hours as I received treatment. His kindness didn't stop there–he continued to check on my recovery and even light-heartedly asked when we'd play golf together again.

Mr. Arjun's actions were a true embodiment of selflessness and compassion. Over time, we became good friends and have shared many rounds of golf since that day. His gesture taught me that even in moments of adversity, there are individuals who carry the light of humanity within them, reminding us that divine help often comes in the form of ordinary people.

Once, I was in Zurich, traveling from Zurich to Interlaken. As I stepped onto an escalator, someone accidentally hit me, causing me to lose my balance. I struggled to stay upright on the moving escalator and eventually fell. A kind lady rushed over and stopped the escalator. Soon, the police and other bystanders arrived, and I was taken to a hospital conveniently located within the railway station.

The doctor examined me, asked me to move around a bit, and assured me that everything seemed fine. However, he advised me to return if I experienced any difficulties.

The next morning, I had a flight to catch, but as I reached the airport, I suddenly felt intense pain in my hip and started limping while pushing my trolley. An airport staff member noticed my discomfort and immediately came to assist me. She helped me to a nearby bench and called for a porter and a wheelchair. With the help of painkillers, I managed to board my flight and reach Delhi.

Upon arrival, I underwent an X-ray, which revealed that my hip was fractured. I chose to go for surgery instead of a hip replacement. It took me four months to recover fully, during which my golf partners continuously wished and prayed for my speedy recovery.

I feel deeply grateful to God for sending those kind-hearted individuals—the lady who stopped the escalator and the airport staff member who assisted me. Their timely help prevented the situation from escalating into something far more dangerous.

As I have written in this book, God is like our travel agent—He decides our journey.

Tour to Europe

In 1980, I decided to travel to London and Brussels for the first time. I purchased air tickets for just Rs. 13,000 (around USD 200 at the time). Foreign currency regulations limited us to carrying only USD 500 for such trips.

Upon landing at London Airport, I unexpectedly encountered Mr. Srivastava, whose baggage I had handled previously. He recognized me, greeted me warmly, and generously offered me accommodation at his place. I gladly accepted. During my stay, I explored many parts of London, including meeting my counterpart there.

When it was time to depart for Brussels, Mr. Srivastava called Mr. Sharma in Brussels and requested him to assist me during my stay. Mr. Sharma met me at the airport, took me to his residence, and thoughtfully planned my sightseeing itinerary in Belgium.

At one point, Mr. Sharma encouraged me to explore more of Europe. I hesitated, explaining that I lacked the funds and planned to return to Delhi. But he insisted, purchased a 15-day Eurail pass for me, and told me to repay him later. He even arranged my stay in Frankfurt, Bonn, Rome, and Geneva. To my surprise, I spent less than USD 300 throughout the entire extended journey!

Even now, when I reflect on this experience, I marvel at God's greatness. How seamlessly my trip unfolded, extending beyond my plans and expectations, all because of the kindness and generosity of people like Mr. Srivastava and Mr. Sharma. I remain deeply grateful to everyone who came forward to assist me during this memorable journey.

Tour to Helsinki

I heard that the people of Finland are friendly and the happiest people in the world. I decided to visit there. I landed and checked in at the Radisson hotel, near the square and railway station. I sent a text message to our Ambassador, Mr. Ashok Kumar, saying that I was in Helsinki and would like to meet the packers on the embassy panel. He was so friendly and called me immediately, telling me he had some work near our hotel and would personally come for a coffee and share the list of packers. It was my second opportunity after Mr. Hear to meet the Ambassador personally in a coffee shop in Helsinki. He was very nice, and we had a good meeting.

The next day we took a walking tour. First, we saw the medieval castle and the beautiful Helsinki Cathedral. We had a good time at Esplanade, a green space right in the middle of the city, where people come for picnics, relaxation, and entertainment in the summer. Next was Uspensky Cathedral, the largest Orthodox church in Western Europe. We also visited the Temppeliaukio Church, where we were surprised to see a person sitting in meditation with many pillows surrounding him. We waited for more than 30 minutes, and he was completely still, seemingly deeply connected to his inner world. It was heartwarming to note that our tradition of meditation is followed by foreigners as well.

Later, we took a taxi to Seurasaari Island, where we saw old workshops, farms, manor houses, and cottages, all connected by a network of walking trails through woodlands and along the coast. We had some difficulty finding a taxi back to the hotel, as the place was a little far from the city. We asked a jogger for help, and he kindly offered to drop us off near the market after finishing his run. True to his word, he helped us, and we easily found a taxi from the market back to our hotel. It was a testament to the kindness and helpfulness of the Finnish people.

On the way back, we told the taxi driver how lucky he was to live in such a wonderful city known for its happy residents. He smiled and said that while they enjoy good financial stability and a good life, the weather could sometimes be difficult – with either 20 hours of light or 20 hours of darkness, which sometimes leads to depression. He mentioned that his life was mostly limited to his house, his dog, and the challenging weather.

I am also grateful to the Ambassador, who advised me to visit Tallinn by ferry for a day trip. It wasn't part of our original itinerary, but it turned out to be a memorable tour. It truly felt like destiny leading us there, and we enjoyed a wonderful cup of coffee in Tallinn.

Tour to Gulf

In 1980, I took a memorable tour to the Gulf. I remember purchasing air tickets for just Rs. 8000 all sector, covering Delhi, Dubai, Doha, Kuwait, and Saudi Arabia. The purpose of this trip was to appoint counterparts for door-to-door services, and I had already requested appointments with the Heads of Chancery (HOC) for meetings with the forwarding agents on their panels.

My first stop was Dubai, where I met Mr. Chawla, Attaché Admin. He introduced me to the local agent, and from there, I took a taxi to Abu Dhabi. In Abu Dhabi, I met Mr. Jain, Attaché Admin, who was equally helpful in introducing me to their packers. I also did some shopping, picking up cosmetics, clothes, and video cassette movies for my kids.

The next day, I flew to Doha. After immigration, I was going through the green channel when my bag was marked with a white cross, indicating it needed to be examined. As I opened my bag, I ran into Mr. Batish, HOC, who was surprised to see me there and inquired about my visit. I explained my mission to appoint counterparts for door-to-door delivery and my preference to work with agents on the Embassy's panel. Mr. Batish requested the customs officer to expedite my clearance, but the officer responded rather curtly, stating that the inspection had to be completed as I was not a diplomat. After the examination, they found nothing objectionable and allowed me to proceed. That evening, I attended a traditional Indian Kathak dance performance organized by the Embassy. It was a wonderful experience, and I truly appreciated the warmth and hospitality of the Embassy staff.

My next destination was Kuwait, and once again, my bag was selected for examination. This time, they only took my video cassettes to ensure there were no religiously sensitive or inappropriate films. After about half an hour, they returned my tapes without issue. As I exited the airport, I was pleasantly surprised to see Mr. R.P. Singh waiting for me. He was equally surprised to see me and kindly took me to his residence, insisting I stay with him instead of at a hotel. He was incredibly helpful in arranging my meeting with the packers on the Embassy's panel. Coincidentally, Mr. R.P. Singh was the same person I had met earlier at Johannesburg airport.

My final stop was Riyadh, where I faced yet another customs inspection. This time, they opened all my cosmetics, including Nivea cream, and even used a knife to check inside the boxes for any contraband. After clearing customs, I went directly to the Embassy and met Mr. Malhotra, Attaché Admin. He was very supportive and called the local agent to the Embassy so I could speak with him directly. Later that evening, Mr. Malhotra invited me to his home for dinner, which was a warm and memorable experience.

This Gulf tour was one of the most significant and rewarding trips of my career. Without the support and kindness of the Embassy staff in each country, the visit would have been far less productive. Even today, the same agents I appointed on that trip continue to work with us, maintaining a professional relationship that has lasted over 40 years.

The Story of Neeraj

One day, Reeta called me and asked if I could help her with something. I warmly replied, "Please tell me, how can I assist you?"

She explained, "Neeraj's son, Ankush is coming to Delhi for two days for some work. Can you help him if he needs anything?"

I assured her, "Don't worry, I'll take care of him. He can stay with me—it's no problem at all." She forwarded me his details on WhatsApp.

As per the schedule, I went to the airport with a placard displaying his name, waiting to receive him. A young, well-built boy wearing jeans and a gold T-shirt spotted the placard and approached me. To my pleasant surprise, he touched my feet as a gesture of respect. I blessed him and thought to myself how wonderful it was that he still valued the rites of Hindu culture, despite living abroad for the past ten years.

He got into my car, and we began our journey to my residence.

We reached my house late, around 2 AM. After helping him shift his luggage to the guest room, I told him, "You can change into something comfortable and rest. See you in the morning."

However, Ankush, with a polite smile, said, "Uncle, can I take a shower before I sleep? And if it's not too much trouble, could you arrange a cup of hot milk? Both will help me relax."

I immediately called my cook to prepare the milk. A little while later, Ankush knocked on my door and said, "Uncle, if you don't mind, could you lend me a book or a magazine to read? I have a habit of reading before bed."

I handed him a recently purchased book, *Kaizen.* He glanced at it and said, "Oh, Uncle, I've already read this one. Do you have any other books?" After checking my bookshelf, I gave him another book, *Desi Girl.* With a thankful smile, he took the book and went to his room.

Since I'm a golfer, I have the habit of waking up at 6 AM. After getting up, I headed to the kitchen for a glass of water and to prepare my tea. To my surprise, Ankush walked into the kitchen as well.

I greeted him, "Why are you awake so early? You arrived so late last night. Go back to sleep!"

But Ankush replied, "No, Uncle, I'm in the habit of waking up early in the morning."

I offered him tea or coffee, but he declined. “No, Uncle, I’d like to go for a walk. Is there a garden nearby?”

I suggested, “Let’s have tea or coffee first, and I’ll take you to a nearby garden. It’s very well-maintained.” He agreed, saying, “I’ll sit on the sofa. You have your tea first, and then we can go.”

After finishing my tea, we headed to the garden. Just at the entrance, a vendor was selling coconut water. Ankush looked at me and said, “Uncle, can I have some coconut water? But I didn’t bring any money.”

I assured him, “Don’t worry. I’ll pay via UPI.” I asked the vendor for two coconuts, and we enjoyed the refreshing drink. When I paid using UPI, Ankush remarked, “Uncle, I’m amazed that even street vendors have QR codes for payment. This is incredible!”

I smiled and replied, “Yes, in India, digital payments are widely accepted—even in the most remote areas. It’s very convenient.”

We started walking on the jogging path. After one round, Ankush said, “Uncle, do you mind if I jog for a bit?”

I assured him, “Not at all. I’ll sit on the bench here. When you’re done, we’ll head back.”

After some time, he returned, saying, “Let’s go home.”

On our way back, I asked, “Ankush, can we stop by the vegetable market to pick up some vegetables?”

“Of course, Uncle,” he replied.

At the market, I purchased some vegetables and asked an elderly vendor, “Where’s your QR code for payment?”

With a smile, she picked up the pot she used for her weighing scale and turned it upside down to reveal a QR code pasted underneath. Ankush burst into laughter, exclaiming, “Wow, Uncle! This is amazing. I’m genuinely surprised. Well done, India!”

This transformation truly reflects the vision of our Prime Minister. All credit goes to his forward-thinking approach. The convenience of digital payments has become a reality in both rural and urban areas.

Initially, many experts doubted the success of this initiative. They argued that it wouldn't work because people were not well-educated, many couldn't afford smartphones, and electricity infrastructure in some areas was lacking.

Yet, the results speak for themselves. Even a street vendor today accepts digital payments with ease. The adoption of technology has empowered people at all levels of society, bridging gaps and making life more convenient for everyone. It's a testament to the power of determination and innovative governance.

As Ankush said while laughing at the QR code under the pot, "This is incredible. India has truly set an example for the world." Moments like these remind me how far we've come as a nation, and I feel a deep sense of pride.

I asked, will you would like to have in breakfast

Yes uncle, I prefer to have cornflower with milk, black coffee and if you have any fruits, I told my wife and she served a butter toast grilled with that breakfast.

Uncle, I had not asked for this toast,

Eat it son.

He did not eat it and I packed it and gave it to him. If you feel hungry, eat it on the way.

He smiled and said, I will take it and started going.

Ok, tell me what time you will come at night and what would you like to eat.

I take very light dinner, you make soup and grilled paneer, salad and I will back by 7 PM

Do not worry, we will be waiting for you.

He left and I started discussing it with my wife.

I mentioned to my wife how impressed I was with Ankush's discipline and health consciousness, despite living abroad. She smiled and replied, "Today's generation is very aware about their health and well-being. You, on the other hand, don't take these things seriously."

I playfully responded, "I'm fine!"

But she wasn't convinced. "Sure, keep filling your body with filth," she said with a touch of humour. "What's the use of it? It'll only make you sick in the long run."

Her words stayed with me, a gentle reminder to prioritize health and be mindful of my choices.

When He came in the evening, I questioned, how was your day? I hope all the jobs are completed.

He said yes Uncle all was good and met my old clients and the meeting was quite fruitful.

Today one gentleman gave a lecture which was very useful. I will send you mail and you can print and read this. I am sure you will like it.

Rediscovering Yourself

"The sculpture is already complete within the marble block before I start my work. It is already there. I just have to chisel away the superfluous material." – Michelangelo

The journey back to being our best selves often feels like this quote. We carry within us all the potential, beauty, and strength we once had. The task is to chisel away the layers of doubt, fear, and pain that have built up over time.

It's hard work. At times, it feels painstakingly slow. We stumble, feel scared, and are tempted to give up. But here's the truth: you can always rebuild yourself, no matter where you are in life.

Not so long ago—or perhaps so far back that we've forgotten—we were confident, joyful, hopeful, happy, and grateful individuals with big dreams.

Then, life happened.

You failed once, and discouragement crept in. You were hurt by someone, and a piece of your confidence was chipped away. Someone broke your heart, and trust faltered. Another failure stole your drive, and you began to let go of your hopes. More hurt followed, and you shut down, becoming numb to shield yourself from the pain.

A few wrong decisions along the way, and the person you once were—the vibrant, confident, and passionate version of yourself—seemed to fade away.

Yet, in fleeting moments, something stirs within you. A memory, a feeling, or a spark reminds you of who you used to be. The real you—bold, joyful, kind, and full of belief in your abilities and dreams—feels just within reach. You wonder: *Where did that person go?*

Here's the answer: that person is still there. Just like Michelangelo's sculpture, your best self is waiting beneath the layers. It takes time, patience, and courage, but you can chisel away the excess and rediscover the masterpiece that's always been within you.

The journey might be long, but it's never too late to start.

I was discussing with my wife that Ankush look how disciplined even while living abroad.

Ankush; Uncle it is not that I don't eat anything, I am in detox from last one year, not only in food but one has to detox in many other areas also, it is very important to maintain balance in your life like food, digital life, keep away from negative people and keep company with negative people also bring distress, depression and it affects your life a lot.

Sometimes, I allow myself a cheat day to enjoy the things I've deprived myself of—it's better to Savor them during a gathering or a wedding, rather than indulging impulsively. Life is about balance.

I've realized that starting the day with negativity can ruin the entire day. For instance, if I check my phone in the morning and see bad news, it sets a gloomy tone. Instead of reacting to every notification, it's far better to check messages just two or three times a day. Over time, you also notice patterns—some people always radiate negativity. It's better to distance yourself from such influences for the sake of your peace.

I work long hours, sometimes 12 to 15 a day. But I ensure I take short breaks to recharge. These moments of rest give me a sense of good energy and positive vibrations—much like the peace we feel when chanting *Om* Similarly, regular detoxing—both physically and mentally—restores balance and clarity.

In today's fast-paced world, people are eager to jump high without building a strong foundation. They chase success recklessly, but without stability, they eventually fall. If not today, then tomorrow. And even if they don't fall, their health deteriorates, and regret sets in—often when it's too late.

If you want to be a horse for the long race, discipline is key. Everything you need is already within you; you just need to connect with it. The soul within us is powerful, pure, and brimming with positivity. The challenge is to awaken it.

Meditation is the path to this awakening. It helps us tap into our inner power, which starts with aligning the mind and heart. When we listen to our inner voice, we discover clarity, peace, and purpose.

Habits are hard to change, especially when it comes to negative attitudes and poor mental patterns. But even these can be transformed—if one learns to connect with their inner voice. And that connection comes through meditation.

Meditation is the key to calming and controlling our restless, "monkey mind." It anchors us, quiets the noise, and allows us to find clarity. Once inner strength is established, happiness flows naturally from within—it doesn't rely on external circumstances.

Each of us possesses the ability to harness the beauty and peace of the *Divine Feminine* within us. It's a profound magic, an unparalleled ecstasy that leads to harmony and joy. When we awaken this inner power, we align with something supreme.

Those who fail to recognize this potential are simply ignorant—fools clinging to chaos. The path to inner peace and fulfilment is available to everyone, but only those willing to listen to their inner voice will experience its transformative magic.

"I am very happy and delighted to see you in this form," I said with genuine joy. "Neeraj must be feeling proud in his heavenly abode, watching your greatness and kindness as you walk your path towards divinity."

As we spoke, I added, "So, you're leaving today. I wish you all the best. Even in your short time here, your presence has left a great impact on us."

Then, with a smile, I asked, "You must be around 35, right? Any thoughts about marriage?"

Ankush paused for a moment before replying, "No, uncle. I've thought about it, but I've seen my father's life. It didn't work out, and in the end, only loneliness consumed him. But I believe we can live happily in this beautiful world if we understand the tools for transforming ourselves. The key lies in knowing how to live fully and find joy within."

To live a long, happy, and purposeful life, we must reconnect with nature. Nature is not just a backdrop; it's a healer, a guide, and a source of endless wisdom.

Take time to visit a garden, a forest, or even a quiet park. Talk to the green trees; let their silent strength inspire you. Observe the vibrant flowers, listen to the soothing sounds of fountains, and watch the birds and butterflies dance gracefully in the air. Spend a moment marvelling at fish gliding effortlessly through water.

Take deep breaths, let the fresh air fill your lungs, and allow the serenity of nature to envelop you. Sit quietly amidst the beauty of the natural world, and you'll feel its magic. Nature has the power to calm your mind, uplift your spirit, and reconnect you with your true self.

His words struck a chord. It was a profound reminder that life's fulfilment doesn't always depend on external circumstances but on our ability to embrace transformation and inner peace.

For a healthier and more vibrant life, it's essential to make mindful choices about what we consume. Avoid stimulants like tea, coffee, and intoxicants such as liquor, beer, and wine. These might provide temporary relief or pleasure, but over time, they can take a toll on your body and mind.

Instead, prioritize hydration and nourishment. Drink plenty of water throughout the day—it's the simplest yet most powerful elixir for your body. Include natural liquids like fresh juices, coconut water, and herbal infusions in your routine to replenish and energize yourself.

Add nutrient-rich dry fruits like almonds, walnuts, and dates to your diet. They provide essential vitamins, minerals, and healthy fats, keeping you fuelled and focused. With these simple changes, you can nourish your body, maintain balance, and feel revitalized every day.

Live in the present. Let go of regrets about the past and stop fearing the uncertainties of the future. The key to a peaceful and happy life lies in embracing the now, fully and wholeheartedly.

Be like a baby—innocent and free from unnecessary burdens. A baby thinks only of today, crying only when hungry or unwell, and otherwise living joyfully in each moment. They don't dwell on yesterday or worry about tomorrow.

When we adopt this mindset, we free ourselves from the weight of unnecessary stress. Life I believe a person should never truly retire. Life is meant to be lived with purpose, and work—whether it's professional, creative, or service-oriented—gives us that sense of purpose. One should remain active, engaged, and contributing until their very last breath.

Retirement often implies stepping away from productivity, but staying mentally and physically active is essential for a fulfilling life. Whether it's through a career, pursuing hobbies, volunteering, or sharing wisdom with the younger generation, there's always something meaningful to do.

Work doesn't just keep the body and mind sharp; it gives us a sense of identity, belonging, and accomplishment. The satisfaction of being useful and making a difference, no matter how small, fuels the spirit and keeps life vibrant.

So, instead of seeing retirement as an end, view it as an opportunity to redefine your work, embrace new roles, and continue growing. Life's purpose doesn't have an expiry date.

Be simpler, lighter, and more fulfilling. Focus on the present, and you'll discover clarity, peace, and a renewed appreciation for the beauty of life.

Some people tend to take hasty steps in life, often driven by impulse or emotion. However, my suggestion is to pause, think carefully, and approach matters with patience and deliberation.

Hasty decisions, though tempting in the moment, can lead to unintended consequences that might be difficult to undo. Taking time to assess the situation, weigh the pros and cons, and consider long-term implications can make all the difference.

Going slow doesn't mean being indecisive—it's about being thoughtful and strategic. Whether it's a personal choice, a professional decision, or a relationship matter, patience allows clarity to emerge and ensures a more balanced and well-informed outcome.

Remember, the journey is just as important as the destination. By moving thoughtfully, you not only make better decisions but also reduce stress and create space for growth and understanding.

Avoid overeating—don't feel your stomach to the brim. Eating until you're completely full can lead to discomfort, sluggishness, and even health issues over time. Instead, practice mindful eating and stop when you feel satisfied, not stuffed.

When we leave some space in our stomach, our body functions better. Digestion becomes smoother, energy levels remain stable, and we feel lighter and more active. This approach not only promotes physical health but also cultivates discipline and self-awareness.

Remember the wisdom: "Eat to live, not live to eat." Moderation is the key to a balanced, healthy, and fulfilling life.

Surround yourself with good friends, for they are the pillars of a meaningful and fulfilling life. The company we keep greatly influences our thoughts, actions, and overall well-being.

True friends uplift and inspire us. They celebrate our joys, support us in challenges, and encourage us to grow into our best selves. Their presence brings positivity, wisdom, and strength, helping us navigate life's ups and downs with grace.

Seek friends who share your values, challenge you to think deeply, and bring out the best in you. At the same time, be a good friend yourself—offering kindness, understanding, and loyalty.

Life is richer and more joyful when surrounded by people who genuinely care for you and want to see you thrive. Choose your circle wisely, for it shapes the person you become.

In short, avoid snacking between meals and reserve a cheat day each week to enjoy sweets and hard drinks. Spend less time on social media and steer clear of negative people. Surround yourself with good, positive friends.

Cultivate hobbies that bring joy and fulfilment–sports, book reading, yoga, knitting, cleaning, painting, or gardening. Don't worry if money is tight; you can always rent things, buy second-hand books, or find affordable parts to pursue your passions.

The Vibrational Impact of Food

Food, like the Om mantra, carries vibrational energy that can influence our physical and mental well-being. Different types of foods offer varying levels of energy and impact:

- High Vibrational Foods: Fruits, vegetables, nuts, seeds, soya, coconut, and whole grains provide the best results. These foods keep you healthy, energetic, and fresh.
- Moderate Vibrational Foods: Milk, butter, fish (non-fried), eggs, sugarcane, wine, and honey have a milder positive impact on the body.
- Low Vibrational Foods: Meat, canned juices, soft drinks, liqueur, processed cheese, white bread, jams, chocolates, and bakery products can lead to negative vibrations. These foods contribute little to your health and can make you feel unwell over time.

A little care and awareness about your dietary choices can significantly enhance your quality of life, keeping you vibrant and joyful. Choose wisely for a healthier, happier life.

It's not about how much you have, but about making the most of what's available and dedicating time to activities that enrich your life.

Here are some simple mantras to live a wonderful life:

- Live in the Present – *"This moment is all I have."* Let go of the past and future. Focus on now and enjoy the beauty of the present.
- Gratitude First – *"I am grateful for all I have."* Start and end each day by counting your blessings, big or small.
- Positive Thoughts, Positive Life – *"I choose positive thoughts and actions."* Shift your mindset toward positivity and believe that good things are possible.
- Take Care of Your Body – *"My body is my temple."* Treat your body with respect through healthy food, exercise, and rest.
- Stay Kind and Compassionate – *"I spread kindness everywhere I go."* A kind heart attracts love and positivity into your life.
- Be Patient – *"Everything happens at the right time."* Trust the timing of your life and allow things to unfold naturally.
- Embrace Simplicity – *"Simplicity brings peace and happiness."* Keep things simple, from your possessions to your thoughts, and find joy in the little things.
- Mind Your Energy – *"I choose to be surrounded by good energy."* Protect your energy by avoiding negativity and nurturing your own peace.
- Learn and grow – *"Every day is an opportunity to grow."* Embrace challenges as chances to learn and evolve.

- Let Go of Fear – *"I release all fear and embrace love."* Trust in yourself and the universe, and let go of anything that no longer serves you.

We were so engrossed in the valuable conversation, exchanging thoughts and ideas, that time seemed to slip away unnoticed. The depth of knowledge Ankush shared was remarkable. As my eyes wandered to my wrist, I suddenly realized it was 2 a.m.

"Oh my God, it's already 2 a.m.!" I exclaimed. "Let's get some rest."

Ankush looked apologetic. "I'm sorry, Uncle, for keeping you awake, but I truly enjoyed our discussion. It feels great to have met my dad's best friend. You're such a kind and knowledgeable person."

Touched, I replied, "It was my pleasure hosting you, Ankush. Thank you for your wisdom and tips about life and happiness."

He smiled warmly. "Uncle, I've shared nothing extraordinary. These insights are readily available through books, online courses, and media. The Almighty sends us guides in life; we just need to recognize them when they appear."

The Foggy Morning and a Missed Flight

Ankush asked me to book an Ola for him since his flight to Mumbai was scheduled early in the morning at 5 AM. Instead, I offered to drive him to the airport myself. We set off in the car, but soon a thick fog descended, reducing visibility to almost zero. At first, I followed the white line painted on the road as a guide, but after a while, even that disappeared.

With no clear line of sight and the fog getting denser, I drove extremely slowly and cautiously. Unfortunately, I couldn't see the median in time, and the car ended up climbing onto the divider. We got stuck there for two hours with no assistance from passersby. Even police patrolling team refused to help. Eventually, we managed to call a crane to lift the car off the divider, but by then, Ankush had already missed his flight.

Naturally, he was upset. Knowing he's a golf enthusiast who plays in the UK; I suggested we head to the golf course practice range to blow off some steam until he could catch a rescheduled flight at 12 PM. We later learned from the airline that due to the fog, only international flights equipped with Instrument Landing System (ILS) Category 3 (CAT 3) certification were able to land or take off. All other flights, including Ankush's, were facing delays or cancellations.

A Light Moment at the Golf Course with Ankush

While practicing at the golf range, Ankush suddenly said, "Uncle, do you know what they call an eggetarian who misses a shot in golf?"

Curious, I asked, "What?"

He grinned and replied, "Scrambled!"

We both burst into laughter. That light-hearted joke lifted our spirits, and it reminded us how humour can brighten even the most frustrating situations. Later, I dropped Ankush at the airport for his 12 PM flight, which ended up being delayed by another hour.

Ankush bore a striking resemblance to Neeraj, and I truly enjoyed his company—short-lived though it was. He possesses admirable qualities, particularly the understanding that while one must do their job diligently, life should never be neglected.

After all, this is *your* life; Savor it. Pursue what you love without fretting over others' opinions. Genuine enjoyment stems from following the principles of discipline. With discipline as your compass, you'll invariably stay on the right track and find fulfilment in whatever you do.

The Next Day at the Golf Course

The following day, I arrived at the golf course but found it closed due to the persistent thick fog. Our group of golfers decided to sit down for coffee until the course opened. This, too, turned into a memorable time, as we shared anecdotes and light-hearted jokes:

A Light Moment at the Golf Course: Jokes

We both burst into laughter, the cheerful start to the day reflecting the joy and wisdom of the time spent together. Finally, I dropped him off at the airport and came to know his flight was further delayed by an hour.

Next day I reached the Golf course and the course was closed due to thick fog and we two groups decided to have a coffee till the course was open. This was also a memorable time as the players shared jokes which were as under;

A Light Moment at the Golf Course, jokes

Interview Joke A man goes for a job interview.

The interviewer asks, "What is your greatest weakness?"

The man replies, "Honesty."

The interviewer says, "I don't think honesty is a weakness."

The man replies, "I don't care what you think."

Golf Jok: During a round of golf, one man says to his friend, "Why do you always carry an extra pair of pants when you golf?"

His friend replies, "In case I get a hole in one!"

Sardar at the Golf Course: Sardar ji goes to play golf for the first time. He swings the club with all his might but misses the ball. Frustrated, he shouts, "What kind of game is this? You stand still, and I still can't hit you!"

Airplane and Golf: Two golfers were flying on a small private jet. One of them looked out the window and exclaimed, "Look at that golf course down there! It's so beautiful!" The other golfer squints and says, "That's not a golf course, that's a cemetery." The first golfer replies, "Ah, same thing. Lots of people lying around who wish they could still play!"

Joke, parrot and SardarOnce a sardar turban boy boarded the plane In the plane he saw a parrot saying to hostess, I love you Whenever she came across parrot, parrot again says I love you Turban man also got courage and said the same thing I love you to the Hostess Hostess came with captain and complaint that this turban man said I love you. Captain to turban man, did you said I love you? He said yes, I did and this parrot also said. Captain order throw both of them out of the plane Throw both of them out of the plan When they were about to throw Sardar ji And the parrot said, Sardar ji you know how to fly He said No Then The parrot said then why did you mess with them

The Hyper Job Interview Candidate During a job interview, a candidate seemed overly excited and hyper about every question.

One panellist asked, "Where do you live?"

The candidate replied enthusiastically, "Sir, I live in Malviya Nagar, near the IIT gate."

The panellist followed up, "What is your name?"

"Sir, my name is Vijay, but at home, my family calls me Bitoo," the candidate responded with a big smile.

Another question came: "What is your father's name?"

"Sir, his name is Hukam Singh."

"And what does he do?"

"Sir, he works for the Indian Agriculture Organisation."

Another panellist chimed in, "Hukam Singh? Is it the same person who just retired?"

"Yes, sir, yes!" the candidate exclaimed. "Do you know him?"

"Yes, we were in the same college," the panellist replied, amused.

The candidate proudly declared, "So nice! I assure you he is my real father!"

On hearing this, the entire panel burst into laughter. The poor candidate looked confused, wondering if he had made a mistake.

One panellist finally explained, "My dear boy, we've heard of real sisters and real brothers, but this is the first time we've heard someone refer to their 'real father'!"

Realizing his unintended blunder, the candidate's face turned red with embarrassment.

I stepped in to comfort him, saying, "Don't worry. Mistakes happen! Just remember to stay calm, listen carefully, and respond thoughtfully."

Even now, whenever I think about that interview, I can't help but laugh at the memory!

Don't Underestimate Others A man would come to the bar every single day and drink heavily.

One day, the bartender couldn't help but comment, "Sir, you drink so much! If you hadn't been drinking all these years, you could have bought a Mercedes by now."

The man calmly replied, "Do you drink alcohol?"

The bartender chuckled, "Of course not!"

The man then asked, "Do you have a Mercedes?"

The bartender replied, "No."

The man smiled and said, "Well, I do. It's parked right outside."

The bartender stood there, stunned and speechless.

Sardar Ji's Beer Ritual: A Sardar Ji visited a bar every day and always ordered four beers at once.

Curious, the bartender finally asked, "Sir, why do you order four beers all at once? If you drink one after the other, they'll stay cold!"

Sardar Ji explained, "Well, we're four brothers–one in America, one in Germany, and one in Canada. We can't drink together, so I order four beers to feel like we're all drinking together."

One day, Sardar Ji came in and ordered only three beers.

The bartender hesitated but served the beers and said solemnly, "Sir, I'm so sorry for your loss. It seems one of your brothers is no more."

Sardar Ji laughed and replied, "No, no! All my brothers are alive and well. It's just that *I've given up drinking!*"

The Clever Lady and the Hotel Bill

A lady was driving on the highway when she got tired and decided to stay at a hotel. She checked in, and the room rate was $100 per night.

The next morning, when she checked out, the cashier handed her a bill for $350.

Surprised, she said, "But the price was $100! Why are you charging me $350?"

The cashier replied, "Madam, the room rate is $100, but additional charges apply for facilities like the sauna, steam room, swimming pool, and breakfast."

The lady protested, "But I didn't use any of those facilities!"

The cashier smiled and said, "Madam, the facilities were available–you *could have* used them. It's not our fault if you didn't."

The lady, being clever, wrote a cheque for $50 and handed it over.

The cashier looked puzzled and said, "Madam, the bill is $350, not $50!"

The lady calmly replied, "I charged you $300 for sleeping with me."

Shocked, the cashier exclaimed, "But I didn't sleep with you!"

The lady smiled and said, "Well, the *facility was available.* That's your mistake!"

Friends Reunited in Midlife

They were the kids racing through streets on scuffed bicycles, Legs barely reaching the pedals, hearts brimming with audacious dreams.

Now they arrive in sleek cars with tinted windows, Carrying the weight of grown-up responsibilities–Triumphs, heartbreaks, and a few wrinkles of hard-earned wisdom.

They once rushed home after school for a glass of Complain, A sweet treat that fuelled endless games and silly laughter. But times have changed, and so have their tastes: Those same friends now gather in cozy bars, Clinking glasses and sharing stories over spirits stronger than childhood's brew.

In their eyes, however, the same mischievous twinkle remains, Recalling the pranks of yesteryear– The chalk-stained uniforms, secret crushes, and scoldings from teachers long forgotten. Between sips and chuckles, they rediscover The unbreakable bond that turned innocent classmates into lifelong confidants.

Here, in the middle of life's steady hum, They peel back layers of daily worries– Mortgages, work stress, school fees for their own kids– To remember simpler days when every worry was solved By a quick ride around the block or a shared bar of chocolate.

Stories of old trophies, handwritten notes, and lost diaries spill out, Tinged with playful jibes and heartfelt confessions.

Conversations drift from childhood crushes to real estate woes, from big career moves to unplanned family vacations– Yet within these moments, nostalgia softly glimmers, whispering of a time when tomorrow felt boundless.

And so, even as they raise their glasses high, they raise their inner voices to toast a past That shaped them all in subtle, profound ways. In every shared smile and retold anecdote, they see echoes of that fearless, bright-eyed youth–The version of themselves who believed anything was possible.

Thus, in this comforting swirl of laughter and memories, they find that old joy once more: Their hearts ride bicycles again, their spirits still sip something sweet. Though the Complan may have changed to cocktails, And the world turned more complicated, Their friendship remains a timeless refuge–A place where the child within them can run free.

A Walk That Connected Two Families

I love walking, and whenever I can't find time during the day, I go to the mall for a 30-minute walk. One evening, while strolling through the mall, I unexpectedly ran into Suresh, a friend with whom I used to play golf in Mumbai. He was with his daughter, Ankita, a charming young lady.

As soon as he saw me, Suresh immediately touched my feet as a gesture of respect and apologized for not attending the club dinner that day. He explained, "We got stuck at the police station that night."

I recalled how embarrassing that evening had been for me. "Yes, it was a terrible experience," I said. "I insisted we go to the club, but the hosts were missing, leaving me in an awkward situation."

Suresh took me aside and finally revealed what had happened. "It was a dispute among some teenagers over a girl from the Vaswani family, and the matter escalated to the police station. We were held up until 3 AM before being released. We couldn't update you at the time—it was a complete mess."

Hearing this, my frustration softened. "It's fine," I reassured him. "Don't keep anything in your heart. Things like this happen."

Then, Suresh introduced me to his daughter. "We are looking for a suitable match for her," he said.

At that moment, Ankush, Neeraj's son, came to my mind. I immediately told Suresh, "I know a boy. Let me speak to his family and get back to you."

He was thrilled and eagerly asked me to let him know the outcome. We took a selfie together, and he forwarded it to me on WhatsApp.

Later, I called Reeta to tell her about the girl. However, she immediately turned down the idea, citing a bad experience with the family and calling them irresponsible. I explained the reason for Suresh absence from the dinner, and she calmed down. "Alright, send me her picture," she said, but added, "You know Ankush—he gets irritated whenever we bring up the topic of marriage."

I forwarded Ankita's picture to her.

To my surprise, Reeta later informed me that Ankush had come to Mumbai from London, met the girl, and liked her! She said, "Let them meet and understand each other. We will accept whatever they decide."

I couldn't help but smile and laugh. I had merely gone for a simple walk in the mall, and in the process, two families got connected. It's amazing how life works—everything is already written by destiny; we are merely the means through which things unfold.

Let's see what happens next!

A visit to Virginia, USA, again connected two families.

Once, I was traveling to the USA for a business conference, and my neighbour requested me to visit her daughter at Virginia University if everything went well. I agreed to meet her.

When I landed at Virginia airport, Mukta Nandwani welcomed me warmly and introduced me to a boy studying in her class. Our luggage did not fit in his car, so she suggested keeping the suitcase in a locker. With great difficulty, we managed to push the suitcase inside and locked it with a digital code.

We then proceeded to the hotel and checked in. The next day, she took us to her PG (paying guest) room, showed us around the university, and later took us to a riverside where we had a picnic and spent a wonderful time together.

Both of them dropped me off at the airport, and I could sense that the boy was interested in her. When I returned home, I informed her parents about him and praised him for all the help he provided. I also mentioned that he seemed like a nice person. They told me that, just the day before, he had proposed to her. Since I had spoken highly of him, they decided to give their approval.

After graduating from university, they got married in India and are now happily settled in the USA.

This experience reaffirmed my belief that stories are written by the Almighty—we are merely the medium through which they unfold.

Ankush Got Engaged

Reeta called me to confirm that Ankush had gotten engaged to the same girl. She told me that they were coming to Delhi and staying at Hotel Hyatt. She added that Ankush would call me for dinner or tea, as he had great regard for you and spoke highly of you.

I replied, "That is his greatness, but I did nothing for him."

Later, Ankush called and invited me for dinner at Hotel Hyatt. Before heading to dinner, I first visited their room, where we had a peg of Scotch. Then, we proceeded to an Italian restaurant. On the way, I noticed them walking hand in hand, and at times, Ankush would pull her close and kiss her.

I thought to myself, "How times have changed! In our days, we could never do this in front of an elder like an uncle or father. But it feels good to see that today's generation is open and clear about their relationships."

At the restaurant, we ordered pizza and pasta, and the food was quite good. During dinner, Ankush said, "Uncle, thank you for introducing me to Ankita. She is amazing, and we share the same hobbies and nature."

I smiled and replied, "That is very good to hear."

Ankita added, "Uncle, my father mentioned that he had planned to have dinner with you once, but he couldn't make it. He still feels bad about it."

I reassured her, "Tell him to forget the past. Now we are not just friends, we are family friends."

She smiled, "Of course, Uncle, that's true."

I then asked Ankush about his future plans. "Are you both settling in the UK?"

Ankush replied, "No, Uncle, I am coming back to Mumbai for two reasons.

First, I don't want Ankita's future to be disturbed. I want her to pursue whatever she wants to do.

Second, you know that Reeta Aunty doesn't have any children. I want to stay with her and my uncle as they are getting older."

I was impressed by his thoughtfulness. "That is very considerate of you, Ankush. It's not easy to relocate after settling somewhere, but you are making this sacrifice for others. Well, done! I truly appreciate it and wish you both all the best for the future."

Jokingly, I added, "I hope you will invite me to your wedding!"

Ankush smiled, "Of course, Uncle! You are like my father, and you must come and bless us."

I laughed, "I was just joking, but I will definitely come.

Uncle you are so experienced give us some advice on our future relationship.

I replied, "Well, today's generation is more knowledgeable than us. However, I can give some suggestions."

"When we live together, love is present, and so is friction. The knots of relationships should be strong. To maintain them, you need to be careful and effectively cultivate understanding, patience, and mutual effort.

Friction can arise for many reasons, such as miscommunication, unmet expectations, emotional stress, financial issues, or lack of time together.

Avoid serious discussions when either of you is tired, stressed, or emotional. Listen carefully and actively. Make small adjustments to accommodate each other. You cannot win all the time, so prioritize the relationship over ego. If an argument escalates, take a pause rather than saying things in anger.

Always focus on mutual respect. A simple hug or kind words can make a difference–and I've noticed that you both already practice this, which is wonderful.

Respect individual space. Avoid bringing up old conflicts. Apologize when needed–there's no harm in saying sorry. Don't dwell on small issues.

In some cases, I have seen friction in families take a serious turn, leading to therapy, counselling, and attending workshops. Sometimes, talking to a trusted elder or mentor also helps resolve misunderstandings.

In the end, I will say this–friction in couples is normal, but how you handle it determines the health of the relationship. With patience, respect, and love, any conflict can be turned into an opportunity for growth and deeper understanding."

Ankush said, "I don't think there will ever be any friction between us. She has settled into every nerve of mine now."

1. **The "I" word holds deep meaning and differences:**
    - "I like you" is temporary.
    - "I love you" is eternal.
    - A saint once explained: "When you like a flower, you pluck it. But when you love a flower, you water it daily."
    - One who understand this, understand life

Both of them looked at each other and smiled, their eyes reflecting the deep bond they shared.

Ankush's great uncle said, *"You have presented and explained everything very well. Thank you for sharing these wonderful tips!"*

I told them, Now, let me leave. I have a golf tournament tomorrow."

Ankush asked, "Where is the tournament, Uncle?"

"At Qutab Golf Course, not far from here," I replied.

"All the best, Uncle!" he wished me.

"Thanks, Ankush."

He then said, "Reeta Aunty told me that you won last year as well."

I corrected him, "I was the runner-up last year."

The next morning, I reached the golf course by 7 AM, and the game started at 7:30 AM. I played well and later received a call from the course officials informing me that the next day, the Lieutenant Governor (LG) would distribute the awards and that I had again won the runner-up trophy.

The following day, I arrived at the venue by 8 AM and had a nice breakfast while waiting for LG B. L. Joshi. When my name was called, I went up to receive the runner-up cup.

As I took the cup, the LG recognized me and said, "You won last year as well! Congratulations again."

I smiled and replied, "Sir, when you were posted in London, we handled your shipments."

He recognized me and smiled.

Recently, in the senior citizen category, I again won a cup, this time presented by Honourable LG Anil Baijal.

Achievements always bring a unique kind of happiness.

Just like in sports, where sometimes you win and sometimes you lose, life is the same—you gain some, you lose some. But if we consider life as a game, then there are no worries, no disappointments.

Good message very inspiring and show the mirror of life received on whatsapp

Live in a Strange Locality

I live in a strange place, where people rarely meet but always peer—Eyes that truly understand you, become friends; Otherwise, even enemies can wear beautiful faces.

Sometimes, it's necessary to taste defeat So we can spot the quiet mistakes we've carried. Even when we lose, refuse to surrender—Prayers are never dismissed, they are only granted at the most fitting time.

Trust me, God's decisions Surpass our own desires. Always beware of two hazards: Ego, which whispers, "I don't need anyone," And delusion, which insists, "Everyone needs me."

In this place of fleeting connections And watchful eyes, Humility and patience guide the heart, Reminding us That understanding and grace Are better companions than pride.

Reflective Steps of Life

Every destination is within reach For the one who refuses to give up. Do not love sleep so deeply That your goals remain only dreams.

Look around; you'll find no shortage Of good people eager to uplift you. Recognize them as God's own messengers, Guiding your steps when you need it most.

The moment your heart decides "I can do this," You're already halfway to victory.

Life won't always hand you reasons to smile, Yet your own smile Could become the spark That ignites joy in someone else's heart.

I ask little from life: Only that each step I take Improves upon the last.

Remember—those who rise from humble ground Often see their names shine in the sky. To make history, you need more courage Than ink.

Never fear the shadows; They prove that somewhere A light still burns.

Life comes with no remote control, so stand up and change yourself.

Victory teaches us so little, while from defeat, we learn so much.

- The fewer the thoughts in your mind, the smoother the journey of life.
- If your eyes are positive, you will love the world. If your words are positive, the world will love you.
- It is not important that we have; what truly matters is that the Lord is with us.
- You can observe people's true colours simply by staying silent and watching.
- Words are the only currency you spend without ever knowing your balance—use them wisely.
- If God takes something away that you never imagined losing, He will surely give you something you never imagined having.
- Until you spread your wings, you will never know how far you can fly.
- Believe in the healing power of laughter, love, and prayer.
- Success hugs you in private; failure slaps you in public.
- A calm mind is the ultimate weapon against all battles.
- As I make more and more positive changes, my life gets better and better.
- God has planned happiness for each of us at the right time in our lives. The only thing is—He does not share His calendar with us.
- Comforts are good, but their addiction is dangerous. Comfort brings ease and relaxation, but overindulgence in

comfort can make us complacent. Growth happens when we step out of our comfort zones.

- Discipline leads to habits. Habits led to consistency. Consistency leads to growth. Success is not achieved overnight; it is built through daily discipline, positive habits, and unwavering consistency.
- Every situation in life is temporary. When life is good, embrace it, celebrate it, and cherish the moments with gratitude. When life is tough, remind yourself that no storm lasts forever—better days are always on the horizon.
- If you have a choice, choose the best. If you have no choice, give your best. Life does not always offer us perfect options, but our attitude and effort determine the outcome.
- Life is never easy—we have to make it easier. Sometimes by letting go, sometimes by embracing. Knowing when to ignore what drains us and when to accept what strengthens us is the ultimate mantra for peace and success.
- The moment you adopt a positive mindset; difficulties start to lose their grip. Positivity does not mean ignoring problems; it means facing them with a mindset that seeks solutions rather than dwelling on setbacks.
- Waves are inspiring, not because they rise and fall, but because they never fail to rise again. Life's ups and downs are inevitable, but resilience is what defines true strength.
- Mistakes, failures, insults, frustrations, and rejections are not signs of defeat; they are stepping stones to success. Nobody has ever achieved anything meaningful without overcoming these hurdles.

- Growth comes from struggles. Every challenge teaches a lesson, every setback builds resilience, and every failure brings you one step closer to success.

I Have Now Learned How to Live

I have learned now How to truly live– I'm happy, pleased, and blissful, Because I've ceased chasing endless desires.

Within me lies an infinite treasure, An inner jewel beyond all measure; Any comparison with the outer world Feels meaningless once you glimpse this light.

The soul within is pure, And so is the God it reflects. If any impurity exists, It's in my actions and my life. So, in this lifetime itself, I must strive to cleanse and grow.

Yet so often we walk the wrong path, Pressing forward aimlessly And gathering only disappointment. But there is a drop of hope–an elixir– Hidden within our own hearts.

Once inner strength expands, Contentment and joy bloom alongside it. Fear and insecurity begin to shrink, Making room for peace.

To awaken that spiritual force, We must first stir our own inner resolve, Releasing the dormant courage and faith within. Only then do we embrace the truth: That real bliss springs from our own depth– A treasure waiting to be discovered.

Oh Life...

Oh life, I don't have many wishes for you. I don't ask for riches, nor do I crave grand victories. I don't seek a life free from challenges, For I know that struggles shape the strongest souls.

I only ask for one simple thing– Let my next step be better than the last.

Let each sunrise bring me a little more wisdom, A little more patience, a little more kindness. Let my mistakes become lessons, not regrets, And my failures become stepping stones, not burdens.

I do not wish for a life without storms, But I hope for the strength to walk through them with courage. I do not wish for a path without obstacles, But I pray for the resilience to rise every time I fall.

I do not ask for perfection, Just progress. Not greatness, But goodness. Not the absence of sorrow, But the ability to find joy even in small moments.

Oh life, I do not demand certainty, For I have learned that change is your only promise. I do not ask you to be easy, But I hope to be wiser, braver, and kinder with every step.

Let me grow, let me evolve, Let my next step always be better than the last.

Humanity is the key of success

In life, whether you are a government officer, businessman, sportsperson, politician, academic, or belong to any other field, humanity and politeness are the true keys to success. These qualities not only help in building strong relationships but also earn you genuine respect from others.

Success can be achieved through both fair and corrupt means–it is a choice every individual has to make. While dishonesty and shortcuts may bring quick success, they often come at the cost of inner peace, reputation, and long-term stability. On the other hand, when success is earned through integrity, hard work, and ethical practices, it brings a deep sense of fulfilment and lasting satisfaction.

True success is not just about wealth, power, or recognition; it is about the peace of mind and self-respect you carry throughout your journey. Those who choose fairness and honesty may face challenges along the way, but in the end, they sleep peacefully with a clear conscience, knowing they have done the right thing.

Ultimately, life is not just about achieving success–it is about how you achieve it. Choose the path that not only makes you successful but also keeps you at peace with yourself.

"In my experience, I've met two kinds of people. Some reach the very top–achieve the highest positions, wealth, and respect–and yet remain grounded, humble, and polite. They carry their success with quiet dignity. And then there are others–who, with just a taste of name or fame, start walking like gods among mortals, forgetting their roots and mistaking applause for immortality. True greatness is silent; it doesn't shout."

"Transformation requires more than just hard work; it also needs good vibes and positive vibrations. While these tips can serve as a starting point, it's essential to find guidance that resonates with you, allowing you to gain control and create the fulfilling life you desire."

A Journey to Transformation: My Assistant Manager's Experience at Isha Foundation

One day, my 28-year-old assistant manager approached me with an unexpected decision–he was resigning to join the Isha Foundation in Coimbatore for six months. His goal? Personality development and self-transformation.

Though surprised, I respected his determination and wished him all the best.

I recalled an interview I had watched, featuring Kiran Bedi, a Supreme Court Justice, and Sadh guru. It was a profound conversation, filled with insightful questions and logical, well-articulated answers.

The Meaning of Bharat vs. India

One point that stood out was Sadh guru's explanation of the names *India* and *Bharat*. He emphasized that *India* was a name given by colonial rulers, lacking any intrinsic meaning. In contrast, *Bharat* carries deep historical and cultural significance. His explanation left no room for doubt–language, identity, and heritage are deeply intertwined with a nation's self-perception.

My Own Spiritual Practice, ISHA Kriya

Inspired by such teachings, I have incorporated a simple kriya practice into my daily routine:

- Every morning and evening, I sit in stillness for ten minutes and focus on my breath.
- I mentally affirm: "I am not in the body. I am not even in the mind."
- After ten minutes, I chant the vibration sound "aaaaa" eight times, which brings a sense of peace.
- I also enjoy practicing with Isha mantras, available on YouTube, which have a profound effect:
- Yoga Yoga Yogeshwaraya Bhuta Bhuta Bhuteshwaraya Kala Kala Kaleshwaraya Shiva Shiva Sarveshwaraya Shambho Shambho Mahadevaya

Translation of the Chant:

"Salutations to the One, The Yogeshwara, who has transcended the physical, Bhuteshwara, one who has mastered the five elements, Kaleshwara, one who has mastered time and is beyond its cycles, Sarveshwara, one who is everywhere, and is the basis of everything, Salutations to Shambho, the greatest of all, the Mahadeva."

These simple yet powerful practices help bring clarity and inner joy.

The Assistant Manager's Return: A New Person

After six months, he returned—a changed person. There was something different in his presence, his way of thinking, and his approach to life. He shared several insights from his time at Isha, highlighting various programs available at the ashram.

Isha Hatha Yoga: A Path to Total Wellbeing

Hatha Yoga at Isha is not just about physical fitness but a holistic process to master the body and mind. The program revives ancient yogic disciplines that have largely disappeared in modern times.

- Upa-Yoga: A set of 10 powerful practices that activate the joints, muscles, and energy system.
- Angamardana: A 30-step process designed to invigorate the body and achieve peak physical and mental fitness.
- Surya Kriya: A 21-step ancient practice that enhances overall well-being and vitality.
- Yoga Asanas: A set of postures that elevate consciousness, stabilize emotions, and decelerate aging.
- Bhuta Shuddhi: A purification process that balances the five elements within the body, leading to harmony and balance.

Beyond Yoga: Isha's Larger Vision

The Isha Foundation is not just about self-improvement; it extends to environmental and social transformation. Some of its well-known initiatives include:

- Save Soil – A movement to restore soil health.
- Rally for Rivers – A nationwide campaign to revitalize India's dying rivers.

- Community Revitalization – Programs for rural health, education, and sustainability.

Inner Engineering: A Solution for Modern Life

With increasing stress, anxiety, and work-life imbalance, Inner Engineering Online is a timely solution. Developed by Sadhguru, this science-based approach enhances physical health, emotional balance, and mental clarity.

Benefits of Inner Engineering:

Maintain high energy levels throughout the day Increase mental clarity, emotional balance, and productivity Reduce stress, fear, and anxiety Attain joy, tranquillity, and fulfilment

An Unforgettable Experience at Isha

My assistant manager described the Isha Ashram as more than just a retreat—it felt like heaven on earth.

- He walked 18,000 feet daily, which became a meditative experience.
- He attended daily yoga sessions, including advanced postures and breathing techniques.
- He listened to wisdom stories filled with life-changing lessons.

"Isha isn't just a place," he told me, "It's an experience that completely shifts your perspective on life."

His journey made me realize how self-transformation is a continuous process—one that requires commitment, discipline, and the right guidance. Whether through kriyas, meditation, yoga, or social work, the path to a fulfilling life begins within.

For those seeking change, Isha Foundation offers a unique opportunity to experience inner growth and balance, not just in body but in spirit.

My manager also narrated a story which I liked it and summery is as under; My Own Spiritual Practice, ISHA Kriya

Inspired by such teachings, I have incorporated a simple kriya practice into my daily routine:

- Every morning and evening, I sit in stillness for ten minutes and focus on my breath.
- I mentally affirm: "I am not in the body. I am not even in the mind."
- After ten minutes, I chant the vibration sound "aaaaa" seven times, which brings a sense of peace.
- I also enjoy practicing with Isha mantras, available on YouTube, which have a profound effect:

Story (ISHA) read, I liked it, good message.

The Illusion of Success and the Reality of Inner Stability

One day, a weak and aging partridge gazed at a towering tree and sighed, *"There was a time when I could fly to its highest branch, but now my wings have lost their strength. I can barely reach the first branch."*

Hearing this, a bull nearby smirked and said, *"Eat a little of my dung every day, and you'll see–within two weeks, you'll reach the top."*

The partridge scoffed, *"What nonsense! How can eating dung make me fly?"*

The bull replied, *"Try it. This is what humanity thrives on!"*

Reluctantly, the partridge pecked at the dung. To its surprise, it gained strength and, within a few days, reached the higher branches. By the fifteenth day, it proudly sat on the highest branch, enjoying the view.

Just then, an old farmer relaxing in his armchair spotted the plump bird sitting atop the tree. He pulled out his gun and shot it down.

Moral of the Story

Dung may get you to the top, but it won't keep you there!

Many people fill their lives with external distractions—false praise, artificial success, and temporary highs—only to realize that these things don't offer lasting fulfilment.

The Illusion of External Security

You can create momentary happiness by gathering wealth, status, or validation from others. But these things are fragile. They can crumble due to economic downturns, personal losses, or the shifting opinions of others. And even if disaster never strikes, the constant *fear* of losing everything is its own kind of suffering.

So long as your inner stability is dictated by external conditions, you remain in a perpetual state of insecurity.

The Real Solution: Turning Inward

True stability and fulfilment come not from external validation but from within yourself.

- Outer circumstances may provoke emotions, but they do not create them—the source of your experience is within you.
- Fear disappears when inner strength grows—when you stop chasing illusions and start strengthening your inner foundation.
- Joy that comes from within lasts—it isn't dependent on circumstances and cannot be taken away by external forces.

Instead of feeding on emotional "dung" to reach false heights, focus on inner growth, clarity, and self-awareness. Success should be built on real strength, not shortcuts. When you cultivate true confidence and contentment within, no storm—internal or external—can shake your foundation.

Story shared by friend of Isha foundation.

I am so fortunate that recently one of friend sent the story of Isha which is worth to read and I have further given meaning of the same.

So the man trekked up the difficult mountain path, finally reached the master's hut and entered. He noticed there were many disciples there already. The master was talking to his many disciples. When he saw this man, the master asked him to come closer and asked him, "What do you want?" The man said, "I am wandering in search of the Buddha's teachings. I have met many scholars, but nobody could fully answer my questions. I heard that you will be able to explain this better than all the others so I came to you." "Oh! Please be seated. I will tell you after all of them leave," said the Zen master. The man was satisfied. He concluded that this master must be really good for so many disciples to gather around him. The master spoke with each of his disciples and then sent them on their way. Finally, he came to the man and said, "Come with me!" He led the man across the slopes. After covering a certain distance, they came upon some vegetation before them. The master pointed to it and asked, "What is this?" The man replied, "Bamboo." The master then pointed to other bamboo shoots that were off to the side and asked, "When you look at these, what do you see?" The man said, "That bamboo is tall. This bamboo has not yet grown up and is short." The master said, "These are bamboos!" and started walking back to his hut. Sadhguru: Let us say you are six feet tall. When you are among people who have not crossed five and a half feet, you will think you are tall. You will walk like a tall person, sit like a tall person, and run like a tall person. If we suddenly transport you to another country, where the minimum height is eight feet, you will suddenly feel short, walk like a short person and sit like a short person.

The conclusions people draw from their five senses are predominantly in comparison with something else. Comparison is only needed to conduct our affairs in day-to-day life. If you touch something that is cold, it just means that your body is hot. Seeing things in comparison like this is not true perception. If you want to perceive life in its true dimension, you must stop comparing and making conclusions that this is high or low, tall or short, beautiful or ugly. Whether you are six feet or eight feet tall, but ultimately you are still yourself. Whether it is Buddha's teaching or the basics of Yoga, it is just about perceiving life the way it is. For this to happen, you have to move beyond what is recorded by the five senses.

Meaning in short

The story is about the difference between true perception and the limited understanding we get through comparison and the five senses.

The man in the story searches for the Buddha's teachings, hoping to find some extraordinary wisdom. But the Zen master teaches him through a simple example of bamboo – some tall, some short – showing that they are all just bamboo. By this, the master points out that our tendency to label things as "big" or "small," "high" or "low," "important" or "unimportant" only comes from comparing one thing to another. But this kind of comparison prevents us from seeing things as they truly are.

Sadhguru's explanation builds on this idea, saying that what we perceive through our senses is always relative. We call something cold only because we feel warmer in comparison. We call something tall only because we've seen shorter things. But these judgments are not reality – they are just our mind's interpretations based on limited information.

True perception, like the Buddha's wisdom, comes when we go beyond this habit of comparing and simply see life as it is – without conclusions, without judgment. Only then can we experience the deeper truths of existence.

In short: The story teaches us that wisdom and higher states of being come from moving beyond comparison and experiencing life directly, without the distortions created by our senses and our minds.

The story is about the difference between true perception and the limited understanding we get through comparison and the five senses.

The man in the story searches for the Buddha's teachings, hoping to find some extraordinary wisdom. But the Zen master teaches him through a simple example of bamboo – some tall, some short – showing that they are all just bamboo. By this, the master points out that our tendency to label things as "big" or "small," "high" or "low," "important" or "unimportant" only comes from comparing one thing to another. But this kind of comparison prevents us from seeing things as they truly are.

Sadhguru's explanation builds on this idea, saying that what we perceive through our senses is always relative. We call something cold only because we feel warmer in comparison. We call something tall only because we've seen shorter things. But these judgments are not reality – they are just our mind's interpretations based on limited information.

True perception, like the Buddha's wisdom, comes when we go beyond this habit of comparing and simply see life as it is – without conclusions, without judgment. Only then can we experience the deeper truths of existence.

More In short: The story teaches us that wisdom and higher states of being come from moving beyond comparison and experiencing life directly, without the distortions created by our senses and our minds.

Blessed to Be in the Land of Divinity

How truly blessed and fortunate we are to live in a country where divinity is present in every corner of Bharat. The spiritual energy that fills this land is unmistakable—whether in the grand celebrations of Ayodhya, the sacred rituals of Varanasi, or the awe-inspiring spectacle of the Maha Kumbh Mela.

Millions of devotees gather at these holy sites, drawn by an unseen force that connects them to something greater than themselves. This profound devotion, expressed through prayers, chants, and selfless service, makes our country not just a geographical land but a spiritual powerhouse.

Following the Teachings of Guru Sri Sri Ravi Shankar

Mind, Body & Soul Meditation

Preparation:

- Sit comfortably with your back straight.
- Gently close your eyes.
- Take a deep breath in... and breathe out.

Awareness of the Mind & Breath

- Bring your attention to the top of your head.
- Recognize that the mind and body are separate.
- Breathe deeply and chant "Om".
- Observe: The breath flows within the body, yet it is not the body.
- Feel the air around and within you—every cell in your body is breathing.

Awareness of the Self

- You exist in the body, but you are not the body.
- Your mind is present throughout the body, yet beyond it.
- Smile gently, take a deep breath, and honour the mind with "Om".

Expanding Awareness

- Become aware of the vast sky above, filled with billions of stars.
- Let your mind expand beyond boundaries.
- Keep smiling and sit in stillness for a few minutes—nothing to do, nothing to know, just relax.

Closing

- Chant "Om Shanti, Shanti, Shanti" (peace, peace, peace).
- Slowly become aware of your surroundings.
- Breathe in with a smile... breathe out... and gently open your eyes.

I have been deeply influenced by Sri Sri Guru and his teachings. His wisdom is both moderate and profound, blending ancient spiritual practices with modern understanding. His approach is not just about rituals or philosophy—it is about bringing spirituality into everyday life with simplicity and clarity.

The Power of Sudarshan Kriya

One of the most transformative practices I have embraced is Sudarshan Kriya. Practicing it daily brings me a sense of clarity, inner peace, and energy that lasts the entire day. It is truly remarkable how such a simple breathing technique can harmonize the body, mind, and emotions.

For those who have not experienced it, I highly recommend exploring Sri Sri Guru's teachings on YouTube and other media platforms. The guided sessions available make it easy to learn and practice, offering a beautiful path to inner transformation and well-being.

Living in Bharat means being surrounded by spiritual richness at every step. By immersing ourselves in the wisdom of great Gurus and embracing life-enhancing practices like Sudarshan Kriya, we not only uplift our own lives but also contribute to the collective consciousness of this sacred land. May we continue to walk the path of devotion, wisdom, and self-discovery.

A story read somewhere delivering good message

Raju and the Vastu Shastra Expert

Raju was a kind-hearted man who had recently retired and built a beautiful house in his village. As is often the case in small communities, friends and neighbours bombarded him with advice—especially about hiring someone versed in *Vastu Shastra* (the traditional Indian system of architecture) to ensure his home's harmony.

Although Raju felt content with his new house, he decided to humour his well-wishers and agreed to meet a renowned Vastu Shastra expert from Delhi. On the day of the consultation, Raju drove the expert to his village. Along the way, the expert observed Raju's driving habits:

- Whenever another vehicle approached from behind, Raju would gently move aside, waving them past with a smile.
- "Why are you letting them overtake you so easily?" asked the expert.
- "They might have more urgent business than I do," Raju replied politely.

Not long after, a child suddenly dashed onto the road. Raju braked at once, patiently allowing the child to cross. The expert, shaken, urged Raju to continue.

- "Let's wait a bit more," Raju cautioned. "Children often play in groups—there might be more coming."

Sure enough, a few more children scampered into the street. Raju waited until they too had safely passed. The expert, now both nervous and intrigued, witnessed another delay as Raju noticed some birds flying nearby.

- "Why have we stopped again?" asked the expert.
- "It looks like those children are picking mangoes," Raju answered. "If I drive ahead, they'll get frightened and could hurt themselves running away."

By the time they finally reached Raju's new home, the Vastu Shastra expert was visibly moved by Raju's patience and empathy. When Raju invited him inside to assess the house, the expert shook his head and smiled.

- "My friend," he said, "you don't need *any* Vastu Shastra. Your heart and your actions already bring harmony to this place."

Raju's kindness on the road—his empathy for other drivers, for children at play, and for nature—proved to the expert that the strongest foundation for a home isn't found in architectural rules alone, but in the genuine goodness of the person who dwells there.

Narrow escape at Gir

It was an adventure we had been eagerly looking forward to—our trip to Gir National Park, the only home to Asiatic lions in the wild. The excitement in our group was palpable as we entered the dense forest in an open jeep at dawn, ready to witness nature in its raw form.

Our guide, a seasoned tracker who had spent years in the jungle, seated me in the front for the best view. "You'll get the best experience from here," he assured me with a knowing smile. The crisp morning air carried the earthy scent of the forest, and as we drove deeper, the silence was occasionally interrupted by the distant calls of birds and the rustling of leaves.

After an hour of searching, we finally spotted them—a pride of lions resting lazily in the shade of a large tree, their golden coats blending seamlessly with the dry grass. The guide pointed them out, whispering, "There they are! Look closely."

Wanting a clearer view, he encouraged me to roll down the glass. I hesitated for a moment, but his confidence reassured me. "They're far away," he said, "It's safe." Carefully, I lowered the window and took in the breathtaking sight.

After spending a few minutes watching them, we moved ahead on a narrow dirt track winding deeper into the jungle. I shifted to the back seat while the driver and guide discussed the next route. The air was thick with the sounds of the wild—birds chirping, leaves rustling, and the distant roar of an animal, probably marking its territory.

Suddenly, we spotted another group of lions resting on the other side of the path. This time, they were closer. We stopped at a safe distance, observing them in silence. Just as we were admiring their majestic presence, an unexpected movement caught our attention.

A lion—**not from the group ahead but from behind us—**had silently emerged from the bushes and was now just a few feet away from our jeep.

Our hearts stopped.

The air felt heavy with tension. None of us had noticed it approaching. It was massive, its golden mane slightly ruffled, its piercing eyes locked onto us. It stood still for a moment, scanning us, assessing the situation.

Then, in a split second, the lion took a step forward.

It was at this moment that we realized the front window was still open.

The driver panicked. Instinctively, his hand shot forward to close the glass.

A grave mistake.

The lion immediately reacted. Its ears twitched, its muscles tensed, and in a flash, its expression changed from calm curiosity to aggression. It let out a deep, guttural growl—so powerful that it sent a shiver down our spines. The guide, sensing the danger, barked in a hushed but firm tone, "Stop! Don't move!"

The driver, frozen in fear, quickly withdrew his hand, but the damage had already been done.

The lion stepped back slightly, positioning itself to charge. Its powerful limbs flexed, its tail twitched sharply—it was preparing to pounce.

At that very moment, a loud rumbling noise shattered the tense silence.

A tracker's tractor, parked nearby, suddenly roared to life. The forest guard, realizing the danger, had swiftly turned on the engine and was now driving toward the lion. The machine's sound startled the beast, distracting it just enough to make it reconsider.

The lion turned its head toward the tractor, hesitating for a fraction of a second. The tracker revved the engine again, edging closer, making the lion reassess the threat.

Then, in one swift motion, the lion backed away and disappeared into the dense foliage.

We exhaled—only then realizing that we had been holding our breath.

The guide looked at us, his face calm but firm. "That was close," he muttered, wiping the sweat from his forehead.

The driver, still shaken, kept his hands clenched on the steering wheel. I could feel my heartbeat still pounding in my chest, the adrenaline refusing to settle.

We thanked the tracker profusely, realizing that if he hadn't been nearby, the situation could have taken a very different turn. His tractor, enclosed with iron fencing, was a necessary protection against such unpredictable encounters.

As we drove back, the guide turned to us and said, "In the jungle, never assume you are safe. Anything can happen in an instant."

That day, we learned a lesson we would never forget: Life is unpredictable, and danger often arrives silently. We must always be alert, respect nature, and above all, be grateful for every safe moment we get.

As we exited the park, I looked back at the dense jungle, still echoing with its own secrets. What had started as an exciting safari had turned into an experience that would stay with me forever.

God Is Great

In today's fast-paced world, everyone is constantly running–chasing goals, meeting targets, and striving for success. Life has become a race where people are consumed by work, responsibilities, and expectations. Some work 10 to 12 hours a day, driven by ambition, while others struggle to find meaning and balance.

However, this relentless pursuit often comes at a cost. Many face stress, anxiety, hardships, insomnia, and fatigue, which lead to irritability, frustration, and emotional exhaustion. The pressure to perform, achieve, and stay ahead can create a deep sense of dissatisfaction, making people feel as if they are merely existing rather than truly living.

The digital era has brought significant advancements, offering convenience, efficiency, and endless opportunities. However, as the saying goes, "Too much of anything is not good for health." While technology has made life easier, it has also contributed to increased mental fatigue, lack of focus, and excessive dependence on digital distractions. Social media, online content, and digital entertainment have flooded our minds, often leading to comparison, self-doubt, and unrealistic expectations.

Today, there is a vast amount of information available on how to handle stress, improve mental health, and achieve success. YouTube videos, self-help books, online courses, and motivational content offer countless solutions. But it is important to remember that these are just tools and guidance—real transformation comes from self-discipline, adopting healthy habits, and making conscious efforts to improve one's behaviour and mindset.

Your Behaviour Shapes Your Life

A person's habits and daily routine play a crucial role in determining their success and overall well-being. It is important to ask yourself:

- Do you complete your tasks or leave them halfway?
- Are you well-organized or messy?
- Do you manage your time effectively or constantly feel overwhelmed?
- Are you patient and resilient, or do you give up easily when facing challenges?

Your behaviour, mindset, and level of self-discipline determine not only how successful you become but also how happy and peaceful you feel. True success is not just about reaching goals—it is about maintaining mental peace, emotional stability, and a sense of fulfilment.

Finding Balance in Life

In the rush of modern life, we often forget that balance is key. Achievements and material success lose their meaning if they come at the cost of our health, relationships, and peace of mind.

To live a truly fulfilling life:

- Prioritize your mental and physical well-being. A calm mind and healthy body will help you achieve more in the long run.
- Develop self-discipline. Stay consistent in your efforts and don't leave things unfinished.
- Cultivate patience and gratitude. Learn to appreciate what you have rather than constantly chasing what you don't.
- Limit unnecessary distractions. Excessive social media, entertainment, and digital consumption can drain your energy and focus.
- Maintain healthy relationships. Success is meaningful when shared with loved ones who support and uplift you.

The key to a peaceful and successful life lies in discipline, balance, and a positive mindset. Learn to manage time, stay focused, and work with dedication—but also remember to pause, reflect, and enjoy the journey. After all, life is not just about achievements; it is about living with contentment, purpose, and inner peace.

Reeta and Ankush side

Reeta called me and told me that the marriage of Ankush has been fixed this February 25th but venue not yet fixed, Ankush wants wedding in London and reception at Mumbai.

I told her, it is not possible for me to go to Uk for wedding but assure you I will be in Mumbai in Reception.

Reeta yes, I am telling him do everything here, In UK hardly anyone will go to UK but today generation, you know have different thinking and different plans.

I told her, Ankush is quite nice buoy, He will agree or should I speak to him.

She declined and said don't worry we are after him to change the idea, let us see.

I will update you.

I told her insist him to in India as our Prime Minister has recently also requested all to do wedding in India and not abroad. It will not only too expensive but lot of foreign exchange will be spent.

She laughed and said, I will convey your message to him, let us see.

I was sipping my evening tea when my phone rang. It was Suresh. His voice was heavy with concern.

"Ashok bhai, these kids have had a fight," he said, exhaling deeply. "Ankush and Ankita are saying they won't get married now. I can't see Ankita like this—she's just crying non-stop. Please talk to Ankush. I don't know what to do."

I could hear the helplessness in his voice. I took a deep breath and thought about how difficult it is to understand today's generation. Just last month, Rita was excitedly talking about the wedding venue. And now, here we were.

These days, it's best not to interfere too much in young people's relationships—if something goes wrong, the one who tries to help often gets blamed. But Suresh was a dear friend, and his worry was genuine. I decided to step in.

Gathering my thoughts, I called Ankush.

"Hello, Uncle!" His voice was warm, as always.

"I'm fine, Ankush," I said. "But tell me, what's going on between you and Ankita?"

There was silence on the other end for a moment. "Uncle, who told you?"

"Suresh just called me," I said. "He's very worried about Ankita."

Ankush sighed. "Uncle, it's nothing major. It's just... Ankita bought me a very expensive gift for my birthday. I refused to accept it. I told her that love isn't measured by the price of a gift. Today she can afford it because her father pays, but tomorrow, when we start our life together, I won't be able to match that. And I don't want to start a relationship where she gets used to things I can't provide in the long run."

I listened carefully. He continued, "Whenever we go out, she insists on paying. She always chooses expensive restaurants, five-star hotels, luxury brands... I don't want her to stop enjoying these things, but I just want her to understand that money isn't everything. Uncle, I love her. But I want her to realize that love is not about spending extravagantly."

His words carried sincerity. He wasn't rejecting Ankita; he was trying to guide her toward a more balanced perspective on life and relationships.

"Ankush, talk to Ankita," I said gently. "She's very upset."

"I will, Uncle," he assured me. "Give me a couple of days. I just want her to reflect on this without feeling pressured. I haven't even told Rita–I'm just acting distant so that she understands on her own."

I nodded to myself. His approach made sense.

After our conversation, I called Suresh back.

"Suresh , don't worry," I reassured him. "It's just a misunderstanding. Ankush loves Ankita, but he wants her to realize the value of simplicity and thoughtful spending. He will talk to her in a couple of days."

Suresh exhaled in relief. "Thank you, Ashok. This gives me some hope. I'll talk to Ankita and help her understand, too."

As I hung up the phone, I reflected on how relationships aren't just about love–they're about understanding each other's perspectives, values, and future expectations. Sometimes, a small disagreement can feel like the end of the world, but with patience and the right guidance, love finds a way to survive.

A Call of Happiness

This morning, my phone rang, and I saw Ankush's name flashing on the screen. As I picked up, his cheerful voice greeted me.

"Uncle, I have some good news!"

I smiled. "Tell me, son. What's the news?"

"Ankita and I are on a date today," he said, sounding relieved. "Everything is sorted now. We have decided that the wedding will take place in Mumbai, not London."

I felt a wave of happiness wash over me. "This is wonderful news, Ankush! God bless you both. I'm truly happy for you."

"Now, Uncle, you just wait for the wedding invitation!" he said excitedly. "You have to come. There's no question about it."

I chuckled. "Of course, son. How could I miss it?"

"Wait, Uncle," he said, "talk to Ankita."

A moment later, Ankita's cheerful voice came through. "Hello, Uncle! You are so wonderful. Ankush and Papa always speak so highly of you. I feel incredibly lucky–after all, I met Ankush because of you. I can't thank you enough from the bottom of my heart."

I smiled warmly. "Oh, dear child, don't say all this. We are just the medium, but everything is written by God. I only wish for you both to stay happy and blessed always."

"Thank you, Uncle," she said sweetly. "You are so kind."

"Alright then, my best wishes are always with you. Take care."

"Right, Uncle! Bye and all the best!"

As I hung up, my heart felt full. Some moments in life remind us that happiness comes from seeing our loved ones find their own joy. And today was one of those moments.

Wedding date venue fixed

Today I received Ankush's wedding card and the wedding was in Maurya Hotel and I reached there a day earlier and checked in at the hotel and told Rita and Ankush that I have checked in at the hotel.

"I noticed that Reeta looked unhappy, so I approached her and asked if everything was okay. She shared with me that despite Ankush's wedding being a joyful occasion, her family was going through a tough time.

Reeta revealed that they had invested around 20 crores in London as part of an incentive program, but the UK government changed policies, leaving them with significant losses. Their home was hypothecated, and they were struggling financially.

Reeta's family had considered postponing the wedding due to their financial situation, but Suresh, Ankush's father, stepped in and took over the project, paying them 10 crores. Although this helped alleviate some of their financial burden, Reeta's family still faced a significant loss.

Reeta confided that the stress of this situation had taken a toll on Neeraj, who unfortunately passed away in London. I offered my sympathy and expressed gratitude that Suresh's support had provided some relief. Reeta acknowledged that while the financial loss was significant, her family might be able to recover in the long term."

What a profound reflection on life!

"Life can be unpredictable and cruel. One moment, everything seems to be going smoothly, and the next, disaster strikes. It's like a tiger stalking its prey, slowly and silently closing in. If you manage to escape unscathed, consider yourself lucky.

This unpredictability is a reminder to cherish every moment, appreciate the good times, and be prepared for the unexpected twists and turns that life can take."

These words evoke the idea that life is fragile and can change in an instant. It's a powerful reminder to stay grounded, appreciate what we have, and be resilient in the face of adversity.

Ankush was firm in his decision. At first, he was not willing to accept any kind of help from Suresh . When the subject came up, Ankush's face tightened with resolve. "My prayer is that you don't even request Ankita's father for any help," he said quietly but firmly. "I will do whatever I can on my own." There was a calm determination in his voice, the kind that only comes from a deep sense of self-reliance.

I looked at him with both pride and concern. "He has become very wise," I thought. But I also knew that sometimes wisdom can turn into stubbornness. "He is just taking over," I said gently. "This happens in business; it's a common thing. Sometimes you have to accept support to move forward."

Ankush sighed and looked down for a moment, as if weighing my words. "I have read books all my life," he said softly. "And my personality has also become like the pages of a book—calm, thoughtful, and sometimes distant. I understand everything in theory, but when it comes to real life... it's different. Still, whatever you feel is right, whatever is true—do that only."

I reached out and placed a reassuring hand on his shoulder. "Son, listen to me," I said. "In sadness, one often encounters many big and good things in the world. And even in those moments, God sends help and consolation from unexpected places."

I paused, letting the words sink in. "Ankita's father has a very big heart," I continued. "And those who have big hearts are always generous. Accepting help doesn't make you any less capable or independent. Sometimes, it takes even greater strength to accept support when it's offered with love."

Ankush didn't reply right away. He was thinking, his eyes reflecting both his inner conflict and his growing understanding. It was a quiet moment, filled with the kind of contemplation that often precedes important decisions.

I narrated story to Reeta and Ankush on this subject

In a small village nestled between green hills, there lived an old man named Ravi. He wasn't wealthy, nor did he hold an important position in the village, but he had a heart full of kindness. Every day, he would do small acts of generosity – feeding stray animals, helping his neighbours with their chores, and offering kind words to anyone who needed them.

One day, a terrible storm swept through the village, destroying homes and flooding the fields. Everyone was busy trying to rebuild their lives, and the air was filled with tension and worry. Despite his own damaged house, Ravi went from house to house, offering whatever little help he could – fixing broken fences, sharing his meagre food, and comforting those who had lost more than he had.

One evening, Ravi sat outside his half-repaired home, exhausted but content. As the sun dipped below the horizon, a group of villagers approached him. They carried baskets of food, tools, and materials. "We've come to help you, Ravi," one of them said.

Ravi was taken aback. "But why? I never did anything special."

A young girl stepped forward. "You always did the little things, Uncle Ravi. When my mother was sick, you brought us food. When my father lost his job, you found small errands for him to do. When I was scared of the dark, you gave me a lamp. Those little things... they stayed in our hearts."

Tears welled up in Ravi's eyes as the villagers worked together to repair his home. The love and warmth they showed him were a reflection of the kindness he had spread over the years.

The village rebuilt itself slowly, but stronger and more united than ever before. And Ravi's story became a gentle reminder that small acts of kindness often occupy the biggest part of people's hearts.

Never stop doing the little things for others. Sometimes, those little things make the biggest difference.

Sehra bandi

Sehra Bandi took place at 4 o'clock in the evening and Ankush sat on the mare from the in gate of the hotel to the out gate and there were not many people, there must have been around 50 Beratis, invitees Rita, her husband, I and our friends danced a lot and had some snacks, then had food and sat down for Lava Pheras (wedding ceremony).

Ankush introduced me to a British woman, Marila, and said, *"Uncle, please brief her about the function. She is keen to understand the details."*

Curious, Marila asked, *"Why is the groom riding a mare?"*

I smiled and explained, *"The tradition dates back to ancient times when marriages were often linked to battles. Wars were fought to win the bride or to display one's bravery. Our scriptures are filled with such instances."*

"For example, in the Ramayana, when Sita Mata's swayamvar was taking place, many powerful kings attempted to lift the divine bow, but none succeeded. Only Shri Ram was able to break it. As Sita moved forward to garland him, the defeated kings, enraged, drew their swords. Shri Ram also prepared to fight. However, when Parshuram Ji arrived, everyone realized that challenging Shri Ram meant inviting death."

"Similarly, in another episode from history, when Lord Krishna first married Devi Rukmini, he had to fight a battle. These incidents reflect how grooms were often warriors who had to prove their strength and valor before marrying."

"During those times, horses were crucial in wars, symbolizing power and bravery. That is why grooms traditionally rode a horse to their wedding. However, as times changed, swayamvars, battles, and wars became things of the past. The modern world adopted this tradition differently–now, the mare is seen as a symbol of good fortune."

"There is also another belief," I continued. *"The mare is considered an intelligent, skilled, and clever animal. Only a healthy and capable person can ride it. Holding its reins symbolizes that the groom is responsible and capable of taking care of his family."*

Marila listened intently, nodding in fascination. It was a reminder of how traditions evolve while still carrying the essence of their origins.

Her second question, Why the people, relative putting garland to each other and bride and bridegroom

The ceremony begins once the groom arrives at the wedding venue with the baraat (wedding procession). As part of the traditional welcome, the bride's mother greets and blesses the groom before the main event takes place.

One of the most cherished moments of the wedding is the exchange of garlands (varmala) between the bride and groom. This ritual symbolizes their acceptance of each other. To add an element of fun, the groom's friends often playfully lift him up or move him away, making it challenging for the bride to place the garland around his neck. Laughter and joy fill the air as guests cheer and celebrate this light-hearted tradition.

Surrounded by relatives, close family, and friends, the couple shares this beautiful moment, marking the beginning of their new journey together.

Regarding relative putting garland to each other it is just to introduce the relations of both sides. Generally, these garlands are exchanged with immediate relatives like brother, uncle, brother-in-law etc.

What is this going on near the fire, what is this lava phera, she said

I replied, well the seven pheras (Saptapadi) are the core of a Vedic Hindu wedding, symbolizing the sacred promises that bind the couple in a lifelong commitment. Each step taken around the sacred fire represents a unique vow, calling upon divine blessings and reinforcing the responsibilities of marriage.

The Seven Vows (Pheras) and Their Significance:

First Phera – Praying for nourishment, food, and a prosperous life together.

Second Phase – Seeking strength and courage to support each other in all aspects of life.

Third Phera – Asking for prosperity, wealth, and a righteous life.

Fourth Phase – Commitment to love, respect, and mutual understanding.

Fifth Phera – Praying for the well-being and happiness of their future children.

Sixth Phera – Seeking a harmonious and long life together.

Seventh Phera – Pledging eternal friendship, loyalty, and companionship.

After completing these seven rounds, the couple is officially considered husband and wife, with their bond blessed by the divine.

The beauty of this ritual is that it emphasizes not just love but also duty, respect, and lifelong partnership—a holistic view of marriage.

The First Phera is Based on Nourishment

- Groom's vow: "You will offer me food and be helpful in every way. I will cherish you and provide for the welfare and happiness of you and our children."
- Bride's vow: "I am responsible for the home and take charge of all household responsibilities."

The Second Phera is Based on Strength

- Groom's vow: "Together, we will protect our house and children."
- Bride's vow: "I will be by your side and be your courage and strength. I will rejoice in your happiness. In return, you will love me alone."

The Third Phera is Based on Prosperity

- Groom's vow: "May we grow wealthy and prosperous and strive for the education of our children. May our children live long."
- Bride's vow: "I will love you the rest of my life, as you are my husband. Every other man in my life will come second to you. I vow to remain chaste."

The Fourth Phera is Based on Family

- Groom's vow: "You have brought sacredness into my life and have completed me. May we be blessed with noble, obedient children. May our children live long."

- Bride's vow: "I will shower you with happiness from head to toe. I will strive to please you in every way I can."

The Fifth Phera is About Togetherness

- Groom's vow: "You are my best friend and staunchest well-wisher. You have come into my life and have enriched it. God bless you."
- Bride's vow: "I promise to love and cherish you for as long as I love."

The Sixth Phera is About Fortune and Fidelity

- Groom's vow: "May you be filled with joy and peace."
- Bride's vow: "I will always be by your side."

The Seventh Phera is About Wisdom

- Groom's vow: "We are now husband and wife and are one. You are mine, and I am yours for all time."
- Bride's vow: "As God is witness, I am now your wife. We will love, honour, and cherish each other forever."
- Reeta told Suresh now your daughter is ours and you need not to worry about her.
- Both flew to London for honeymoon next day and I came back to Delhi
- In the plane I was thinking how the time is flying, it looks and feels just few years back I attended Neeraj wedding and now attended his son wedding.
- Now more than two years have passed, there was no communications from Ankush and Reeta. The life has become too busy and hectic, no person has time and, in these days, togetherness is visible only in wedding or death. This is true what I am saying.

- Thanks to our tradition customs, we at least family member meets on occasion like
- Dewali, Holi, bhiya dooaj etc.

They say that if you truly remember someone, they appear before you.

Just then, Reeta called. "Everything is fine," she said. "Ankita has also become friendly now. Both are happy, and I am very thankful to you on behalf of all of us."

Only one issue with her is that she eats very little – mostly soup, juice, salad, nuts, and occasionally one bread, chapati, vegetables, dal, or pulses. Sometimes I worry that one day her stomach might touch her back! A person should neither be too thin nor too fat. But I've realized it's best not to intervene in their personal choices – with time, she will understand what's best for her.

Have you ever heard of newlywed couples wanting space even at the beginning of their new life together? Recently, my friend's son got married, but the boy and the girl are living separately. She says she needs space and only meets him occasionally."

It really is a reflection of how much relationships – and people's expectations from marriage – have changed over time. This new generation often values personal space and independence just as much as togetherness. For some, even after marriage, keeping separate spaces helps them maintain their individuality and avoid feeling overwhelmed.

But yes, it can be surprising for those of us who grew up seeing marriage as a partnership where people share not just their lives but their daily routines. Maybe the girl feels that having her own space helps her balance her own needs and identity – or maybe they both believe that meeting occasionally keeps their relationship fresh and less strained.

Still, it's important that both partners are on the same page about this arrangement. A marriage works best when both people's emotional needs are respected. If the boy is okay with it, maybe they've found a balance that works for them – but if he's feeling neglected or confused, they'll need to communicate openly about what they both want.

What do you think? Do you feel this approach is sustainable in the long run? She asked me.

"What can I say – this is the reality of 21st-century life. I've come across similar stories, but I truly believe such arrangements aren't sustainable in the long run. It's painful for parents to see their children drift this way, but there's little they can do when kids are unwilling to listen. Thankfully, these cases are still few – most couples find ways to adjust and build beautiful, fulfilling lives together."

As soon as Reeta hung up, Suresh called. He, too, expressed his heartfelt gratitude.

I replied, *"All this is in the hands of the Almighty. We are merely His vessels."*

"No," Suresh insisted, *"I am grateful to you from the depths of my heart."*

He then asked, *"I hope you enjoyed the wedding. If I have made any mistake, please forgive me."*

"Oh, Suresh, why do you embarrass me?" I laughed.

But as I reflected, I thought–*Look at this life. Anything can happen, yet we remain so entangled in it. Whether life is going well or badly, a person is stuck in this world just like a bee in honey–unable to free himself from its grip.*

Reeta, can I speak to your husband as he is turning 75 years old tomorrow? Let me wish him a happy birthday and know how you are celebrating.

He is doing puja, worshipping, and will speak to you once he finishes his puja," *she said.*

I told her, "But he was a non-believer before. How did he move toward devotion?"

Reeta replied, "He has totally changed. Whenever I see him, he is sitting in meditation, chanting mantras, and reading religious books. He is very quiet now, hardly speaking or discussing things. I can sense and feel the wonderful vibes he is radiating. He is in a state of ecstasy, always happy and smiling. Touch wood, I am also following him, and here we are–two souls doing well."

I replied, "Well, it's wonderful to know about the change in your life. This is essential in today's hustle and bustle. Generally, people say they don't have time. They are willing to pay doctors' fees and spend on medicines but will not give time to themselves to connect with the creator who is within us. Everyone must spare some time for meditation and self-reflection instead of consuming energy on overthinking. The connection within is a treasure mine of peace, joy, and ecstasy. If you are good from the inside, you are a hundred times better in the outer world."

She said, "I think someone is knocking at the door. Let me see, and I will speak to you later."

Many months passed, and I had not received any call from them. I tried two or three times, but there was no response. Finally, I called Suresh to check if all was well with them. He told me they were on a pilgrimage journey for three months. "Don't worry–they are enjoying themselves, and all their losses have been recovered. Their company in London is doing well."

He thanked him again for introducing the family. My daughter is very happy with her husband and their family. A sigh of relief after talking to him.

This is the end of the story

But I would like to continue to write on spirituality, messages, idioms, saying which give great impact on our life. This I am keep writing in between the story just to draw attention that there is other world also of ruhaniyat , spirituality

दुःख में सुमिरन सब करे सुख में करै न कोय।
जो सुख में सुमिरन करे दुःख काहे को होय ॥

"Everyone remembers God in sorrow, but no one does so in happiness. If one remembers God in happiness, then why would there be sorrow?"

Kabir Das Ji emphasizes that most people turn to God only in times of trouble, seeking comfort and solutions. However, when life is smooth and joyful, they often forget to express gratitude or stay connected with the divine.

He suggests that if a person remembers and remains devoted to God even in times of happiness, they will cultivate inner strength, peace, and wisdom—preventing sorrow from affecting them deeply. A heart that stays spiritually connected through all phases of life remains balanced and unshaken by hardships.

This doha, couplet, serves as a reminder to practice gratitude, devotion, and mindfulness at all times, not just in difficult moments. “Everyone remembers God in sorrow, but no one does so in happiness. If one remembers God in happiness, then why would there be sorrow?"

Kabir Das Ji emphasizes that most people turn to God only in times of trouble, seeking comfort and solutions. However, when life is smooth and joyful, they often forget to express gratitude or stay connected with the divine.

He suggests that if a person remembers and remains devoted to God even in times of happiness, they will cultivate inner strength, peace, and wisdom—preventing sorrow from affecting them deeply. A heart that stays spiritually connected through all phases of life remains balanced and unshaken by hardships.

This doha, couplet, serves as a reminder to practice gratitude, devotion, and mindfulness at all times, not just in difficult moments.

maatee kahe kumhaar se, too kya ronde mohe, ek din aisa aaega, main rondoogee tohe

माटी कहे कुम्हार से, तू क्या रोंदे मोहे,
एक दिन ऐसा आएगा, मैं रोंदूगी तोहे ।

The clay speaks to the potter, questioning why he kneads, beats, and molds it harshly. It then reminds the potter that one day, when the potter himself turns to dust (after death), the clay will cry over him.

This highlights two key lessons:

- Impermanence of Life – Just as the clay is shaped today, one day the potter (like all human beings) will return to the earth. Nothing is permanent.
- Karma & Humility – Those who mistreat others should remember that fate eventually comes full circle. The strong today may become weak tomorrow.

आये हैं तो जायेंगे, राजा रंक फ़कीर,
एक सिंघासन चडी चले, एक बंदे जंजीर ।

No matter who we are–a king, a pauper, or a beggar–our ultimate fate remains the same: we all must leave this world one day.

- A king may depart while sitting on a grand throne, surrounded by luxury.
- A pauper or a beggar may leave in chains, in hardship and suffering.

Yet, death does not discriminate–it comes for all, regardless of status or wealth. The only thing that truly matters is how we live our lives, the deeds we perform, and the legacy we leave behind.

This thought echoes the wisdom of saints and philosophers who remind us to live humbly, do good deeds, and not be attached to material possessions

No matter who we are—a king, a pauper, or a beggar—our ultimate fate remains the same: we all must leave this world one day.

- A king may depart while sitting on a grand throne, surrounded by luxury.
- A pauper or a beggar may leave in chains, in hardship and suffering.

Yet, death does not discriminate—it comes for all, regardless of status or wealth. The only thing that truly matters is how we live our lives, the deeds we perform, and the legacy we leave behind.

This thought echoes the wisdom of saints and philosophers who remind us to live humbly, do good deeds, and not be attached to material possessions

दुर्बल को ना सतायिये, जाकी मोटी हाय,
बिना जीब के स्वास से लोह भसम हो जाए ।

- One should never oppress or harass the weak, thinking they are powerless.
- The curse of the helpless and oppressed carries immense weight—it may not be spoken aloud, but it reaches the divine.
- Even without a tongue (without verbalizing it), their silent plea can be so strong that it turns iron into ashes—symbolizing destruction and karmic retribution.

This reminds us that true strength lies in kindness, and that harming the weak may bring unforeseen consequences upon the oppressor. It aligns with the philosophy of karma—what goes around, comes around.

चलती चक्की देख के दिया कबीर रोये,
दो पाटन के बीच में बाकी बचा ना कोई ।

- The "running mill" (chakki) symbolizes the world, constantly in motion, grinding everything in its path.
- The "two millstones" represent the dual forces of life–joy and sorrow, birth and death, fate and free will, attachment and detachment.
- Kabir laments that no one is spared from this relentless cycle; everyone eventually gets caught between the grinding forces of time and destiny.

Deeper Message:

This couplet teaches us about detachment, self-awareness, and spiritual wisdom. To escape being "crushed" by life's dualities, one must rise above worldly attachments and seek inner enlightenment.

It aligns with the idea of transcending the material world and finding peace beyond the cycle of suffering.

पत्ता टूटा डाल से ले गयी पवन उडाय,
अबके बिछड़े कब मिलेंगे दूर पड़ेंगे जाय ।

- "The wind took away the leaf from the branch" → The leaf represents a human being, and the branch represents life, relationships, or home. → Just as a leaf detaches from a tree when the time comes, humans also part ways–whether due to fate, distance, or even death. → The wind symbolizes time, circumstances, or destiny, which carries people away in different directions.

- "When will we meet again?" → Once separated, there is no certainty of reunion. Just like a leaf that drifts away, humans too may never meet again after parting.
- "When we are separated, we will fall far away." → Once we drift apart, the chances of coming together become even slimmer. → This reflects how life takes people on different journeys, scattering them like fallen leaves.

Deeper Message:

This verse teaches us:

- Cherish relationships while they last – Since separation is inevitable, value the moments you share with loved ones.
- Life is unpredictable – Just as the wind can blow a leaf in any direction, life can take unexpected turns.
- Detachment & acceptance – Recognizing that everything is temporary helps us embrace life with peace and wisdom.

आए हैं तो जाएँगे, राजा, रंक, फकीर
एक सिंहासन चढ़ी चले, एक बँधे जंजीर

- "If we have come, we will go" → Life is temporary. No one is immortal; death is the ultimate reality.
- "Be it a king, a pauper, or a fakir" → Wealth, status, or spirituality do not change this truth. → A king may have all the riches and power, but he must leave one day. → A pauper may struggle his whole life, but he too will depart.

→ A fakir (saint), who renounces worldly desires, also cannot escape death.

- "One goes on a throne, the other tied in chains" → Some people leave this world with dignity and honour, while others leave in suffering or disgrace. → A king departs in comfort and grandeur, while a prisoner or a troubled soul departs in hardship. → This line reminds us that how we live our lives determines how we will be remembered.

Philosophical Message:

- The Illusion of Power & Wealth - No matter how rich or powerful we are, death spares no one.
- Live with Humility & Purpose - Instead of chasing material things, focus on kindness, wisdom, and good deeds.
- Make Your Life Meaningful - Since we all must go, our actions define our legacy.

Modern Relevance:

- Today, people often get caught up in status, fame, and material success—forgetting that none of it will last forever.
- This verse encourages us to live a life of value, peace, and contribution rather than just accumulating wealth or power.

jab Dukh Ki Ghadiya Aaye
Sach Par Jhuth Vijay Paae
Is Nirmal Paavan Man Par
Jab Kalank Ke Ghan Chhaaye
Anyaay Ki Aandhi Se
Kaan Uthe Jab Tere Dol
Tab Manav To Mukh Se Bol
Buddham Saranam Gacchami
Tab Manav To Mukh Se Bol
Buddham Saranam Gacchami
Dhammam Saranam Gachchhaami
Sagham Saranam Gachchhaami
Jab Duniya Se Pyaar Uthe
Nafarat Ki Divaar Uthe
Maa Ki Mamta Par Jis Din
Bete Ki Talawaar Uthe

This passage conveys a deeply philosophical and emotional reflection on the state of the world, the triumph of falsehood over truth, and the search for refuge in Buddhism when injustice prevails.

Interpretation & Meaning:

- "Now the clouds of sorrow have come" → The world is experiencing pain, suffering, and turmoil.
- "Falsehood has won over truth" → Deception, lies, and corruption seem to have overpowered honesty and righteousness.
- "On this pure and pure man, when the clouds of disgrace have covered" → Even the good and innocent suffer in times of moral decay.

Turning to Buddhism in Times of Suffering:

- "From the storm of injustice, when your ears have risen" → When oppression and injustice become unbearable, people seek spiritual refuge.
- "Then man speaks from his mouth: Buddham Saranam Gachchhami" → In despair, people turn to Buddhism for peace and guidance.
- "Dhammam Saranam Gachchhaami, Sangham Saranam Gachchhaami" → These are the Three Jewels (Triratna) of Buddhism:
  - Buddha – The Enlightened One (seeking wisdom and truth).
  - Dhamma – The Teachings (living a righteous life).
  - Sangha – The Community (finding support in like-minded people).

Loss of Love and Rise of Hatred:

- "When love rose from the world, the wall of hatred rose" → The absence of love leads to division, enmity, and chaos.
- "The day the son's sword rose on the mother's love" → When a child turns against a mother, it signifies the ultimate breakdown of values, love, and humanity.

Deeper Message:

- This passage reflects Buddhism's core teaching that suffering (Dukkha) exists in the world due to human greed, ignorance, and hatred.

- When injustice and hatred take over, people seek peace in spiritual wisdom.
- The world needs compassion, truth, and righteousness to overcome the storm of falsehood and suffering.

Modern Relevance:

- Conflicts, dishonesty, and suffering are increasing in today's world, just as the passage describes.
- Turning to spirituality (like Buddha's teachings) can help find inner peace and guide humanity toward wisdom, kindness, and unity.

God of India
Buddha's song
Every home is precious
This man speaks with his mouth
Buddham Saranam Gachami
This man speaks with his mouth
Buddham Saranam Gachami
He got angry when he heard
Whom should I ask
I could recognize the love
This innocent world
When I take shelter
When I get the blessings
When this little man
He was happy with his God

This passage beautifully captures a spiritual awakening, the search for refuge in Buddha's teachings, and the deep yearning for peace and love in a troubled world.

Interpretation & Meaning:

Faith and Refuge in Buddha:

- "God of India, Buddha's song" → Buddha, one of India's greatest spiritual figures, represents wisdom, compassion, and enlightenment. → His teachings are like a song of peace, guiding humanity toward inner harmony.
- "Every home is precious, this man speaks with his mouth: Buddham Saranam Gachchhami" → Every home, every individual is valuable, but people still struggle and suffer. → Seeking refuge in Buddha is a way to escape suffering and find meaning in life.
- Repeating 'Buddham Saranam Gachchhami' (I take refuge in the Buddha) → Shows deep faith and a realization that spiritual wisdom is the only way forward.

Struggle and Realization:

- "He got angry when he heard, whom should I ask?" → Confusion and frustration arise when one sees injustice and suffering. → People wonder, "Where can I find answers? Who can guide me?"
- "I could recognize the love, this innocent world" → Love and kindness exist, but they are often hidden beneath pain, anger, and worldly distractions.

Finding Peace & Happiness:

- "When I take shelter, when I get the blessings" → Taking shelter in Buddha, Dhamma (teachings), and Sangha (community) brings blessings and inner peace.
- "When this little man was happy with his God" → A simple, humble person finds true happiness not in material wealth, but in divine wisdom and spiritual connection.

Deeper Message:

- Human suffering leads to spiritual search – When people feel lost, they seek guidance in faith and wisdom.
- Love is the ultimate truth – The world is innocent, but greed, anger, and ego blind us from recognizing love.
- Real happiness comes from within – Taking refuge in spirituality, not worldly desires, leads to lasting peace.

Modern Relevance:

- In today's world of stress, conflict, and uncertainty, Buddha's message of peace, mindfulness, and compassion is more relevant than ever.
- People are still searching for love, wisdom, and meaning, just as the passage describes.

Satya Teraa Jab Ghabraye Shradha Ho Jab Daanvadol Tab Manav Tu Mukh Se Bol Buddham Saranam Gacchami

Tab Manav Tu Mukh Se Bol Buddham Saranam Gacchami

This verse beautifully captures the essence of seeking spiritual refuge in times of uncertainty and doubt.

Interpretation & Meaning:

1. Fear and Doubt in Truth & Faith

- "When your truth is afraid" → When standing by the truth becomes difficult, when honesty is challenged, and falsehood seems to dominate.
- "When your faith is shaky" → When belief in goodness, justice, and spirituality begins to waver due to life's struggles.

2. Seeking Refuge in Buddha

- "Then, human, you should say with your mouth: Buddham Saranam Gachhami" → In these moments of fear and doubt, seek guidance in Buddha's wisdom and teachings. → This phrase means: "I take refuge in the Buddha." It symbolizes a commitment to wisdom, self-realization, and inner peace.

Deeper Message:

- Truth and faith will be tested, but spiritual wisdom offers strength.
- Buddha's teachings guide us through suffering, confusion, and moral dilemmas.
- Reciting 'Buddham Saranam Gachhami' is a call to self-awakening, reminding us to seek clarity, peace, and righteousness.

Modern Relevance:

- Injustice, deception, and hardships often make people question their beliefs.
- The solution is spiritual resilience—not giving in to fear but turning to wisdom and inner strength.
- Buddhism teaches mindfulness, detachment, and self-control—key to overcoming life's struggles.

Bulleh Shah,

Makkay gayaan, gal mukdee naheen
Pawain sow sow jummay parrh aaeey

Ganga gayaan, gal mukdee naheen
Pawain sow sow gotay khaeeay

Gaya gayaan gal mukdee naheen
Pawain sow sow pand parrhaeeay

Bulleh Shah gal taeeyon mukdee
Jadon May nu dillon gawaeeay

This beautiful poem by Bulleh Shah, a Sufi poet and mystic, speaks of true spirituality beyond rituals and emphasizes ego dissolution as the ultimate path to enlightenment.

Interpretation & Meaning:

1. Religious Rituals Alone Do Not Lead to Liberation

- "Going to Makkah is not the ultimate, even if hundreds of prayers are offered"
- "Going to the River Ganges is not the ultimate, even if hundreds of cleansing baptisms are done"

- "Going to Gaya is not the ultimate, even if hundreds of worships are done"

◆ Bulleh Shah critiques blind faith in rituals and pilgrimages, suggesting that physical acts alone cannot bring true spiritual realization if the heart remains unchanged. ◆ He challenges the idea that salvation lies in external religious practices, whether Islamic, Hindu, or any other faith. ◆ True spiritual growth happens within, not by mere rituals.

2. The True Path to Liberation—Destroying the Ego ("I")

- "Bulleh Shah, the ultimate is when the 'I' is removed from the heart!"

◆ The ego (self-importance, arrogance, attachment to identity) is the biggest barrier to spiritual freedom and divine connection. ◆ True self-realization happens when we let go of ego, pride, and attachment to material or religious identity. ◆ Bulleh Shah suggests that God is not found in places, rituals, or scriptures, but within a humble, ego-free heart.

Modern Relevance

- Ritual vs. Spirituality → Many people focus on external acts of worship but lack true kindness, humility, and self-awareness.
- Ego Blocks Growth → Personal conflicts, wars, and suffering often stem from ego-driven desires.
- True Connection with God is Internal → Love, humility, and surrender—not rigid rituals—bring us closer to the Divine.

This poem is a powerful call for self-awareness, inner transformation, and love beyond boundaries.

Sant Paltu das poem

UlaTaa kuaan gagan mein, tisame jarai chiraag Tisame jarai chiraag, binaa rogan bin baatee chhah ritu baarah maas, rahat jaratain din raatee Sataguru milaa jo hoy, taahi kee najar mein aawai bin satguru kou hoy, nahee waako darashaawai Nikasai ek awaaj, chiraag kee jotinhi maanhee Jnaan samaadhee sunai, aur kou sunataa naanhee Paltoo jo kol sunai, tAke pUre bhAg UlaTA kuAn gagan mein, tisame jarai chirAg

This mystical verse speaks in deep metaphors, using paradoxes to convey spiritual truths. It resonates with Sant and Sufi traditions, where the 'inverted world' represents higher spiritual understanding beyond logic.

Interpretation & Meaning

1. The Well in the Sky & the Lamp Without Oil

- "Ulata kuAn sky mein, tisame jarai chiraag" → "The well is in the sky, and in it, the lamp is burning."
- "Tisame jarai chiraag, binaa rogan bin banatee." → "The lamp burns without oil and wick."

◆ These lines describe a mystical truth that defies logic—a spiritual light that does not need fuel and a well that exists above, not below.
◆ This points to divine wisdom—it is not found in material logic but in higher consciousness beyond the physical world.

2. The Power of the Satguru (True Master)

- "The moment you meet Satguru, you will never see him again. Without Satguru, you are the one who sees me."

◆ This suggests that the True Guru (Satguru) removes duality–the idea of 'I' and 'You' disappears. ◆ Once enlightened, there is no difference between the seeker and the divine. ◆ Without the Satguru, one remains trapped in illusion (Maya), thinking they are separate from the divine.

3. The Sound Without a Source & The Light Without a Lamp

- "One voice was released, no light was left on the lamp. I heard you every day, and you heard me without you."

◆ This refers to the divine sound (Shabad, Naad, Aum) that exists eternally and is heard only in deep meditation. ◆ The idea of hearing without hearing and light without a lamp suggests spiritual awakening beyond physical senses.

Deeper Meaning & Connection to Mysticism

- Paradox as a Teaching Tool → Many spiritual masters use paradoxes to shake people out of their usual way of thinking.
- Inner Awakening vs. External Rituals → The divine is not in outer actions but in inner realization.
- Merging of Self & Divine → Once enlightened, duality disappears, and the seeker becomes one with God.

Benefits of Yagya (Vedic Fire Ritual)

Yagya (also spelled Yajna) is an ancient Vedic ritual that involves offerings to the sacred fire while chanting mantras. It is considered a powerful spiritual, mental, and physical purifier with scientific and metaphysical significance.

1. Spiritual Benefits

◆ Divine Blessings: Yagya is considered "Yajóoaya Sarvakamdhuk", meaning "it fulfills all desires" by pleasing divine forces. ◆ Purification of Karma: Helps in removing past sins (Prarabdha Karma) and accumulating good karma. ◆ Increases Positive Energy: The vibrations of Vedic mantras elevate consciousness and create a spiritually charged environment. ◆ Connection with the Cosmos: Aligns individual energies with universal cosmic forces, enhancing spiritual growth.

2. Mental & Psychological Benefits

◆ Calms the Mind: The rhythmic chanting of mantras and focus on fire helps in reducing stress and anxiety.

◆ Enhances Concentration: The disciplined process of Yagya improves focus and mindfulness. ◆ Emotional Cleansing: Creates a positive mental state, removing negative emotions like anger, fear, and depression.

3. Physical & Environmental Benefits

◆ Air Purification: The medicinal herbs and ingredients (like ghee, sandalwood, and camphor) release purifying substances into the air, which can kill harmful bacteria and viruses. ◆ Healing Properties: Scientific research suggests that Ayurvedic herbs burned in Yagya produce medicinal fumes that can help in curing respiratory and skin diseases. ◆ Eco-Friendly Impact: Yagya neutralizes air pollution and increases the oxygen level in the surroundings.

4. Social & Cultural Benefits

◆ Fosters Unity & Harmony: Yagyas are often conducted in groups, promoting social bonding and collective well-being. ◆ Teaches Selflessness (Yagna Spirit): The philosophy of "sacrifice for the greater good" inspires people to work for society's welfare rather than self-centred goals. ◆ Preservation of Ancient Wisdom: By performing Yagyas, we keep the rich traditions of Vedic knowledge alive.

Scientific & Vedic Perspective on Yagya

The Rig Veda states: 🔥 "Agni Mode Purohitam" – Fire is the priest, the purifier, and the divine messenger.

◆ The first revelation of the Vedas was about fire and energy, highlighting its importance for material and spiritual growth. ◆ Fire is the fundamental source of all transformation in the universe—whether it is the fire of digestion, the fire of the sun, or the fire of knowledge.

In many religions, fire is worshipped because of its divine, transformative, and purifying qualities.

The Gayatri Mantra: Meaning, Benefits, and Practice

The Mantra:

Om Bhur Bhuvah Swaha Tat Savitur Varenyam
Bhargo Devasya Dhimahi Dhiyo Yo Nah Prachodayat

Meaning:

O Divine Mother, may your radiant light illuminate all realms of our being. Remove darkness from our hearts and grant us true knowledge.

Significance & History:

The Gayatri Mantra, mentioned in the Rig Veda, is considered the essence of all mantras. It is personified by Goddess Gayatri, who embodies wisdom, protection, and strength. The mantra was revealed to Sage Vishwamitra after his deep spiritual practices.

Benefits of Chanting:

- Enhances concentration and mental clarity
- Promotes inner peace and spiritual growth
- Dispels negativity, fear, and bad karma
- Raises vibrational energy, benefiting both the individual and the world

How to Chant:

- Best recited at sunrise and before sleep
- Begin with deep breathing and focus on each word
- Repeat silently for the most profound impact
- Visualize the sun's light entering your heart and radiating outward

Regular chanting of the Gayatri Mantra brings peace, prosperity, and divine connection, leading to a more enlightened life.

Story

A Farmer's Fortune – All's Well That Ends Well

In a quiet village nestled between rolling hills, lived a humble farmer named Ramesh. He worked tirelessly on his small piece of land, providing for his wife and two children. Life was simple but tough.

One year, an unexpected drought struck, leaving his crops withered and his hopes shattered. With no other option, Ramesh borrowed money from the village landlord, promising to repay it after the next harvest. Unfortunately, fate had other plans. A violent storm arrived just before harvest season, destroying whatever little he had left. The landlord, known for his greed, demanded repayment and threatened to seize Ramesh's land.

Broken and desperate, Ramesh turned to the village temple and prayed, "Oh Lord, I have nothing left. If I lose my land, I lose everything."

The next day, determined not to give up, he went to his barren field and began ploughing once again. Suddenly, his Plow struck something hard. Digging further, he uncovered a large earthen pot filled with gold coins and ancient jewelry. His heart pounded—was this a blessing or a test?

News of the treasure spread like wildfire. The landlord, sensing an opportunity, rushed to claim it. "This land is mortgaged to me. The treasure is mine!" he declared.

The village elder, a wise old man, intervened. "The land belonged to Ramesh's ancestors for generations. The treasure was hidden long before the debt. Justice must prevail!" After much debate, the village council ruled in Ramesh's favour.

With the treasure, Ramesh repaid his debt, invested in better farming tools, and helped other struggling farmers in the village. Over time, his farm flourished, and he became a respected and generous man. The landlord, on the other hand, lost his influence as people saw his true nature.

Standing in his lush green fields a year later, Ramesh smiled, realizing how life had tested him only to reward him in the end. Indeed, all's well that ends well.

Story giving good massage, moral,
The Old Monk and the Young Pupil

A young monk, proud and full of arrogance, arrived at a monastery seeking wisdom. Hoping to deepen his knowledge, he approached an old, wise monk, who agreed to teach him.

One day, as they walked through the forest, the young monk spotted a rabbit. With his quick reflexes, he caught it easily. Holding it up triumphantly, he said, "This rabbit will make a great meal."

The old monk looked at him calmly and said, "Release the rabbit." But the young monk refused, his pride getting the better of him.

The old monk then asked, "If you won't release it, at least take me to its home." Curious, the young monk agreed and led the old monk to the rabbit's burrow.

Once there, the old monk gently said, "Now, set it free." After a moment of hesitation, the young monk obeyed and released the rabbit, watching it disappear into its home.

As they walked back, the old monk asked softly, "How do you feel now?"

The young monk lowered his eyes and said, "I feel sorry for what I did."

The old monk smiled and said, "That is the beginning of wisdom— when compassion takes the place of pride and kindness replaces arrogance."

In that moment, the young monk realized his mistake. He apologized sincerely and from that day forward, began treating all living beings with greater respect and humility.

Lessons:

- Realizing your mistakes is the first step to true growth.
- Compassion and kindness lead to peace and harmony.
- Humility and empathy enrich both our character and our relationships.

Moral:

- Treat all living beings with respect and care.
- Learn from your mistakes and grow wiser.
- Cultivate compassion and empathy in your daily life.

Another story on greed giving good moral and lesson

The Goose That Laid the Golden Eggs

Once upon a time, a farmer owned a miraculous goose that laid a golden egg every day. At first, the farmer was overjoyed with his good fortune and eagerly collected the golden egg each morning.

But soon, greed took hold of him. He thought, "Why wait for one egg a day when I could have them all at once? If I cut the goose open, I'll be rich beyond my dreams!"

Driven by his impatience, the farmer killed the goose – only to find nothing inside. No stash of golden eggs, no treasure – just an ordinary goose now gone forever.

In his greed, the farmer lost both the goose and the golden eggs, ending his fortune with his own short-sightedness.

Lesson:

- Greed often leads to loss.

- Patience and contentment bring long-term rewards.
- Rash and selfish decisions can destroy what's most valuable.

Moral:

- Be content with what you have.
- Value steady, consistent gains over immediate gratification.
- Greed and impatience can lead to irreversible regret.

The Idle Mind and the Mischievous Devil

Once upon a time, in a peaceful village, there lived a man named Rohan. He was kind-hearted and well-off but had one big flaw – he was lazy. He spent his days lying around, daydreaming, and doing nothing productive.

One day, an old wise man visited the village and noticed Rohan's idle behaviour. He warned him, "An empty mind is the devil's home. Keep yourself busy with good work, or trouble will surely find you." Rohan just laughed and ignored the advice.

Days turned into weeks, and slowly, strange things started happening. Negative thoughts filled Rohan's mind. He became suspicious of his friends and jealous of their success. He started gossiping and creating conflicts. His peaceful life turned chaotic, and his relationships soured.

One day, when Rohan was sitting alone, the same wise man returned. He asked, "Do you see now what happens when your mind is left empty and idle?"

Rohan realized his mistake. He decided to change his life. He started helping villagers, learning new skills, and working hard every day. As his mind filled with purpose and positivity, his life transformed. Peace and happiness returned, and the devil of negativity found no place in his heart anymore.

Lesson:

- An idle mind becomes a breeding ground for negativity.
- Purpose and productivity bring peace and happiness.
- Staying engaged in good work keeps harmful thoughts away.

Moral:

- Keep your mind active with meaningful work.
- Positivity thrives in a busy, focused mind.
- Idleness invites unnecessary trouble.

Story

The Date Palm Tree and the Little Sparrow

In a vast desert, there stood a tall and proud date palm tree. It stretched high into the sky, its long, slender trunk rising above the sands. Its fruit was sweet and precious, but the tree's branches gave no shade, and its fruit grew so high that no bird or small animal could reach it.

One day, a little sparrow flew through the scorching desert, tired and thirsty. She spotted the tall date palm and thought, "Surely this grand tree will offer me some rest and relief." But when she landed on its branch, there was no cool shade, only the harsh heat of the sun.

"Dear tree," the sparrow chirped, "may I sit in your shade for a while?"

"I offer no shade," the palm tree replied proudly. "I grow high and bear sweet fruits, but they are for those who can reach them from faraway lands. My worth lies in my height and my rare fruit – not in providing comfort."

Disappointed, the sparrow flew away, struggling against the hot wind. Nearby, she found a small, humble neem tree. Its branches were low, and its shade was cool and wide. The neem tree welcomed the sparrow warmly, offering her rest and shelter.

"Thank you, kind tree," the sparrow whispered gratefully. "You may not have sweet fruits, but your shade is life-saving."

The date palm watched from afar. Though tall and proud, it began to wonder – what was the point of its sweetness if it couldn't help those nearby? It stood there, bearing fruit that no one close by could reach and giving no comfort to those who needed it.

Lesson:

- True greatness lies not in how high we rise but in how much we help those around us.
- A generous heart and kindness are often more valuable than rare treasures.
- Providing comfort and support to those near us is a gift in itself.

Moral:

- Be like the tree that gives shade, not just the one admired from afar.
- Success is sweeter when it benefits others.
- Compassion and kindness leave a more lasting impact than distant riches.

Another nice story

The Monk and the Sculptor

In a peaceful village nestled between mountains, there lived a humble sculptor named Arun. He was known for his skillful hands and beautiful statues, but his work lacked something – a soul. No matter how hard he tried, his sculptures never felt truly alive.

One day, Arun heard of a wise monk meditating in a nearby monastery. It was said the monk had found the secret of true devotion and discipline. Hoping to learn from him, Arun travelled to the monastery and asked the monk, "Master, my hands create, but my heart feels empty. How can I bring life into my work?"

The monk smiled and said, "Stay with me for a while. Follow my ways, and you will find your answer."

Days turned into weeks. Arun woke before sunrise, swept the monastery floors, fetched water, and meditated with the other disciples. At first, he grew restless. "When will I learn the secret?" he wondered. But the monk only instructed him to focus on his tasks with patience and dedication.

One morning, as Arun quietly swept the courtyard, he noticed the gentle rustling of leaves, the soft warmth of the sun, and the rhythm of his own breath. He felt calm and connected to everything around him.

That evening, the monk said, "Now, sculpt something." Arun picked up his chisel and began carving a statue of the Buddha. But this time, something was different. His hands moved with grace, his heart poured love into every detail, and his mind stayed focused and still.

When the statue was finished, the other monks gathered around, awed by its beauty. It radiated peace and life. Arun realized the secret at last

– true art, like true life, comes from devotion and discipline. Through patience, focus, and love for his work, his creations gained a soul.

The monk placed a hand on his shoulder and said, "When your heart is steady and your mind is pure, everything you create becomes a reflection of your inner peace."

Lesson:

- Devotion and discipline bring true mastery.
- Patience and focus lead to excellence.
- A peaceful heart gives life to every action.

Moral:

- Success is not just about skill but the love and dedication you put into your work.
- Discipline shapes your character; devotion gives your work meaning.
- When you cultivate inner peace, it reflects in everything you create.

Another story (hustle-bustle)

The Village of Restless Winds

In the heart of a lush green valley lay a village called Jivanpur. But unlike its serene surroundings, the village was always buzzing with noise and chaos. The streets were crowded with merchants shouting their prices, children running wildly, and people rushing from one task to another. Everyone was in a hurry – always chasing something, yet never seeming satisfied.

Among them lived a man named Ravi, who was no different. From dawn to dusk, Ravi ran his small shop, managed his household, and always had a hundred things on his mind. His days passed in a blur, and his nights brought little rest. He believed that if he worked harder and faster, one day he would finally have peace.

One day, an old sage arrived in Jivanpur and set up a small camp by the river. Curious, Ravi went to see him and asked, “Master, I work so hard, but I never feel happy or peaceful. How can I find peace when life is so demanding?”

The sage smiled and said, “Come with me tomorrow at sunrise, and I’ll show you the answer.”

The next morning, Ravi met the sage, and they started walking toward a nearby forest. As they walked, the sage moved slowly, pausing to admire the flowers, listen to the birds, and feel the wind on his face. Ravi grew impatient. “Master, why are we wasting time? We have a long way to go!”

The sage chuckled. “But where are we trying to go so fast, my son?” he asked.

Ravi had no answer.

They reached a calm, clear lake. The sage asked Ravi to look at his reflection. But when Ravi looked down, the ripples on the water distorted his face. “The water is too restless!” Ravi complained.

“Exactly,” the sage said. “When your life is full of hustle and bustle, you can never see your true self clearly. Just like this water, your mind needs stillness to reflect peace.”

The sage sat by the lake and closed his eyes, breathing slowly. “Sit with me,” he said. “Let’s just be still.”

At first, Ravi struggled. His mind raced with thoughts of his shop, his errands, his unfinished work. But gradually, as he listened to the soft rustling of leaves and the gentle lapping of water, his breath slowed. The tension in his body eased. For the first time in years, Ravi felt the sweetness of stillness.

When he opened his eyes, the lake had become calm – and his reflection was clear.

The sage said, "The hustle and bustle of life will never end. But if you don't pause, you will miss the beauty around you and the peace within you. Make time to slow down. In stillness, you will find clarity and joy."

From that day on, Ravi changed. He still worked hard, but he no longer rushed. He made time to watch the sunset, laugh with his children, and sit quietly by the river. And in that balance, he found the peace he had been searching for.

Lesson:

- Life's demands will never end – but your well-being shouldn't wait.
- Stillness brings clarity; rushing only creates confusion.
- Peace is not found in doing more but in being present.

Moral:

- Slow down, breathe, and enjoy the journey.
- In the quiet moments, you'll discover what truly matters.
- Balance work with rest, and your life will feel richer and more fulfilling.

Let me know if you'd like me to add or tweak anything!

Guruma Anandmurti explains the intricate relationship between the mind, body, and intellect with remarkable clarity.

It is not difficult to understand that we are not the body. The changes in our physical form over time make this evident. If you place your photographs from childhood until now side by side, it becomes obvious how much the body has transformed. Yet, when you look in the mirror every day, you don't perceive these gradual changes. The body alters slowly, but the transformation is undeniable when you reflect on the past.

The greater challenge lies in understanding that we are not the mind either. This is because we experience everything through the mind—our identity, our relationships, and our understanding of the world are all filtered through it. Your sense of caste, family, and personal history are perceived by the mind, making it difficult to separate yourself from it.

But how do you observe the mind? Unlike the body, there is no external mirror for it. To see the mind clearly, you must develop a subtle and refined intellect.

Consider a simple example: when you woke up in the morning, your mind was joyful because you were excited to meet someone important. Later, when that person became busy and couldn't meet you, disappointment set in. The next day, when you finally met them, your happiness returned. Throughout this experience, you observed the shifting states of your mind—joy, disappointment, and joy again. But did the mind see these emotions, or did you see them? The fact that you can observe your mind's changing states suggests that you are something beyond the mind.

In close relationships, where emotional stakes are higher, the fluctuations of sorrow and happiness become more intense. This cycle of attachment often brings greater joy and deeper sorrow. By observing these changes with a subtle intellect, you begin to understand the distinction between the observer and the observed—the true self and the ever-changing mind.

Through this awareness, you realize that peace lies not in the mind's fleeting emotions but in the stable presence of the observer within. This insight is the key to true wisdom and lasting contentment.

Story, opportunity by chance or change

In a small town nestled between rolling hills, there lived a man named Arjun. Arjun was known for his kindness and simplicity, but his life was stuck in a routine. Every day, he followed the same schedule – waking up early, going to his modest shop, returning home tired, and spending his evenings in front of the television. Though content in some ways, a quiet dissatisfaction always lingered in his heart. He often dreamed of a better life, but he believed that luck and fate determined success.

One evening, Arjun sat with his old friend Ravi, who had recently started a successful business. As they talked, Arjun sighed and said, "You're so lucky, Ravi. Your life has changed so much for the better. I wish something like that would happen to me."

Ravi smiled and replied, "Your life doesn't get better by chance, Arjun. It gets better by change. I wasn't lucky – I took risks, learned new things, and worked hard. If you want a better life, you have to step out of your comfort zone and make it happen."

Those words stayed with Arjun. That night, he thought deeply about his life and realized he had been waiting for opportunities instead of creating them. The next day, he decided to make a change. He started by learning about new products he could sell in his shop and experimented with different marketing ideas. He also began attending business workshops and networking with other shopkeepers.

Slowly but surely, things began to improve. His shop attracted more customers, and his earnings increased. Encouraged by this progress, Arjun expanded his business, introduced home delivery services, and even launched an online store. With every step, his confidence grew, and so did his success.

A year later, Arjun met Ravi again. This time, it was Ravi who admired Arjun's transformation. "You've come so far, my friend," Ravi said.

"See? It wasn't luck – it was your willingness to change that made all the difference."

Arjun smiled, remembering his old self. He realized that life indeed gets better not by chance but by the courage to embrace change. And with that understanding, he continued to grow, knowing that every new day was an opportunity to become better than before.

Story, on light and dark days

In a bustling village, there lived a young man named Karan. He was loved by everyone – his friends admired him, his family praised him, and his life seemed perfect. With success in his work and joy in his personal life, Karan felt invincible. When he walked through the village, people greeted him warmly, and his presence always attracted attention.

One day, an old sage visited the village and watched Karan from a distance. In the evening, the sage approached him and said, "Young man, remember this – when you are in the light, everything is with you. But when you enter the dark, even your own shadow will not stay with you."

Karan laughed off the sage's words, too confident in his bright and happy life. "That's not possible," he said. "I have my family, friends, and my success – I will never be alone."

But life, as it often does, took an unexpected turn. A business decision went wrong, and Karan faced heavy losses. The once-thriving business started falling apart, and his financial situation became dire. As his wealth disappeared, so did the warmth around him. Friends who used to celebrate with him became distant. Even his close companions started avoiding him. The respect and admiration he once enjoyed faded.

One evening, feeling defeated, Karan walked alone on an empty road. The sun began to set, and as darkness fell, he noticed something strange – his shadow, which had been walking alongside him, slowly disappeared into the night. At that moment, the sage's words echoed in his mind. "When you enter the dark, even your own shadow will not stay with you."

Karan realized the truth in those words. In times of light and success, people surround you. But when darkness falls – when hardship and failure come – you often find yourself alone. Yet, in that solitude, Karan found something even more powerful: his inner strength. He understood that the only true companion in both light and dark is one's own resilience and self-belief.

Determined to rise again, Karan worked harder than ever. He rebuilt his business slowly, not for admiration or applause but for his own dignity and peace. This time, he cherished the people who stood by him in his darkest hours and learned not to rely on the fleeting presence of those who only stayed for the light.

And so, when the light returned to his life, Karan stood stronger – not because of the crowd around him but because of the strength he had discovered within himself.

Today it's me. Tomorrow it's you

In a peaceful little town, there lived a kind-hearted girl named Meera. She was known for her gentle nature and the way she cared deeply for everyone around her. Her feelings were pure and delicate – when she loved, she loved with all her heart, and when she trusted, she did so completely.

One day, Meera became friends with a boy named Arav. They spent a lot of time together, sharing their dreams, fears, and hopes. Over time, Meera started developing feelings for Arav. One evening, gathering all her courage, she expressed her feelings to him. But Arav, surprised and unsure, brushed it off lightly.

"Oh, Meera, don't take things so seriously," he said with a laugh. "We're just friends. Don't complicate things with all these emotions."

Meera felt a sharp pain in her heart, but she smiled through it, not wanting to show how hurt she was. From that day on, a distance grew between them. Meera remained kind, but her delicate feelings had been wounded.

Months passed, and life took its course. Arav eventually met someone he truly cared for. When he confessed his feelings, he faced an unexpected response. "I'm not sure," the girl said, brushing him off much like he had done to Meera.

That night, as Arav sat alone, feeling the sting of rejection, he remembered Meera's quiet pain. The words of an old saying echoed in his mind: "Feelings are the most delicate things in life. When someone truly shows them to you, never hurt them – because today it is me, tomorrow it could be you."

Realizing his mistake, Arav sought out Meera. He apologized, not because he felt obligated but because he now understood the weight of unacknowledged feelings. Though life had moved on, their friendship found a new depth, built on understanding and respect.

From that day forward, Arav learned to treat people's emotions with care – knowing how fragile and precious they truly are.

Inspiring story (never given up)

In a small village, there was a boy named Rohan who dreamed of becoming a great artist. He spent hours every day sketching and painting, pouring his heart into his work. But no matter how hard he tried, his paintings were never selected for exhibitions, and his talent went unnoticed.

One day, after yet another rejection, Rohan sat by the river, tears streaming down his face. "Maybe I'm just not good enough," he whispered. He felt defeated and thought of giving up his dream.

As he sat there, an old fisherman named Kashi approached him. "Why so sad, my boy?" Kashi asked gently.

Rohan shared his disappointment, and Kashi listened patiently. When Rohan finished, the fisherman smiled and said, "Let me tell you something, son. I've been fishing in this river for over 30 years. Some days, I catch nothing. Other days, the nets come up full. But I never stop going out on the water because I know the next day could bring the best catch of my life. Everyone has bad days – the secret is to never give up."

Rohan thought about Kashi's words. Inspired, he picked up his brush the next day and started painting again. He experimented, learned new techniques, and kept improving. Even when his work wasn't recognized, he kept going, remembering the fisherman's advice.

After years of perseverance, Rohan's hard work finally paid off. One of his paintings was selected for a prestigious exhibition. Soon, people began to see the beauty and emotion in his art. His talent was finally acknowledged, and his dream started coming true.

Standing in the gallery, looking at his painting on the wall, Rohan remembered the days he almost gave up. And he smiled, knowing that it was his persistence – his ability to pick himself up after every bad day – that had brought him this far.

Good message story (I replace by we)

In a quiet neighbourhood, there lived an elderly man named Mr. Mehta. He had been a lively and cheerful person once, but after his wife passed away and his children moved abroad, loneliness slowly crept into his life. Over time, his health began to decline – his once-bright spirit faded, and illness took hold of his body.

His neighbour, a young woman named Asha, noticed the change. She often saw him sitting alone on his porch, looking lost in thought. One day, she decided to visit him. "How are you, Uncle?" she asked kindly.

"I'm fine," Mr. Mehta replied with a weak smile, but Asha could see the sadness in his eyes.

Over the next few days, Asha started visiting more often. She brought home-cooked meals, shared stories, and even convinced a few other neighbours to join them for evening tea. Slowly, the quiet porch began to fill with laughter and conversations.

One afternoon, as they sat together watching the sunset, Mr. Mehta said, "You know, I never realized how much I missed this – being part of something, being cared for." His health, though still fragile, began to improve. The joy of companionship brought back his appetite, and his strength returned bit by bit.

One day, Asha said something that stuck with him: "When 'I' is replaced by 'we,' even illness becomes wellness. You don't have to face anything alone – we're here for you."

Those words stayed with Mr. Mehta. The warmth and support of his new-found family filled the emptiness in his life. With their love and care, his recovery became not just physical but emotional too. And in that shared journey, they all discovered the true power of togetherness.

Another good story, face, fight and finish

In a bustling city, there lived a young man named Kabir. He had big dreams of starting his own business, but life kept throwing challenges his way. Despite his ambitions, his path was filled with obstacles – financial struggles, self-doubt, and people who didn't believe in his vision.

One day, Kabir's mentor, Mr. Sharma, gave him a piece of advice that stuck with him. "Whenever a problem arrives, do three things: face it, fight it, and finish it."

Soon enough, life tested those words. Kabir finally gathered enough savings to start a small café. But just weeks after the opening, a sudden economic slowdown affected businesses across the city. Customers became scarce, bills piled up, and the dream he had worked so hard for seemed to slip away.

Kabir remembered Mr. Sharma's advice. First, he faced the problem. Instead of denying the reality or giving in to fear, he acknowledged the situation and analysed what was going wrong.

Next, he decided to fight it. He revamped his marketing strategy, introduced special discounts, and reached out to local influencers to spread the word about his café. He worked day and night, refusing to let the circumstances defeat him.

Finally, he finished it. With his persistence and smart efforts, the café slowly started attracting more customers. His unique menu and warm atmosphere won people over. Within months, the business not only survived the crisis but flourished.

Looking back, Kabir realized that every problem he faced had made him stronger. By facing, fighting, and finishing his challenges, he turned his obstacles into stepping stones. And his café stood as a symbol of resilience and determination for everyone in the neighbourhood.

Another story, Silence to happiness

In a small town, there was a quiet girl named Anaya. She wasn't one to speak much, and most people mistook her silence for shyness. But behind that quiet demeanour was a heart carrying burdens she never shared – the loss of her mother, the pressures of her studies, and the loneliness she often felt.

One day, a new boy named Aarav joined her school. He was lively and friendly, always surrounded by people. But something about Anaya's silence intrigued him. While others overlooked her quietness, Aarav noticed the sadness in her eyes.

Instead of pushing her to talk, he started sitting next to her during lunch, sharing funny stories without expecting a response. He'd leave little notes with silly jokes on her desk and bring her favourite books without being asked. Slowly, a change began – a small curve appeared on Anaya's lips, and the heaviness in her eyes softened.

One afternoon, as they sat under a tree, Anaya finally spoke. "Why are you so kind to me when I hardly say anything?"

Aarav smiled and said, "Because the best translator is the one who can translate someone's silence into a smile. And your smile – it's worth the wait."

From that day on, Anaya began to open up, and their bond grew stronger. Aarav never asked for her words – he understood her through her quiet moments. And in his patient kindness, he became the reason her silence slowly turned into laughter and happiness.

Sometimes, it's not words that show we care. It's the ability to hear what's unsaid and bring warmth to someone's world without demanding their voice. Aarav did just that – and in doing so, he gave Anaya the courage to smile again.

Story, confidence

In a lively town filled with noise and chatter, there was a quiet boy named Neel. He wasn't the most popular, nor the most talented – at least that's how he saw himself. He often felt invisible, blending into the background, unsure of his worth.

One day, a new girl named Riya joined his class. Unlike Neel, Riya was confident and full of life. But what set her apart was her warmth. She made everyone around her feel seen and heard.

Riya noticed Neel sitting alone during lunch and decided to join him. She didn't just talk – she listened. She asked about his drawings, his favourite books, his dreams. And slowly, Neel started to open up.

Over time, their friendship grew. Riya would cheer him on when he doubted himself and remind him of his strengths when he forgot them. When Neel shared his sketches with hesitation, she admired them with genuine enthusiasm. "You have a gift, Neel," she'd say. "Why don't you show them to others?"

Because of Riya's encouragement, Neel entered an art competition – something he never would have dared before. To his surprise, he won first prize. But more than the award, it was the belief in himself that felt like the real victory.

One day, Neel told Riya, "You've been such a good friend to me."

Riya smiled and said, "The true measure of friendship isn't just how you feel about someone. It's about how that someone makes you feel about yourself. And you deserve to feel proud of who you are."

In Riya's reflection of his strengths, Neel discovered his own confidence. And in that friendship, he realized his true worth.

Shivani Didi, Braham Kumari

That's a beautiful observation – the essence of what all true masters, preachers, and saints teach is indeed the same: inner peace, clarity, and connection with the self. Their methods may differ – some emphasize meditation, some prayer, some self-inquiry – but the goal remains aligned: helping people reach a state of balance, joy, and wisdom.

Listening to their words attentively, repeating their teachings, and truly absorbing them creates a powerful inner transformation. When the master is genuine and experienced – like Shivani Didi, for example – their guidance can act like a healing balm for the restless mind. It helps us disconnect from the noise of the outer world and tune in to our inner silence and strength.

As you rightly said, a sound mind leads to a sound life – health, happiness, and energy naturally follow when we're at peace within. Consistent practice of this inner connection brings more and more benefits over time. It's like a daily medicine for the soul – simple, powerful, and transformative.

Sit straight and relax yourself.

While meditating, exactly in the middle of the forehead where we apply tilak, see yourself as a very powerful, shining star. I am the soul, the power that runs this body. I am the master of the mind. I am the master of the senses. I am the soul, the power that makes every resolution. I am the soul who always thinks good. I am the soul who thinks less.

I am the power that speaks every word. I am the soul; I speak less. I am the soul; I speak softly. I am the soul; I speak sweetly. My every word is a blessing. My every action is the best. I am the soul; there is light in every existence. I give respect and love to everyone. I make every impossible possible. I am a powerful soul; rays of power spread all around me. I am an angel; the souls that come in contact with me are very good.

They are very good. They are powerful souls. Their behaviour is perfect. Our relationship is strong. I am a soul who gives love and respect to every soul and gives blessings to every soul. I am a soul who is full of love. Whatever is happening for me is happening for my welfare. I am a soul who is full of happiness. Rays of happiness are spreading all around me. I put a dot on past things. I finished them. I lighten them. I forgive myself. I accept myself. I love myself. I am a soul who is full of peace. Rays of peace are spreading all around from my soul. I am an angel. I am close to the formless God. God is always with me. God is my companion. I share everything in my mind with Him. If I have any question or need advice, or if I have to make a decision, I tell Him. I get answers to everything from Him. Every mean becomes lighter after talking to Him. The powers of the Almighty God are coming into and going from my soul. Old habits have been destroyed. I, the soul, am filled with the powers of the Supreme Soul. The Supreme Soul is the ocean of love. He accepts me as I am. He loves me. I do not need anything from anyone else.

I am filled with God's love. The powers of every soul are emanating from me, the soul, and reaching every soul. Every soul is filled with the powers of the Supreme Soul. Every soul is peaceful. Every soul is happy. Every soul is healthy. The rays of the Supreme Soul, the ocean of purity, are giving power to all the five elements of nature. Nature is pure. Nature is powerful. Nature is my companion. There is a protective shield of the powers of the Supreme Soul all around me. Everything is peaceful. I, the soul, am an angel who gives power. I am an angel. Om Shanti.

Any preacher's main aim, target, destiny is one, to connect yourself to your inner world, their path, their way may be different but destiny is the same.

Story

Once upon a time, in a bustling kingdom, there lived a proud and mighty swordsman named Veer. Known for his strength and skill, Veer was admired by all and often boasted of his power. "Strength is everything," he would say. "With my sword, I can conquer anything."

One day, the kingdom announced a grand competition of skill and strength. Eager to prove his superiority, Veer entered without hesitation. Among the participants was an elderly tailor named Ratan. The crowd laughed when they saw the frail old man with nothing but a needle in his hand. "What can a needle do against a sword?" they jeered.

The competition consisted of many challenges – breaking stones, slicing through logs, and feats of strength. Veer excelled in them all, his sword flashing brilliantly. Finally, the last task was announced: the contestants had to mend the royal banner, which had been torn by a storm. The banner was enormous and delicate, made of fine silk.

Veer stepped forward confidently and slashed at the banner with his sword, only making the tear worse. Frustrated, he tried again, but the sword was too rough and powerful for the delicate fabric.

Then Ratan quietly approached. With his needle and thread, his hands steady despite his age, he carefully stitched the silk. The crowd fell silent as they

watched the old man's patience and skill. Soon, the banner was whole again, the stitches so fine they were almost invisible.

The king rose from his seat and addressed the crowd. "Let this be a lesson to all," he said. "Power has its place, but so does patience and skill. The sword may win battles, but it is the needle that mends what is broken."

From that day on, Veer learned to respect not just strength, but wisdom and gentleness. And the people of the kingdom never again underestimated the quiet strength of the humble needle.

Conclusion and Gratitude

As this book comes to an end, I reflect on the journey of writing it and the purpose it serves. Life is a continuous learning experience, shaped by our thoughts, actions, and the people we meet along the way. The wisdom shared in these pages is a humble attempt to inspire, guide, and bring clarity to those who seek understanding.

I bow to all incarnations, saints, masters, preachers, and deities whose teachings have enlightened countless souls and continue to illuminate our paths. Their wisdom transcends time, offering us guidance and peace in our moments of doubt.

A heartfelt thank you to all my readers, supporters, and well-wishers. Your encouragement and interest in my work are the true motivation behind my writing. To those who have shared their insights, experiences, and love, I am deeply grateful.

A special acknowledgment to my beloved wife, Lata Khanna. I am truly blessed to have found not just a life partner, but a companion, a friend, and a guiding force in my journey. Her wisdom, patience, and unwavering support have been a pillar of strength in my life. Through her, I have learned countless invaluable lessons—whether in the small routines of daily life or in the deeper philosophies of love, kindness, and resilience. She has nurtured in me the virtues of patience, discipline, and gratitude, and her presence has made every challenge easier to face and every joy even more meaningful.

Her love is not just a source of comfort but a profound inspiration. She has been my silent strength during difficult times, my loudest cheerleader in moments of achievement, and my steady companion in all the in-between moments of life. Her ability to bring peace in chaos, her boundless generosity, and her unwavering belief in me have given me confidence to pursue my dreams and overcome obstacles.

Lata is not only my partner but also my greatest teacher. From her, I have learned the importance of humility in success, resilience in adversity, and gratitude in everyday life. Her selflessness, warmth, and innate kindness have not only shaped me into a better person but have also created a home filled with love and positivity. She has made every shared experience richer, every celebration more joyful, and every difficulty more bearable simply by being there.

Words may never fully capture the depth of my gratitude for her presence in my life. But if there is one thing I wish to express in this acknowledgment, it is my sincere appreciation for the love, care, and wisdom she has given me. This book is as much a result of her support as it is of my efforts, and I dedicate it to her with all my heart.

May this book serve as a source of reflection, strength, and wisdom in your life. Keep growing, keep learning, and keep spreading positivity.

Radha Swami!

With gratitude and respect, Ashok Kumar